# the
# wine club

Editor: Tricia Laning
Associate Design Director: Chad Jewell
Contributing Writer: Winifred Moranville
Illustrator: Mark Marturello
Photoprapher: Tanya Braganti

First Edition. Printed in the United States of America.
Library of Congress Control Number: 2005921344
ISBN: 0-696-22543-3

For Mom and Dad: Thanks for giving me a taste of
the good life and teaching me that it's mine for
the taking. I love you both.

For Michael: There's no one in the world I'd rather
share a bottle of wine with than you. Thank you for
making me so happy. I love you more every day.

When I started writing this wine book, I never imagined I'd complete it while typing with one hand and taking turns feeding two beautiful baby boys with the other. It has been an experience I'll never forget, and there are a ton of people without whom I could never have done this. From the bottom of my heart—thank you, thank you, thank you, all.

Michael, there aren't enough words to express how thankful I am that you are in my life. Thank you for always telling me that this would be a great book; it wouldn't have been without you. You are more to me than I could have ever dreamed.

To my mom and dad, Peg and Dave Christian, thanks for giving me so many opportunities including the best education and a chance to travel the world. Mom, I credit you for all the creative ideas swimming in my head; Dad, for instilling in me the drive and determination. Thank you both for showing me that indeed it is a wonderful life.

Thank you to my sister, Coleen, for always being my biggest fan and a great friend to me; my little sister, K.C., for making me laugh; and my brother, David, for reminding me you only live once, so go for it. To my grandparents, Marge and Ed Todd, Pop, for being a die-hard Riunite fan; Gram, for telling me you only drink your wine with ice cubes. You both inspired me to write this book. To my in-laws, Donna and John Petrosky, and to Maeve, Jay, Brenna, and Jerry Burke, Sarah, John, Monica, and Kenia, for all the support and love you've given me.

To Sarah Murphy, for starting the book club in Atlanta and giving me the foundation for this story. Emily Miles Terry, for asking me to write the essay which then became this book. Kathleen Daelemans, for making me see this was finally the perfect idea for my book. To my talented agent at Trident Media Group, Melissa Flashman, for understanding and protecting my original vision. To my agent Scott Wachs at William Morris, for believing in me.

I can't thank the people at Meredith Publishing enough. First, to Leah Karliner, and Laura Sigman, for making my first experience with Meredith wonderful. Paul Hunt, for the kind words. My team—Jan Miller, Tricia Laning, Wini Moranville, and Chad Jewell, for all of the great work and for being so kind.

The culinary team—Vanessa Parker, I knew you were an amazing cook when you made me love lima beans. Iri Greco, for making coconut crème brûlee a million and one times. Megan Twining, for teaching me how to pronounce those fancy French wines. To my food friends in Hotlanta—Todd Immel, Marty and Lynn Ticar, and Oscar Morales. To my research team and best gals—Tamie Cook, Susie Manning, and Amara Wagner.

To the all of you at the Food Network—Susan Stockton, for giving me my first job. Jill Novatt, for being a great friend. To Robert Bleifer for always being good for a laugh. Emily Reiger, for those forever indelible words, "Never be afraid to ask for what you're "worth." Amy Stevenson, for proving you can have a family and still work in this crazy business. And Derek Flynn, for showing me how to find any ingredient in New York City, no matter how obscure!

To all my friends at CNN and CNN Headline News—Diedre Wenokur, for inviting me to talk about wine on TV. To Kay Jones and Erin Vaughn, for working on all of those segments! To Kate Underwood, for being an incredibly creative producer and friend. To Steve Rosenberg, for showing me that guys will definitely be into the wine club.

To Barbara Fairchild, for being an awesome role model to women in this biz. To you, Marcy MacDonald and Amara Wagner, for giving me the chance to represent *Bon Appétit* magazine.

To all of my friends in TV who gave me a shot at proving myself—Rainy Farrell at the *TODAY* show, Laurie Weiner at FOX, and Susan Durrwachter at MSNBC.

To Gil Kulers, for giving me the chance to grow as a writer. To Lisa Frederick and Oma Ford, for publishing my first article. To Diane Jackson, Marisa Palmisano, and Athalie White, for being so great to work with. And a quick shout out to Robert's Road.

To all of the wonderfully generous wineries, for sharing your wine.

And last but not least—to my boys Christopher and Elliot, thank you for showing me there is so much more to life. Kisses and Hugs XOXOXOXO.

# contents

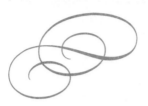

\* \* \* \* \* \* \* \* \* \* \* \*

# JOIN THE CLUB

***It's*** *time to put on your favorite music, indulge in some great food, and fall in love with wine on your own terms. Perhaps you've been a faithful white Zinfandel fan and want to branch out but don't know how. Maybe you've begun to notice how wine makes your food taste so much better—and want to learn more. Or perhaps you had a recent jaunt to Europe and noticed what a good time everyone seemed to be having at the*

table with family, friends, great food, and a bottle of wine smack in the center of it all. Whatever your reason for becoming more fascinated by the world of wine, you've come to the perfect place.

That's right. Step out of the stuffy wine shop, put down the textbook, close that encyclopedic wine list, and head home. I'm sure you have some wineglasses and a corkscrew (if not, pick some up before you start) and a few friends to boot. So, you see, you've already gathered the makings of a wine club without even trying. That's how easy learning about wine should be! A little more fun, fewer boundaries, and wine is your oyster.

\* \* \* \* \* \* \* \* \* \* \* \*

Starting a wine club is the ideal way to casually integrate wine into your life. Learning about wine in your home, surrounded by friends, eliminates stress and highlights enjoyment—and that's what this book is about. In fact, the inspiration for this book came from a series of informal get-togethers a few years ago in Atlanta.

### Here's My Story

While living in Atlanta, I met Sarah, Vanessa, Tamie, and Susie: a hilarious hypochondriac, a sharp beauty queen, an inspiring chef, and a sassy writer. Sarah was a television production assistant who desperately wanted more from life; Vanessa slung drinks at hot clubs in town, working her way through school; Tamie had left an unhappy marriage after 10 years to follow her dream and become a professional cook; and Susie was a wine writer who just happened to be having a fabulous French love affair. As a freelance culinary producer and wine writer, I worked with each of them in some capacity.

It was the beginning of football season, and Sarah's boyfriend (now husband), Derek, was spending Sundays and Mondays with the boys. Sarah wanted something of her own, so she started a book club. At first it was a tough sell, and attendance was low. But once we decided to bring some wine, the book club took on a life of its own. Work was how we met, but wine was how our friendship grew.

I remember an interview with Heather Locklear where she said, "The truth is, women only go to book clubs for the wine." Before too long, our get-togethers couldn't begin until the cork left the bottle. If we got around to discussing the book, all the better! Mostly we talked about ourselves. There was Sarah's freakish obsession with eating dessert and her main course at the same time, Susie's hot tub rendezvous, and Vanessa's bartender gossip. Wine opened our mouths, our hearts, and our minds, and we became closer to each other than we were to the girls we had grown up with or our college roommates.

It's hard to find time to cultivate meaningful friendships. But as we drank in colors as rich as velvet and inhaled swirling aromas, we had a new passion for life. Wine allowed each of us to rediscover friendship and network careers, all while enjoying the best-tasting therapy around. And while we bonded over wine, we were learning to love it too.

I graduated from the Culinary Institute of America, passed my sommelier certification, and still had butterflies when I entered a large wine shop or attended a stuffy wine tasting. Did I smell the right things? I was afraid to say the "wrong" thing. But what was I afraid of? Wine appreciation isn't rocket science. A little bit of taste-testing among friends gave an electric charge to my wine confidence. Wine became more memorable in my living room than it had in any classroom or lecture hall.

Now with ease I recommend rare bottles to my sister as gifts for her boss and explain the difference between Syrah and Shiraz to my mom, and I've convinced my grandpop to sip chilled Riesling instead of his ice cube-laden Riunite. Even my beer-drinking friends are taking risks and buying wine. Rarely does a week go by without a friend phoning in for wine advice, and if I don't know the answer, I'm OK with admitting it.

So, you see, my wine club has inspired me to inspire people everywhere to start their own wine clubs. Learning about wine with friends removes the fear factor. It doesn't matter what you smell or whether you like the wines the critics rave about. It just matters that you're having fun. Entertaining with wine is wonderful for bonding with friends, seeking other singles, and networking. Mostly it's an opportunity to build your wine confidence in a relaxed social setting. While sipping with friends and creating new memories, you'll also be gaining a deeper understanding of wine and a lasting appreciation for what you may have once thought was just a drink.

Maybe you already love wine. Maybe you drink beer or your beverage of choice is a Manhattan. Whatever the case, we've all experienced a snooty wine lover. Unfortunately, there is an atmosphere of exclusivity in the world of wine, and often it's perpetuated by those working in the industry. Perhaps these gatekeepers think that shrouding the wine world in an air of mystery somehow adds to its allure, but I say "Nonsense!" No matter how accessible wine may become, no matter how many people drink it, wine will always be fascinating. Wine is about lifestyle—not lifestyles of the rich and famous but those of everyday people. Fakes, posers, elitist wine drinkers—this book isn't for you. It's for the rest of us who'd like to kick back, relax, and enjoy a glass of vino with friends. Throughout all the laughter and clinking glasses, we'll be nibbling on good food and feeding an appreciation and understanding of the world of wine.

✳ ✳ ✳ ✳ ✳ ✳ ✳ ✳ ✳ ✳ ✳ ✳

# baby sips

*Wine may be daunting at first, but with baby steps (or baby sips, as I like to call them), you'll be up and running in no time. Here's how it works.*

## Wine of the Month

Pick your poison—or better yet, let me pick it for you. Each chapter in this book is devoted to one meeting (fete, soiree, party, gathering—whatever you want to call it) of your wine club. At each monthly gathering, your club will focus on one style of wine (like Champagne) or one varietal (that is, a wine made from a particular grape, such as Pinot Noir or Cabernet Sauvignon).

I've chosen each wine with baby sips in mind. We'll start off with some wines you may be familiar with and, I hope, some you've never heard of. The wines also go with the weather. For example, you would never want a big, full Cabernet Sauvignon on a hot August day, so in that month we'll be sipping a crisp, chilled Sauvignon Blanc.

One week before the wine club meeting, the host/hostess should call to let everyone know what wine he or she should be seeking. One bottle will serve up to 10 people. Remember, everyone gets just enough to get a good taste, one to two ounces. If you have more than 10 participants, you need to account for that when assigning the wine. Also, don't forget to assign a nonalcoholic beverage.

Each month, you will throw in a ringer; for example, if you're tasting Cabernet Sauvignon, sneak in a Merlot too. This will help you pick up on the differences between the grape varieties. The host purchases this ringer (I'll give suggestions), and only the host should know which bottle it is. Keep bottles under wraps until you've tasted them all (see "How to Taste Blind," page 12).

## Party Favors

You'll notice that each month you learn a little more about wine—beyond the characteristics of the grapes. In February, I'll tell you about Cabernet Sauvignon, the exciting world of wine flights, and the importance (or not!) of vintages. I've tucked these painless little lessons in here and there. Don't worry—they won't get in the way of the fun; think of them as party favors that keep on giving.

I'll lead you through the tasting process for each wine. You'll look at appearance, aroma, taste, body, and finish. I'll tell you specific characteristics to look for in each wine.

## Step-by-Step to a Great Tasting

Before you get started, introduce club members to the art of tasting (as opposed to merely guzzling) wine. Remember, one person's Monet is another person's Picasso. There aren't any rules per se, but here are a few guidelines to keep your tasting on track:

**Appearance:** Hold your glass against a white sheet of paper or a white tablecloth and take a look. Is it a sunset or a velvet robe? Murky or bright? The appearance is the first clue to what's in the glass. Is it red, white, rose colored, or shades therein? Does it look watery or thick? Do you see bubbles? Is there something floating in your glass or something dark settling to the bottom? Take note of everything you see. Your eyes will not deceive you.

**Aroma:** You've seen that dramatic swirling of wine in the glass—now it's time for you to get in on the show. Before you get swept up in swirling, sniff your wine and make a mental note of what you smell. Now place the base of your glass flat on the table and gently move it in a circular motion, swirling it just enough to let the wine work its way up the sides of the glass. If you're overzealous you'll end up with more wine on the table than in your mouth.

Go ahead and take a whiff. Stick your schnoz right in the glass. Note the difference from what you smelled before you swirled. That's because you aerated the wine— mixed in air. Month by month, you'll learn how to recognize different smells in the wines you drink. This all translates to the "nose" of the wine. And you only get better at it by doing it over, and over, and over again.

Don't feel bad if you can't identify smells right away; smelling is tough, and often people disagree, but basically whatever you smell is correct. I'm not up your nose, so how can I tell you what you smell? A visit to the spice rack, the grocery store, the florist, and even a local farm will awaken your nose to what you may smell in the glass. I promise you will eventually smell more than alcohol!

* * * * * * * * * **WHEN IT'S YOUR TURN TO HOST** * * * * * * * *

I suggest that all wine club members be willing to take turns hosting the gathering. Here's what to do when it's your turn to host:

**Plan ahead.** I recommend reading the chapter in the book two weeks in advance. This will give you enough time to assign wines to guests and to prepare little by little for your gathering.

**Prepare the food.** You can shop a week in advance, and every recipe has steps that can be done ahead of time. The more you do in advance, the more you can wind down and relax before the wine club get-together.

**Assign the wines.** Keep in mind that some months the wines may vary in price range, so if one wine is significantly higher priced, split it between two members. On average, wine club members should be prepared to spend about $20 a month, though each month's host will spend more due to the food (that's why I recommend taking turns).

**Purchase the ringer.** This is always the host's responsibility. It is to be kept a secret so that all guests are challenged to test their palates.

**Conduct the tasting.** I highly suggest holding a blind tasting (with the bottles wrapped in foil and revealed only at the end of the night). If you wish, you can make it a more casual affair. The element of surprise that comes with revealing each wine's identity is much more fun.

**About the glasses:** It's always OK to ask other guests to bring wineglasses if you don't think you'll have enough. Just make sure you're sipping from glass, not plastic, not foam—and by no means from mugs!

* * * * * * * * * * * * * * * * * * * * * * * * * * * * * *

**Taste:** Take a sip. What does it remind you of? For me, the easiest way to taste what's in the glass is to associate it with food—flavors like blueberry jam, cherry pie, and pepperoni. We're trying to get more out of you than "That's delicious." Think about fruits, spices, and other foods you can relate it to. Wines carry flavors of everything from sweet to savory, fruit to nuts. Compare the taste to what you smelled (sometimes they aren't the same). And sometimes, wine doesn't taste like pie or jam—but *terroir*. Don't worry. I'll explain. There's nothing terrifying about *terroir*.

**Body:** Wine experts compare wine to what is familiar. The easiest way to describe the difference in light-, medium-, and full-bodied wines is to think in terms of cow's milk. If your wine is watery like skim milk, and it doesn't leave a coating on your mouth, consider it light-bodied. If it's heavier like whole milk, it's fuller bodied. Is full-bodied better than light-bodied? That's up to you. Only you know what your mouth prefers.

**Finish:** The way your mouth feels after you swallow the wine and the few moments following is called the finish. Acid, tannins, and alcohol may present themselves in the finish— some wines leave your mouth watering, while others have you all puckered up. You'll notice that some finishes may stick around longer than others. Start counting after you take a sip (count slowly: one Mississippi, two Mississippi, three Mississippi, four Mississippi ...). If the taste remains for three seconds or less, that is considered a short finish. If it lingers past 10 seconds, that is considered a long finish.

**Price Value:** After you've tasted the wines, the host will unveil the bottles and reveal the prices. Now's the time to discuss what you expected to pay for a wine versus the actual cost. As you taste more wines, you'll start to learn a few of the characteristics of finer wines. And with luck, you'll experience the distinct thrill of discovering a wine that tastes expensive—but is really, really cheap.

Be sure to take notes about the wine as you go; otherwise, you'll never remember what you tasted and loved (and finding wines you love is a major goal of this club!). You can photocopy the tasting notes sheet on page

### * * * * * * * HOW TO TASTE BLIND * * * * * * *

For those of you who want to go all the way and test yourselves, the host should wrap all of the bottles in aluminum foil or brown bags. Be sure to remove the entire foil capsule at the top of the bottle so there are no signs of what lies beneath. Then number each bottle with a permanent marker. The host should keep a list of names, numbers, and prices of the bottles to be revealed once the tasting has finished. This is called a blind tasting, and it eliminates preconceived notions about the wine. If you can't see the name and don't know the price, you are more likely to taste true to your palate and not be swayed.

Even Master Sommeliers have been tricked! There have been tastings where the expensive wine has been removed from the bottle and replaced with inexpensive wine. But the spotting of a rare bottle or a famous vineyard on the label has turned educated sommeliers into blubbering idiots as they rave about the wine's complexity—when actually they are sipping a less common juice. By covering the bottles, you learn to trust yourself.

* * * * * * * * * * * * * * * * * * * * * * * *

219 and keep your notes in a file for future reference. Better yet, I recommend a bound notebook—something small that you can keep in your pocket or purse. With all your notes in one place, you can easily refer to them on your next trip to the wine shop. Before you know it, your wine notebook will become a diary full of notes on great wines—and memories of the good times you had tasting them.

## Guests Can Google™

Because the host provides the atmosphere and the food and also assigns the wine (guidelines are outlined in each chapter), I suggest each guest bring a li'l something extra in the way of a few interesting tidbits about the assigned wine.

This is simple. Get online and Google the wine you're bringing. Most wineries have websites, and every wine has a story behind it. It's not essential to know this info, but it does add flavor to the mix. Give eBay a rest, already!

## Pairing Wine and Food

What's the best way to become an expert on pairing food and wine? Certainly not by studying boring grids and memorizing long, dull lists, but by tasting, sipping, tasting, and sipping. And tasting and sipping.

We've heard it millions of times: Red wine goes with red meat, and white wine goes with white meat or fish. There is some basis to this theory. But it wasn't until one chilly fall evening when I bit into a juicy New York strip steak, hot off the grill, followed by a gulp of California Cab, that I saw the light. Until I tasted the two together, it had never really clicked. The steak's fatty juices softened the heavy tannins in the wine, letting its ripe fruit flavors take center stage. Those same fruity flavors then highlighted the smoky grilled meat flavors. That night I understood that steak and Cab are truly a match made in heaven.

* * * * * * * * * * * * * * *

### YOUR WINE CLUB MEMBERS

Having a wine club is the best way to taste lots of wines without going broke. First, find out how many people will be interested in coming to the wine club (or, I should say, how many people you are interested in hosting). I recommend no more than 10 to 15. For those of you living in tight spaces, like my Manhattan box in the sky, I strongly suggest capping the list at 10 guests. Smaller gatherings are better for learning and making conversation. If you want your gatherings to be less formal, go nuts and invite the whole neighborhood.

My number-one tip for a successful wine club is to drink only with people you like!

Unfortunately, my first wine club was hijacked after I left. An insidiously irritating invitee penetrated the club—it was only after she joined that she revealed her nightmarish tendencies. No matter how good the wine, her way of turning any conversation to focus on herself left a bad taste. Her incessant blabbering about her car, her house, her job, her new husband, her wedding, her driveway (yes, her driveway!) ultimately led others in the group to form a new, underground wine club. As with any gathering, the guest list is key to a fantastic time or a flop—so choose your wine companions wisely.

* * * * * * * * * * * * *

For each of your meetings, I'll give you recipes that provide memorable wine and food pairings. These will often tap into three classic pairing strategies: bridging, complementing, and contrasting the flavors. For example, in April you'll see how using Merlot in one recipe bridges the flavor between the food and the wine. You'll notice how Merlot's soft tannins complement beef tenderloin skewers in another recipe, and how its fruity flavors contrast the heat you'll feel from the horseradish in yet another.

I'll also give you some tasty no-cook alternatives for when time is crunched. You can combine homemade dishes with no-cook options to keep the gathering stress-free.

Oh—and by the way—if you don't want to commit to a monthly meeting, just pick and choose among the chapters to create fun get-togethers anytime. Consider each chapter a complete menu for a fabulous wine and hors d'oeuvres party. And if you learn something about wine in the process, all the better!

## Coming Your Way—Every Month

Each chapter is full of features including tips that key you into shopping for wine, collecting wine, and wine trends. There's no need to stress over deciphering wine vocabulary; I'll give you a little taste at a time. And I find things I learn from my mistakes stay with me far longer than those I try to memorize. So, like it or not, you'll be doing a few things backward for the sake of moving forward. I'll also arm you with some tricks for when it's your turn to host.

Look for these:

**Bang for Your Buck:** I'll recommend a value-priced wine for the budget-conscious.

**The Mona Lisa:** When I started at culinary school, my new best friend, Megan Twining, was previously an art major. I asked her how she ended up there, and she looked at me like I had two heads. "Because food and wine are the ultimate art forms. They appeal to every sense," she replied. We won't be buying priceless bottles at auction, but the *Mona Lisa* pick is definitely a splurge that will encapsulate the essence of that month's wine club pick.

**The Salvador Dalí:** The Salvador Dalí pick, like the painter, won't be so mainstream. Quirky, funky, and definitely not for everyone, these wines are esoteric. They bring something a little different—maybe even a little off—to the table.

**Wine Trend:** We'll look at gizmos, gadgets, and trends—from the question of screw tops to the answer of Wine-Away (a lifesaver when wine gets spilled).

**You'll Never Forget It:** I offer a fun trick, tip, or activity for remembering an important wine lesson. For example, one month I ask you to ask your wine shop for a corked bottle. Once you've gotten a whiff of a good wine gone bad, you'll know what it means to be "corked."

**Wine Speak:** We must include some technical terms—but you're going to love the way they help you expand your mind and palate.

**If the Glass Fits:** We'll explore what each type of glass adds to the enjoyment of wine, as well as how to select glassware.

That's it—all you need to know to get started. So get your sipping shoes on—you're in for a party (12 of them, in fact).

# calendar

**23** DAYS BEFORE
Snoop around local wine stores—any good buys this month?

**22** DAYS BEFORE
Make photocopies of wine tasting sheets.

**21** DAYS BEFORE
E-mail wine club members with a teaser about this month's meeting.

**20** DAYS BEFORE
Mark your calendar with wine club to-do list.

**19** DAYS BEFORE
Assign wines to be brought.

**18** DAYS BEFORE
Create your menu.

**14** DAYS BEFORE
Organize music for party.

**12** DAYS BEFORE
Polish your wineglasses, but pour yourself a glass before you begin.

**7** DAYS BEFORE
Make a shopping list—be sure to check your menu.

**5** DAYS BEFORE
Google™ your wine pick.

**3** DAYS BEFORE
Organize your bar area.

**2** DAYS BEFORE
Hit the store.

**1** DAY BEFORE
Prep any food ahead of time.

**WINE CLUB MEETING**

**1** DAY AFTER
Save memorable labels. Download digi pics.

**2** DAYS AFTER
E-mail thank-yous to wine club guests; include digi pics.

*become a*
*bubblehead*
champagne

*Forget* empty promises of weight loss, quitting smoking, or getting out of debt—this year's New Year's resolution is right there bubbling up under your nose: Resolve to become a die-hard bubbly drinker (or bubblehead, as we say in the wine world). It's a resolution you'll love to keep, and

all that's required is that you take an oath to drink sparklers all year round.

These ticklers are not just for weddings or New Year's Eve—as you're about to discover. Champagne and sparkling wines almost always guarantee a good time every time you drink them, and that makes them the perfect way to kick off your wine club. And you'll be surprised how well sparklers pair with food.

So start the New Year with a pop—and don't stop!

### Getting to Know Champagne

Really. How much do you need to know to enjoy Champagne? Not a lot, that's for sure—you've probably already raised a glass or two in your life and had a fine old time with it no matter if you could pinpoint Champagne on a map (yes—it's a place). Ready to delve a little deeper? Here's a crash course.

### First—the Word on Champagne

Ever notice how sometimes wines that bubble

Bubble Bubble
Bubble Bubble Bubble Bubble
Bubble Bubble Bubble Bubble Bubble
Bubble Bubble Bubble Bubble Bubble
Bubble Bubble Bubble Bubble Bubble
Bubble Bubble Bubble Bubble Bubble Bubble
bble Bubble

are called Champagne, and other times they're called sparkling wine or even something else? What's with that? Any wine that sparkles can be called sparkling wine, but not all wine that sparkles can be called Champagne. Technically, to be called Champagne—with that all-important capital "C"—the bubbly must come from Champagne, a region in the northeast of France. So out of respect (and because French Champagne makers tend to get a weensy bit territorial about these things), we call all other bubblies "sparkling wines." Specific sparkling wines from other parts of the world go by different monikers, including

**Cava:** Bubbly from Spain.

**Vin mousseux:** French sparkling wine produced outside the Champagne region.

**Spumante:** Fully sparkling bubbly from Italy.

**Frizzante:** Lightly sparkling bubbly from Italy.

**Sekt:** Bubbly from Germany. Never heard of it? Don't worry—most people haven't. It's not

### ✦ ✦ ✦ $$$$ AND SENSE ✦ ✦ ✦

Whenever you do a wine tasting, there will be some wines that are more expensive than others. For example, whoever brings a traditional French Champagne will surely shell out more dough than the person assigned to bring the Spanish Cava. Work this out among your friends, perhaps with a rotating schedule of who will buy the most expensive wine each month. Or let two wine club members pitch in on the month's most expensive pick. Keep it fair—you don't want to start the club off with any hard feelings!

widely available, so plan on learning about this one somewhere down the tasting line.

Note that bubbly from California, Australia, or anywhere else not listed is simply referred to as sparkling wine. Sparkling wines produced in particular winegrowing regions often go by more specific names. For example, Prosecco is an Italian sparkling wine made in the Veneto region of Italy. I could tell you more—but the best way to learn about these sparklers is to taste them, not to read about them. And you'll be doing that soon enough.

### Make Mine Méthode Champenoise

Sure, now and then it's great to pop the cork on a bona fide Champagne—from the Champagne region of France—but most of us can't afford these world-renowned bubblies on a regular basis. Happily, it's easy to find high-quality sparkling wines from elsewhere in the world that can bring a lift to the occasion without emptying your wallet. To find one, it helps to look for the words *méthode champenoise* on a bottle's label. This means that the sparkling wine inside has been produced using the intricate, labor-intensive methods used to make true Champagne. Such sparklers will generally be better than those made by the less expensive *charmat* method (sometimes called "bulk process" in the United States), which involves bulk fermentation of the wine in tanks.

### Blanc de What?

Another tidbit that's helpful to know about sparkling wines is this *blanc de blanc* business. If you see these terms on a bottle, they're telling you—in that sexy and mysterious (OK, baffling) French way—what grapes were used to make the wine:

**Blanc de blanc:** This term literally means "white from white" and refers to white Champagne made from Chardonnay, a white grape.

**Blanc de noir:** This term literally means "white from black" and refers to white Champagne made from Pinot Noir, a red grape.

**Rosé:** If you see "rosé" on a bubbly's label, what's inside will be pink and sparkling.

### Oh, You Brut!

What about that word "brut" you sometimes spot on the label? No, it doesn't mean the stuff inside is going to slap anyone around. What it does mean is that what's inside is dry. Here are other terms that clue you into the level of sweetness, from sweet to dry:

**Doux or dolce:** This means "sweet" in French and Italian, respectively.

**Demi-sec:** This literally means "half dry"—which is really pretty sweet.

**Extra-dry or extra-sec:** This, confusingly, is not quite as dry as brut.

**Brut:** The word to look for if you want something really dry.

**Ultra brut, extra brut, or natural:** This is as brut as it gets—really, really dry.

Please don't sit around and try to memorize this stuff. Just remember to look for the word "brut" if you don't like any tinge of sweetness in your wine. The rest you'll learn as you drink.

### Was It a Good Year?

When you see a date on a wine bottle's label, this is its vintage; it refers to the year the grapes were harvested. However, you might

* * * * * * * * * * * * * * * * * * * * * * * * * * * * * * * * * *

## IF THE GLASS FITS …

So how are you going to get those bubbles into your mouth? There are lots of styles of champagne glasses out there. Which one's the best? Here's my take:

**The coupe:** Very old-school. It's been said that these glasses were fashioned after Marie Antoinette's breasts; while that makes a great story, the glasses are a lousy home for bubbles. The wide mouths let the bubbles escape too quickly.

**The trumpet glass:** Sleek and oh-so-now, but you're choosing fashion over function (a good move with a slinky party outfit, a not-so-good move with a champagne flute). With this stemless glass, the wine warms up in your hand, and the bubbles escape too quickly from the wide mouth.

**The flute:** We're getting closer. Look for a long and slender stem and a small mouth so those beautiful bubbles cannot escape so quickly.

**The tulip:** Best yet. With its slender stem, good-size bowl, and slightly curved lip, this is my top pick for appreciating the aroma of your bubbly.

* * * * * * * * * * * * * * * * * * * * * * * * * * * * * * * * * *

notice that many Champagnes and sparkling wines do not have a vintage listed on them. Such sparklers are nonvintage (NV), which means they're made of grapes harvested from a variety of years. This does not mean they're bad or even mediocre sparklers; in fact, even well-known French Champagnes like Moët & Chandon White Star are often nonvintage. That's because producers pick and choose among the grapes from a variety of years to achieve the style of Champagne or sparkling wine they desire.

Some years—including 1990 and 1995—the quality of the grapes is so amazing that the winemaker may deem it a vintage year and bottle some wines that highlight this year. Vintage Champagnes and sparkling wines are usually considered higher quality and thus command a higher price; California

### * * * * SHAKE IT UP * * * *

What about that celebratory way of hosing someone down with a bottle of Champagne? Do it with the cheap stuff. And remember— wait until AFTER you've uncorked the bottle to shake it. If you shake first you're guaranteed a renegade cork, likely to send someone to the emergency room.

winemakers often designate vintages for many of their top-quality sparkling wines.

Curious about vintages? In general, vintages are more important for red wines than white, so let's leave the topic there for now. You'll learn more about vintages where they really matter—in the Cabernet Sauvignon chapter, ahead.

### * * * THE MONA LISA * * *

Taittinger Brut Millesime 1998, France; $70. A vintage Champagne is always a special treat because it is usually made in small batches and only from outstanding harvests. At first glance of this wine, you can't miss the very dense mousse (the white foam at the top of the glass) and ohh-sooo-many petite bubbles. Layered aromas of floral perfumes, grapefruit, and toasty notes, and yummy citrus flavors leave your mouth watering. Remember, this is a real splurge, so invest only if you plan on savoring every sip.

### * * * THE SALVADOR DALÍ * * *

Rosa Regale Brachetto d'Acqui, Italy; about $19. A totally sexy sparkling wine, this one's on the sweeter side and is the essence of romance, with its raspberry-colored juice, its rose petal aroma, and the way that it pairs perfectly with chocolate anything. It's great as an aperitif (a drink to start off and get your taste buds dancing), as a dessert wine, or anytime for a romantic rendezvous. I bought this one for my husband on our first Valentine's Day, and he still remembers it. At this price, it's a steal, and you'll remember each and every teeny, tiny, seductive little bubble.

**Dom and the Veuve—Ever Heard of Them?**
Two of the most famous of all French Champagnes are named after people—a monk and a widow. By name you know the monk, Dom Perignon. And by sight you probably know the widow Clicquot, or Veuve Clicquot—that loud yellow label that makes its way to plenty of parties. These two wines are named for people who, as history has it, played major roles in the development of the bubbly we drink today.

It may be the rich history or the name recognition, but whatever the reason, Dom P. and Veuve C. can break the bank. French Champagne is always more expensive, but you don't have to spend a fortune to learn about bubbles. Once you've tasted your way through the rest, you may find yourself craving a French tickle—and by all means indulge. As with all wines, French Champagne prices are driven up by reputation and availability. There are California sparklers that have been said to be just as good as, if not better than, some French bubbly. Whether you prefer fuller bubbles or tiny bubbles, a sweet note or an extra-dry finish, your personal preference should drive your purchase, not famous names or location of origin.

### Chill Out—at the Right Temperature
Most wine books recommend serving sparkling wines at 41 to 47 degrees. I think around 43 to 50 is more like it. You see, the colder a wine is, the more flavors are masked—and believe me, you'll want to taste the flavors of your Champagne and sparkling wines.

Keep in mind that most refrigerators are set at about 40 degrees F, so you may need to do some adjusting before you serve your sparklers. If you think they're too cold coming directly from the fridge, then keep the bottle on the countertop for about half an hour before serving. Remember, too, that once wine is poured it will continue to warm up as you sip and talk and eat and laugh and do all those wonderful things you do at parties. And while you're doing all those things, stop and take a sip and notice your wine—because it's doing something too: Its flavors and aromas are changing as it warms in your glass. When this happens, that's a good thing—it helps you notice flavors in wine.

But you know what? If you prefer your sparkler supercold, go ahead and serve it that way, straight from the fridge. But do give my slightly less frigid way a try at least once. I think you'll like what you notice.

A warning about warm sparkling wine: It will explode upon opening. Don't believe me? I'll never forget the day I was going to make a Champagne sorbet with a bottle that had been sitting on my countertop for a couple of hours.

**✷✷ BANG FOR YOUR BUCK ✷✷**
Cava from Spain is the way to go here, as most will be under $20. If you're hosting a party on a budget, lay in a supply of Cristalino Brut; at around $9 a bottle, it's a true bargain. For an inexpensive but festive gift, look for Segura Viudas at $20; it comes in a beautiful metal-crested bottle.

Champagne is so extraordinary, it comes with its own special lingo. These words aren't essential to know, but you'll love the way they roll off your tongue as you sip your newfound favorites:

**Mousse:** The foam on top when you pour the bubbly.

**Perlage:** The small strings of tiny bubbles you see streaming through your wine. Think of tiny pearl necklaces.

**Pètillance:** French for "that little buzz in the mouth that's so exciting when you drink Champagne."

**Cuvée:** Refers to a blend of wines. Many sparklers are made from a blend (or cuvée) of still wines from different years. Sometimes you'll see the word cuvée on a label; this simply lets you know that it is a blend of juices and not 100% Chardonnay like a blanc de blanc.

---

I began to open it, and as soon as the cage was loose, that cork popped up faster than a Google IPO and left a dent in my kitchen ceiling as an ever-present reminder to keep it cool.

### Pulling the Plug with Finesse

People often talk of "popping a cork," but making the cork go "pop" is just one way to do it. Certainly that popping sound is festive, but the downside is that you'll lose a little of the bubbly as the cork sails out. Not a good thing when you're drinking Dom.

Instead of going for the pop, coax the cork out with a whisper—it's sexier, and you'll save more of the good stuff for sipping. To do this, first gather the gear. You'll need:

**A linen napkin,** a serviette, or a clean dish towel. Placing the linen between your palm and the cork creates more of a pocket to catch that cork—a surefire way to keep your eyesight for the New Year!

**The appropriate number of glasses.** Have them ready and waiting—once the bottle's open, you'll want to pour it on!

Next, follow these steps:

**Hold It!** It's important to be comfortable

---

### YOU'LL NEVER FORGET IT

Wash one flute in the dishwasher and another by hand. Now, pour one of your favorite sparkling wines in that hand-washed glass. Oh, that's beautiful! OK, now try your sparkler in the machine-washed glass. Oh, that's ... weird. What happened to the bubbles? That's right— once you taste what residual soap does to your sparkling wine's bubbles and body, you'll never put your glasses in the dishwasher again.

Another tidbit I've learned along the way: Bob Iantosca, winemaker at Gloria Ferrer vineyards in Napa, once noticed that the bubblies they poured at home into their hand-washed and hand-dried glassware were looking a little flat and lacked that ring of foam that looks so nice. The culprit? "The fabric softener on the sheets used in the dryer," says Iantosca. He explains that when they started to dry glasses with paper towels as opposed to cloth, the problem vanished—the bubbles were beautiful again.

Moral of the story? Hand wash. And hand dry—with paper towels or lint-free cloths.

Sparkling Shiraz? Yes, they've done it down under. Hardy's Sparkling Shiraz is a brilliant red wine with bubbles. I'll be honest—it confuses me a little bit. The first thing I see is the deep, dark color, which tricks me into thinking I'm having a glass of red wine. Then when it hits my mouth, it bubbles—my brain just can't comprehend it. It's a novelty item—and like many novelty items, some people will love it, some won't. I don't, but you might—so give it a go if you're intrigued. Besides, with its rich red color, it may be just the thing for Valentine's Day.

with the bottle in your hands. You should grip the bottle in your weaker hand at the base, placing your stronger hand on top of that cork to fight the pressure in the bottle.

**Peel Away:** Remove the foil from the wire cage that wraps the cork; underneath, you'll see the cage and a little round tab. Holding down the cork with a cloth napkin or a kitchen towel, bend the tab down and unwind it to loosen and remove the wire cage. Do this very carefully because once you loosen the cage, the cork can go at any moment.

**Do the Twist:** Tilt the bottle away from you (and everyone else!) at a 45-degree angle.

### * TO SWIRL OR NOT TO SWIRL? *

With Champagne that is definitely a question! Once, I was on a trip with a group of wine journalists when one rudely said to another, "You shouldn't swirl Champagne; it just isn't done!" The swirler's jaw dropped. Well, the truth is that when you're a wine geek, after a while you'll start swirling everything—even glasses of water! So live lightly and don't take yourself or your wine so seriously, and swirl if you want to swirl.

With the cloth still over the top of the bottle, grasp the cork with one hand and gently twist the bottle—not the cork—with the other. Let the pressure in the bottle gently force out the cork, and let your cloth catch the cork and any small sprays of foam. Remember—twist the bottle, not the cork, because twisting the cork can cause it to tear and break.

**Hiss or Pop?:** The amount of pressure you keep on the cork will determine whether you create an elegant hiss or a head-turning pop. For a seductive hiss, make that baby wait—that is, keep more pressure on the cork as you let it slowly make its way out.

**Pour It On:** We've all underestimated the bubbles in bubbly and ended up with a volcanic eruption from our champagne flutes. If you want to drink this stuff (as opposed to wear it), pour your sparkler in two steps. Start with a 1-ounce pour (called "priming the glass"). Let the bubbles settle, then finish off pouring until the glass is about two-thirds full. This leaves a place for those boisterous bubbles to go.

### Save the Bubbles!

I recommend drinking sparkling wines as soon as you open them—life's short, and those bubbles won't last forever. However, if

*A toast to you!*

I recommend drinking sparkling wines as soon as you open them—life's short, and those bubbles won't last forever.

you do find yourself with leftovers, there are a couple of ways to save the fizz. If you drink a lot of sparkling wines, you may want to invest in a gizmo called a Champagne clamshell, available at wine shops and gourmet stores. To use, place the rubber stopper on the bottle with the two stainless-steel side clips open, then press the clips down firmly to lock the stopper in place. Or take some of the foil you used for the blind tasting and put

it into the neck of the bottle, bunching it up so that it fits in the bottle about an inch down but still hangs over the mouth.

Either option will help you save your bubbles. The clamshell will save your bubbles for three to four days, and the foil will preserve them until lunch the next day, and maybe even dinner. If your bubbles go flat, cork the bottle and keep it in the fridge to use for cooking when a dry white wine is called for (as long as your sparkler was dry).

### January's Picks

Kick off your wine club with a "world tour" of Champagne and sparkling wines. This way, you can get a taste for the variety of styles available from countries famous for their bubblies. Here are my picks:

**1. Cava from Spain:** Look for a bottle in the $6 to $12 range.

**2. Prosecco from Italy:** In the $10 to $15 range.

**3. Sparkling wine from California:** In the $20 to $25 range.

**4. Champagne from Champagne, France:** These will be more expensive; look for a bottle in the $30 to $45 range.

**5. Blanc de blanc:** In the $20 to $30 range.

**6. Blanc de noir:** In the $25 to $40 range.

**7. Ringer:** It's more than perfect to include a sparkling white grape juice or nonalcoholic sparkling wine in your tasting. In fact, doing so will help you see what alcohol contributes (besides a buzz!) to wine. Also, it's always appropriate to offer a nonalcoholic beverage for guests who don't drink or who drink very little.

# GET YOUR DRINK ON

*Once you have your chilled bubblies lined up, foil wrapped, numbered, opened up, and ready for drinking, get out your tasting note sheets and take some sips. I've listed, in each category, some qualities you might notice while you're tasting. Feel free to follow along as you taste, or wing it!*

**COLOR:** Sparkling wines will range in color most significantly because of style. For example, blanc de noirs range from having a hay color to a pinkish tint, and rosés will look salmon colored to pink. You'll notice that even the clear or white sparklers will range in color; some Proseccos may look incredibly clear and light—almost watery. Other sparklers, like vintage Champagne, will have deeper golden hues. Take note of the bubbles—if they are large or small, or if there are lots of streams or just a few. The amount of bubbles and their size are really manipulated by each winemaker. Not all tiny bubbles are attributed to Champagne, France. Some California bubblies are just as elegant with endless streams of teensy-weensy bubbles. In the same respect, there are sparklers from both France and California that come bearing big bubbles.

**AROMA:** Some of the things you'll smell in sparklers include yeasty or toasty scents, citrus, pears, apples, and florals. Prosecco is often noted for its peach and apricot scent, while French Champagne and California sparklers bring to the table aromas of freshly baked bread, yeast, and toast along with fruity aromas. And often aromas of dried strawberries, ripe raspberries, and cherries show in blanc de noirs.

**TASTE:** Sparklers show every taste from citrus to spice. Depending on the winemaker, the aging process, and where the grapes grow, you can look for everything from toast flavor to grapefruit notes. The important thing is that the flavors balance one other. Sweetness shouldn't mask acid, for example—the two should play well together.

**BODY:** Think of milk again. When it comes to sparklers, unless they are dessert wines, they should be light-bodied. Other words you may be searching for are clean, crisp, or, my favorite, "twinkly"—like little stars in your mouth. Look at those bubbles again—do the wines with more bubbles make your mouth feel different? You'll notice that, in general, the Italian sparklers have less assertive bubbles. Some sparklers barely fizz, while most French and California sparkling wines maintain strong necklaces of bubbles from your first sip to your last.

In general, the more elegant the wine, the more you'll see a lasting mousse and numerous strands of tiny bubbles. While bigger bubbles are fun, it's the finesse of millions of tiny bubbles that really tickles my fancy.

**FINISH:** Bubblies will never linger as long as big red wines. Most will be clean and crisp. Some will linger sweetly, and with age you'll find a longer finish. In general, bubblies will make your mouth salivate or maybe even pucker up. And most French Champagne and California sparklers that carry aromas of baked bread will usually end with a creamy midpalate finish. When thinking about the finish of a sparkler, you should pay attention to how your mouth feels as well as how long those sensations linger.

**RINGER:** At first sight, nonalcoholic sparkling wine and grape juice will look more viscous in the glass. When you smell the nonalcoholic spritzer, you will notice the absence of alcohol, and you will get a very fruity nose. Upon sipping you will surely notice the sugar content. Nonalcoholic sparklers and sparkling white grape juice tend to be heavier on the palate and a bit cloying.

**T**hese tempting tastes have been designed to enhance your bubbly experience by bridging, contrasting, or complementing the flavors of the food and wine. You'll see some dishes, such as the Macerated Berries, call for Champagne or sparkling wine in the recipes themselves to bridge what you're eating with what you're sipping. Other tastes offer a contrast to the wine; for example, when sipping sparkling wine after nibbling on the Creamy Onion Tart, you'll find the bubbly cleanses the palate.

With the oysters, you'll get a delicious exercise in a food-and-wine paring strategy called complementing the flavors. Freshly shucked oysters create a clean feeling in your mouth; so does Champagne. The Classic Mignonette will cause your cheeks to salivate and give you a craving for more; sparkling wines do pretty much the same thing. There's also something ritualistic about eating oysters—and the same goes for drinking Champagne. Yes—these two are a match made in heaven.

\* \* \* \* \* \* \* \* \* \* \* \* \* \* \* \* \* \* \* \* \* \* \*

# STRAWBERRIES TIRAMISÚ

*I'm a tiramisu addict. I've tried mascarpone cheese, cocoa powder, and confectioner's sugar on almost everything. Strawberries and Champagne are a classic match, but I made things a little more interesting. With one bite you get the juicy strawberry, creamy cheese, and sweet chocolate. Alone these are delightful, but with bubbly they're straight-up addictive.*

| | |
|---|---|
| 12 | large strawberries |
| ½ | cup mascarpone cheese, softened |
| 2 | teaspoons confectioner's sugar, sifted |
| 3 | ounces dark chocolate, chopped |

1. Using a small, sharp knife, remove a small slice from the bottom tip of each strawberry; hollow out the center. Keep the green stem end intact.

2. In a small bowl combine mascarpone cheese and confectioner's sugar. Spoon cheese mixture into a piping bag fitted with a small round tip. (Or place cheese mixture in a resealable plastic bag with a corner snipped off.) Pipe a little bit of the cheese mixture into the center of each strawberry.

3. Melt the chocolate in a double boiler. Dip the strawberries into melted chocolate; let excess chocolate drip off. Place dipped strawberries on a cookie sheet lined with parchment paper or waxed paper. Let stand until set. Refrigerate for up to 6 hours.

**Makes 12 appetizers**

Note: If you don't have a piping bag and a few tips, I encourage you to buy them. You can find them in most grocery stores or online. They make hors d'oeuvres so much cuter. And having the right tool for the job is much easier than wrangling with a plastic zip-top bag.

# OYSTERS ON THE HALF SHELL
## with Classic Mignonette

*What's sexier than Champagne and caviar? Champagne and oysters! The briny oysters and the Classic Mignonette will explode with acid in your mouth, and a follow-up sip of bubbly is sure to keep that sensation lingering a little longer. It's one of those life experiences everyone must try at least once!*

| | |
|---|---|
| 1 | cup diced shallots (5 medium shallots) |
| ¾ | cup red wine vinegar |
| ¼ | cup dry red wine |
| ¼ | cup fresh lemon juice (2 medium lemons) |
| ¼ | teaspoon kosher salt |
| ⅛ | teaspoon cracked black pepper |
| 20 | oysters in shells |
| ¼ | cup chopped fresh chives |

1. In a medium bowl combine shallots, vinegar, wine, lemon juice, salt, and pepper. Let stand about 20 minutes or until shallots are softened. (The shallot mixture can be made a week in advance.)

2. Meanwhile, clean all your oysters under cold running water. Hold an oyster in a clean, heavy hand towel. Insert the tip of an oyster knife (or other blunt-tipped knife) into the hinge of the shell. (This is where the top and bottom shells come together.) Move the blade along the inside of the upper shells to separate the top and bottom shell. Slide the knife under the oyster to sever it from the bottom shell. Repeat with remaining oysters. Discard the flat top shells; wash the deep bottom shells. Place each oyster in a shell. (If you like, instead of discarding the liquid in the shells, called oyster liquor, slurp it out.)

3. To serve, use a small spoon to top each oyster with some of the shallot mixture. Sprinkle lightly with chives.

**Makes 20 appetizers**

Note on vinegar: The traditional mignonette, that tangy vinegar mixture above, is made with red wine vinegar. But since we're talking Champagne here, you may want to use Champagne vinegar. And just like the rules with the one you drink, real Champagne vinegar should be made with Champagne from Champagne … you following me here?

# SPICY SAUSAGE–STUFFED MUSHROOMS

*My husband comes from an Italian-American family in New Jersey and waits all year for his uncle Al's stuffed mushrooms at Thanksgiving. I decided he shouldn't have to long for them and came up with my own version. The spicy sausage stuffed into an earthy mushroom is full of flavor, but it's also full of heat. You'll notice your mouth go up a few more degrees when you follow it with a sip of Champagne.*

36 large fresh white button mushrooms

1 pound uncooked spicy Italian sausage links (remove casings)

1 tablespoon olive oil

½ cup grated Parmesan cheese

¼ cup Italian-seasoned fine dry bread crumbs

1 slightly beaten egg

1. Preheat oven to 350°F. Rinse and drain mushrooms. Remove stems and discard. Set mushroom caps aside.

2. For stuffing, in a large skillet cook sausage in hot olive oil over medium heat until brown. Use a wooden spoon to break up the sausage as you cook it. Drain off fat. In a bowl stir together ¼ cup of the Parmesan cheese, the bread crumbs, and egg. Stir in the sausage.

3. Use a small spoon to fill the mushroom caps with the stuffing. Place the stuffed mushrooms in a large broiler-proof baking pan. Bake for 20 to 25 minutes or until heated through. Remove from oven. Drain off any liquid from the bottom of the baking pan.

4. Preheat broiler. Sprinkle mushrooms with the remaining ¼ cup Parmesan cheese. Broil for 2 to 3 minutes or just until cheese melts and browns.

**Makes 36 appetizers**

Note: You can make the stuffed mushrooms (without the Parmesan cheese topping) up to three days in advance. Cover and chill until ready to serve. Reheat in a 300°F oven about 20 minutes and finish under the broiler as instructed above. If you prefer a milder bite but still want the flavor, use sweet Italian sausage instead of the spicy Italian sausage.

# CREAMY ONION TART

*Oscar's Restaurant in Atlanta, Georgia, serves this for all of its special parties. The chef, Todd Immel, was kind enough to share some of his secrets so that I could transform it for the home cook. The creamy consistency, the sweetness of the onions, and the delicate crust add up to a delish bite.*

| | |
|---|---|
| 1 | rolled refrigerated unbaked piecrust |
| 1 | tablespoon unsalted butter |
| 2 | cups diced sweet onion (such as Vidalia) (1 large onion) |
| 1 | teaspoon kosher salt |
| | Dash black pepper |
| 2 | egg yolks |
| ¼ | cup plus 1 tablespoon half-and-half or light cream |
| ½ | teaspoon freshly grated nutmeg |

**1.** Preheat oven to 400°F.

**2.** For crust, line an 8×8×2-inch baking pan with a 12×14-inch piece of parchment paper. This will make removing the dough easier. Press the piecrust into the pan. Trim dough so that it is only ¾ inch high on the edges. Using a fork, prick the bottom and sides of the dough. Bake for 9 minutes. Cool on a wire rack.

**3.** Reduce oven temperature to 375°F. For onion filling, in a medium nonstick skillet melt butter over medium heat. Add onion, ½ teaspoon of the salt, and pepper. Cook and stir for 10 to 12 minutes or until onion is translucent. Remove skillet from heat.

**4.** In a small bowl combine egg yolks and ¼ cup half-and-half; stir into skillet with onion filling. Transfer filling to a bowl; stir in the remaining 1 tablespoon half-and-half, the remaining ½ teaspoon salt, and nutmeg. Place in the freezer for 5 minutes to cool; stir. Return to freezer for 5 minutes more. The mixture should be slightly warm but not hot.

**5.** Pour filling over crust. Bake about 12 minutes or until filling is set. Remove baking pan from oven. Preheat broiler. Broil for 2 to 3 minutes or just until top is golden brown.

**6.** Let stand for 5 minutes. Use the parchment paper to lift tart out of pan; cut into 24 to 48 pieces.

**Makes 24 appetizers**

Note: The filling can be made and refrigerated 2 days in advance. Let the filling come to room temperature before using.

# CHERRY-GLAZED BRIE

*This recipe is so simple and delicious, it will make even an anti-cook want to get into the kitchen. The creamy cheese counters the sweet yet tart cherry topping. And both are better paired with the bubbly.*

| | |
|---|---|
| 2 | small rounds Brie cheese (4 to 6 inches in diameter) or 1 large round (8 inches in diameter) |
| 1 | 12-ounce bag frozen unsweetened, pitted dark sweet cherries |
| 3/4 | cup water |
| 1/2 | cup sugar |
| 1 | tablespoon pure vanilla extract |
| 1/8 | teaspoon freshly grated nutmeg |
| 1/8 | teaspoon cayenne pepper |
| 1 1/2 | tablespoons cornstarch |
| 1 1/2 | tablespoons water |

1. Slice both of the small rounds of Brie into 12 pieces each, keeping them in a round shape. (If using a large round, slice into 24 pieces.)

2. For cherry glaze, in a saucepan combine cherries, the ¾ cup water, and sugar. Bring to a boil. Reduce heat and cook for 5 minutes. Stir in vanilla, nutmeg, and cayenne pepper. Remove from heat. Cool slightly. Transfer to a blender. Cover and blend until pureed. (Make sure to hold a towel securely over the blender lid before turning on the power. Keep your hand in place until you are finished pureeing to prevent any messy explosions. Or use an immersion blender to puree cherry glaze right in the saucepan). Return glaze to saucepan.

3. In a small bowl combine cornstarch and the 1½ tablespoons water; stir until smooth. Using a whisk, combine cornstarch mixture with cherry glaze in saucepan. Bring to a boil. Boil for 1 minute. Remove from heat. Cover and chill. Pour as much or as little of the cherry glaze as you like over the Brie; chill. You can freeze any remaining glaze for up to 1 month. You can also make the cherry glaze 1 week in advance.

**Makes 24 appetizers**

# MACERATED BERRIES
## *and Whipped Cream*

*This recipe is foolproof and will make your guests glad they came. We all eat with our eyes, so presentation is key. A little nip of bubbly with the berries creates a nice bridge to the sparkler you're sipping. This also makes a fantastic dessert in the middle of summer.*

| | |
|---|---|
| 2 ½ | cups raspberries |
| 2½ | cups blueberries |
| ¼ | cup sugar |
| 2 | tablespoons sparkling wine |
| 1½ | cups whipping cream |
| 1½ | tablespoons confectioner's sugar |
| 2½ | tablespoons rose water* |

1. Place the raspberries and blueberries in separate bowls. Sprinkle each with 2 tablespoons of the sugar and 1 tablespoon of the sparkling wine. Toss berries gently; let stand at room temperature for 1 hour.

2. Meanwhile, chill a medium mixing bowl and the beaters of an electric mixer. In chilled bowl beat whipping cream, confectioner's sugar, and rose water on medium speed until soft peaks form.

3. In 10 champagne flutes layer raspberries, piped whipped cream mixture, and blueberries. Fill glasses half full. (If you don't have enough champagne flutes, serve this in any wineglass, preferably a dainty dessert wineglass.) Use a pastry bag with a large tip to pipe the whipped cream into the flutes. (Or place the whipped cream in a resealable plastic bag with a corner snipped off.) This way is much neater than using a spoon. But if you have neither a pastry bag nor a plastic bag, by all means use a spoon. Just be careful not to get whipped cream all over the glasses.

**Makes 10 servings**

### NO-COOK OPTIONS

A few no-cook options for this month:

★ Try serving fresh strawberries to complement the clean, crisp sparkling wine.

★ Serve a plate of rich, dark chocolate to contrast the fruit flavors of the wine.

★ Serve purchased vanilla or tapioca pudding in wineglasses. The vanilla flavor of the pudding will balance the vanilla notes in the bubbly. The crispness of the sparklers will cut through the creamy puddings. And the textural explosion of serving bubbly with that pearly tapioca makes for a phenomenal match.

On the savory side, you can always serve a platter of spicy and salty cured meats, like salami, pepperoni, and prosciutto.

*Note: If you can't find rose water, you can flavor your whipped cream with any flavor of extract. Vanilla, lemon, mint, and almond all work well. Just make sure that you reduce the amount to 1 tablespoon.

# cabernet
## *by the flight*

***With*** *Valentine's Day smack-dab in the middle of February, this month is about roses, romance, and all things red. Tap into the spirit by getting to know red wines. Cabernet Sauvignon is a great place to start because this red wine is widely available and wildly popular. This month you may*

simply sip the vino or mix it up with a little numbers game (involving vintage—the year the grapes were harvested). Then you can decide for yourself whether vintage is an important factor when you're purchasing wine. Along the way you'll learn about tasting flights of wine and why Cabernet Sauvignon is king in California. You'll also be tempted with some aphrodisiacs.

If you prefer not to have this month's gathering focus on the romantic holiday, no

problem. You need nothing more than a good bottle of red and some good company to make February fabulous.

### Getting to Know Cab

First of all, let's get hip to the lingo. Cabernet Sauvignon is a mouthful to say, so it's often just called Cab for short. No one will confuse it with that other Cabernet—the lesser-known Cabernet Franc—because that one's called Cab Franc for short.

### The Grape That Grows Just About Anywhere

Not long ago, I got a call from Kelly Brown, a friend of mine (who also happens to be a wine freak). I mentioned that I was in the process of exploring the wines of Spain.

"So you're drinking some Cabs then, right?" she asked.

I told her that indeed I was.

"There's just nowhere that grape doesn't grow," she laughed. "I bet you could throw it in the desert, and before you know it, vines would be everywhere."

She even bet me I could grow them in the window box of my Manhattan apartment and use them to make my own wine, "Vin de Midtown." I seriously thought about it, until I realized I'd have a little difficulty finding rootstocks at my neighborhood market.

However, it's true. Cabernet Sauvignon grows just about anywhere; nearly every wine-growing country has its Cab. Many of the famous wines of France's Bordeaux region are based on Cabernet Sauvignon. California is definitely Cabernet country (some of California's Napa Valley Cabs have been awarded top honors—even by the French). Chile and Australia are particularly well-known for great Cabs, and South Africa is right on their heels. Now even the East is red, with China producing—yes, you have it—Cab.

### Time to Talk Tannins

Now that we're talking Cab, this is the perfect time to tell you about tannins, because Cabernet Sauvignon is full of them. When you sip a red wine and you are left with a dry feeling in your mouth—sometimes on the roof, sometimes on the sides—that is the tannins at work (or shall we say play?). The sensation is similar to the feeling you get if you drink a cup of very strong tea.

What are these things—and what are they doing in your wine? Tannins come from grape seeds, stems, and skins and from the oak barrels used to age wine. In young red wine, the tannins can be very strong and astringent, but

---

* * * * * * * * * * * * * **WINE TREND** * * * * * * * * * * * * *

Here are a couple of gadgets, priced under $20, that will help keep your wine drinkable after you've opened the bottle.

Vacu Vin Vacuum Wine Saver: My brother-in-law gave us one of these a few years ago, and we've been using it ever since. To use, you place the small reusable rubber stopper into the mouth of the bottle and then use the small hand pump to pull out the remaining air in the bottle. This slows down the oxidation of the wine. I find we get at least one and a half more good days on from open bottle of red and up to a week from an open bottle of white.

Wine Saver Concerto: This is the same product as the Vacu Vin but with a newer, sleek style. The difference is that this one's pump makes a clicking noise once you have reached the correct vacuum level. At around $17 you're really paying only for the new look, as I find the original does just as good a job.

What about those small canisters of nitrogen that you spray in the bottle before recorking, allegedly to help save the wine? I've never had a good experience with them and don't know anyone who has.

* * * * * * * * * * * * * * * * * * * * * * * * * * * *

as the wine ages, the tannins soften and round out. Tannins give structure to red wines along with added sensations; they are an important part of the personality of big reds and make red wines so perfect for pairing with heavier foods like steak and grilled meats.

*Tannins give structure to red wines, along with added sensations as you sip; they are an important part of the personality of big reds and make red wines so perfect for pairing with heavier foods like steak and grilled meats.*

As you sip Cabs this month, notice the tannins. If your mouth feels like cotton after you sip a big red wine, that means the tannins are very strong; if you just slightly feel that dryness in your cheeks or across the roof of your mouth, then the tannins are soft. This isn't just wine-geek speak—the level of tannins is important, because if the tannins are too heavy and not balanced correctly with the fruit of the wine, they make big reds unpalatable with food.

One more thing about tannins: Ever pour out the last sips from a bottle only to see clumps of dark purple or brown sediment plunk into your glass? Those are from tannins too. As wine ages, tannins clump together, and along with the pigments and tartrates in the wine, they form a sediment that settles to the bottom of the bottle. It usually happens only in red wines, and if the clumps gross you out, you can decant the wine to remove them (see "Gunk in Your Glass," page 39).

### Vintage Matters—Or Does It?

In January, I told you a little bit about vintage—a term that refers to the year the grapes were harvested. I mentioned that many Champagnes are nonvintage; that is, they're made of a blend of wines from grapes harvested in different years. That's why you don't see a date on the bottles label.

On the other hand, still wines (ones without bubbles) are almost always labeled with the year the grapes were harvested.

The year the grapes were harvested. That's the definition of vintage on paper. Does the year matter to what's in the bottle—and in the glass?

It can matter a lot. The summer of 2003, for example, was so hot in France that the grapes shriveled up like raisins, leaving little juice and more overripe fruit flavors and

### ✳ ✳ BANG FOR YOUR BUCK ✳ ✳

In Italy and France, you can drink great wines for a couple bucks a bottle, but in the United States, we often pay more for juice from our own shores. If you dig deep, you are bound to find some picks that will pique your palate and please your wallet. For under $15 any of the following California Cabs deliver: Beringer "Founders' Estate," Liberty School Winery, and Ravenswood "Vintners Blend," and Trinchero Winery "Family Selection."

aromas. On the other hand, too much rain can plump up volume and dilute flavors and body. Grapes drowned by a sudden rainfall can burst, causing them to rot.

Think of weather as a "three bears" deal: It can't be too hot, too wet, or too dry. For a great vintage, it needs to be *just* right.

### Aging Wines

Vintage also matters because wines change as they age. For example, in a young red Cab, sometimes, though not always, alcohol can be the first thing you taste and smell. With time in the bottle, that harsh heat you experience on the palate from the alcohol mellows out. This allows all the flavors to meld and creates a more balanced wine.

Also, those in-your-face tannins in young red wines that make your mouth pucker like a fish will actually soften over the years, rounding out the mouth feel and balance of the wine. Because Cabernet Sauvignon has lots of tannins, it's often suggested that it age awhile in the bottle before you drink it. Some vintages need to be aged more than others simply because of qualities present that year. So when buying a Cab for your tasting, you might want to ask your wine merchant for one that's ready to drink now. Other than that, don't sweat the aging thing yet. After you've decided if collecting wine is your thang, then by all means dive in.

### Another View of Vintages

Even wine professionals don't agree on the importance of vintages. During one of my recent wine tastings, I was struck because I wasn't able to tell the difference between a '99 and a '00 Cab. A wee bit concerned (I mean, I do wine for a living—I should know these things!), I called a friend of mine, W. R. Tish, who also writes

---

### ★ ★ ★ THE MONA LISA ★ ★ ★

When celebrating Valentine's Day this month, why not pick up a super special Cab? I fell in love with Cosentino Wines on my first visit to Napa Valley. Try The Poet and M. Coz, two wines made in the Meritage style (that is, by blending grape varieties normally used in Bordeaux wines). With Cabernet, Merlot, and Cab Franc all mingling to create a complex structure with velvety colors, these wines epitomize the art of blending.

### ★ ★ ★ THE SALVADOR DALÍ ★ ★ ★

Diamond Mountain Cabernet Sauvignon is in the collectible category, though with small amounts made at higher price points, these gems may be hard to come by (some bottles command up to $175 upon release). No worries—there still are deals to be had on the mountain. Graeser Diamond Mountain Cab at around $35, Sterling Vineyards Diamond Mountain Ranch Cabernet at $40, and Dyer Vineyards at about $70 a bottle are steals considering that at auction some of these wines go for more than $400 a bottle.

Wanna know what you'll get for your money? How about saturated colors; ripe extracted fruit; chewy texture; smooth tannins; full palate; and aromas of black cherry, currant, violets, and a clean, mineral-like earthiness? At first glance you'll know why these wines have developed a strong cult following.

about wine. He had a different (and very reassuring) view on the topic:

"Vintages, eh? Variation from year to year is utterly overrated, in my humble palate's opinion. Age and variation from producer to producer matter more than differences in the mere vintage. And price matters most of all. A $65 2000 Napa Cab is a world away from a $10 2000 California Cab. And how many people in the world can truly spot the difference between a $10 Cab from 2000 and one from 2001? Again, it's not the year that's going to make or break anything. If you don't like a 1993 Barolo, you probably won't like a 1997 Barolo."

Some wine lovers obsess over the vintage on the label; others ignore it altogether. I fall somewhere in between. And you? If you can't tell the differences in vintages, don't worry. Instead, pocket the extra cash next time you head to the wine store, or spend it on something you absolutely love.

But before you know whether vintages matter to you, you've got to take a closer look … and taste.

## A Flight of Wine

In the wine world, a "flight" is a sampling of smaller pours of wine tasted side by side. Usually at least three and as many as eight wines are sampled in a flight. I love when restaurants offer flights of wine because it is so much more fun to taste your food with different wines. One flight is usually three small glasses of wine and costs a little more than one glass. Believe me, it's worth the trip.

There are generally two types of flights:

**Vertical Flight:** Tasting different vintages from the same producer; for example, you might taste a Hess Select Napa Valley Cabernet Sauvignon from the years '90, '91, '92, '96, '97, and '98.

**Horizontal Flight:** Tasting a particular varietal from different producers but all from the same vintage. For example, you might get California Napa Valley Cabs from Charles Krug, Sterling, Franciscan, and Cakebread, all from 2002.

Flights can vary even more. If you want to compare well-known varietals, smell and

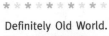

**Breathe:** You'll often hear people say to open a bottle of red well before it's poured so it can breathe. This is especially important for high-alcohol wines like Cabs and Zinfandel, and it helps young red wines to open up and show you what the future may hold once they have been aged. By exposing it to air you allow some of the alcohol to blow off and truly show the aromas of the wine. With swirling and decanting, big reds really breathe, bringing out their best characteristics.

**Extracted Fruit:** Extract refers to what is left over when you take the liquid away from the wine. When you see the words *"extracted fruit"* in tasting notes, this refers to a big, fruity, in-your-face kind of wine. A lot of California Cabs are described as having extracted fruits—which is exactly what the American palate loves. However, not all wine lovers agree. Some say that overextraction takes away from the delicacy and balance of a wine.

**Old World Wine:** A general term used for wines produced in Europe. Those Cabs from Bordeaux?

Definitely Old World.

**New World Wine:** A general term for wines produced in the Americas, Australia, New Zealand, and South Africa. Basically anywhere except Europe is New World.

**BIG:** When it comes to wine, this term is used for those that fill your taste buds with big flavors, your nose with big aromas, and your mouth with full body. They hold their own when paired with heavy foods and are too big to pair with delicacies of the sea. Cabs, Zinfandel, and Syrah are the ringleaders in the "big wine" arena, and depending on the winemaker, sometimes Merlot can be a big-boy wine too.

**Balance:** When a wine is balanced, the sugar, acidity, fruit, tannin, alcohol, and wood are all present without hiding or dominating each other. If you sip a Cabernet Sauvignon and taste only tannins, it is far from balanced. But when you taste a Cabernet that is balanced, you will note each of the components and see how, when in harmony, the wine feels rich and elegant.

---

taste three major reds (try Cabernet Sauvignon, Merlot, and Shiraz) and three major whites (try Chardonnay, Sauvignon Blanc, and Riesling). Or taste varietals country by country or region by region.

You get the picture.

### Temperature Forecast

If Cab is too cold, the flavors and aromas will be muted, but if it is too warm, it will feel flabby when you sip it. Remember Goldilocks—we're going for "just right."

Therefore, aim to serve your big red wines at between 63 and 66 degrees. To do this, don't put your reds in the fridge before pouring and don't keep them in the trunk of your car on a hot summer's day. A cool, dry basement is "just right" for storing your wines.

Keep in mind that it is always easier to warm wine up a few degrees than to cool it down. The bulb-style glasses used to serve red wine allow you to cup the glass with your palm; in doing so, you can bring the temperature up a few degrees.

Yes, yes. You've probably heard along the way that you're supposed to hold a wineglass by its stem, and that's particularly true of whites and Champagnes when you want to keep a chill on. But in this case holding by the bulb is OK. Most places store their reds at too low a temperature, and your body heat is a quick fix to a too cool red. One more thing—red wine should never be served warm. If you order a bottle in a restaurant and it comes out warm, even slightly warm, send it back.

## To Decant or Not to Decant?

When you open a bottle of red wine, you might notice one of two things. If it's a young wine, the first whiffs may smell of alcohol, hair spray, or nail polish remover. If it's an old wine, you might find those gross clumps of sediment lurking in the bottom of the bottle.

In either case, decanting the wine will help. To do this, simply pour the wine from the bottle into a decanter; this lets the wine breathe and allows some of that alcohol scent to blow off. If you're decanting to remove the sediment, stop pouring when the sediment reaches the bottle's neck—the idea is to leave the sediment in the bottle.

Unless you're feeling fancy, there's truly no need for a crystal decanter—you can use a glass carafe or pour that wine into a big glass

### * * GUNK IN YOUR GLASS * *

Ever pour out the last sips from a bottle only to see clumps of dark purple or brown sediment plunk into your glass? Those are from tannins. As wine ages, tannins clump together, and, along with the pigments and tartrates in the wine, they form a sediment that settles to the bottom of the bottle (or to the side, if the wine is stored on its side). It usually happens only in red wines, and if the clumps gross you out, you can decant the wine to remove them.

bowl! To help blow off the alcohol scent, swish the wine around in the bowl; you'll achieve the same success as if you were a sommelier in a schmootzy restaurant.

## February's Picks

For your wine club's Cabernet Sauvignon tasting, I suggest you do a vertical flight of wine. Because vintage can matter noticeably when it comes to Cab, doing a vertical flight is a great way to get a taste of what vintage is all about.

For your vertical tasting, the host should assign five Cabernet Sauvignon wines made

### * * * * * * * * * * * * * *
### YOU'LL NEVER FORGET IT

A big no-no for big reds? Spicy food. Try serving something spicy, such as a big bowl of spiced nuts or your favorite hot-spiced chicken wings. Then taste them against a glass of Cab and—watch out! Big reds, like Cabernet Sauvignon, are usually higher in alcohol. On its own, higher alcohol produces heat, and when you pair it with spicy food, you're adding flame to the fire.

Go ahead—give it a go. Learning by mistake is more memorable than studying flash cards, and once you serve Cab with spicy foods, your guests will remember that next time things get a little fiery on the tongue, the beverage to reach for is something low in alcohol or one that's got a little sweetness to it to balance the heat. Like Riesling, for example—but we'll be all over that in June.

### * * * * * * * * * * * *

Big reds, like Cabernet Sauvignon, are usually higher in alcohol. On its own, higher alcohol produces heat, and when you pair it with spicy food you're adding flame to the fire.

by the same producer but from five different years. This may take a little legwork, so plan ahead. I recommend that the host call the local wine store to find out what it has available or what may be the easiest to obtain. If you can't find five different years from one producer, you could conduct two separate flights using three vintages from two different producers.

**This month's pick:** A Cabernet Sauvignon from Napa Valley—they're widely available and highly regarded in the wine world. They can range in price from $15 to more than $100 a bottle. I'd say plan to spend from $15 to $20 per bottle. You may need to dish out a little more for the older vintages.

**Ringer:** If you really want to throw a wrench into the game, include a Merlot. And if you choose to do a flight of Napa Valley Cabs, include a Napa Valley Merlot.

# GET YOUR DRINK ON

*Get your tasting sheets ready—we're finally going to start sipping. These Cabs are sure to warm you and make your cheeks rosy—red wines have a funny way of doing that. Take your time and take account of all the things you see, smell, taste, and feel. Here are a few things you might notice about Cabernet Sauvignon.*

**COLOR:** Cabernet Sauvignon hues range from dark red and ruby red to purplish red. While young Cabs will have vibrant red hues, a 20-year-old bottle of Cabernet Sauvignon may appear more lucid, be lighter in color, and have brownish hues.

You should never use the term *watery* to describe a Cab—if what you have in the glass is watery, I'd be skeptical that Cab is truly what's in the bottle. What you are looking at should be deep, dark, and rich in color.

**AROMA:** If you're tasting Cabs from California, the wines in your glass will most likely smell fruitier than those from Bordeaux would smell. You may smell black cherries, cassis, asparagus, red bell pepper, vanilla, clove, black pepper, and even cocoa and licorice. The 1998 vintage of California Cabs is marked by its vegetal aromas—some of the wines smell just like the vegetable drawer in your refrigerator. While not all of the wines from that year fell prey to this vegetable-drawer drama, it set '98 far apart from the highly esteemed '97 vintage, which was full of fruit. The bad reviews also drove the price of '98 Cali Cabs down, so you're more likely to find a price break, but not necessarily a quality Cab.

See if you can detect these other elements as you inhale: eucalyptus, mint, chocolate (milk or dark), or any other aroma that comes to mind. Remember, the longer the wine is exposed to the air, the more the aromas will change.

**TASTE:** Cabernet Sauvignon is what I call a "big-boy wine." It is luscious looking and takes over in your mouth. As you sip, notice its big aromas, big flavor, big body—and big alcohol.

The alcohol in Cabernet Sauvignon can range from 12 percent to more than 14 percent (check out the label—it will tell you the alcohol content). If at first you smell and taste only the alcohol, let the wine breathe (see "Wine Speak," page 38).

**BODY:** I have never had a Cabernet Sauvignon that wasn't medium- to full-bodied. The grape is made for big impressions, and that includes a big, juicy, full body that comes from the tannins in the grape's thick skin and the aging in oak vats. Think about milk again—Cab usually falls somewhere around whole milk in the spectrum. Most Cabs are blended with a little Merlot to achieve a mid-palate softness. In California, the bottle has to be only 75 percent Cabernet to call itself a Cab. But some Cabs are truly 100 percent Cab. These are sure to present very full-bodied reds with a more tannic mouth feel.

**FINISH:** Sticking with the "big" theme, Cabs usually have a big finish. Whether it's a burning throat from the high alcohol or a feeling of cotton mouth from the tannins, you are sure to know you just sipped a Cab. Take note of how many seconds these feelings linger. A well-balanced Cab will leave your mouth feeling like you want another sip, not like you need a glass of water.

**PRICE VALUE:** Don't be discouraged to find that domestic Cabs are not always a bargain, especially those from Napa and Sonoma. Basically, if you think the $40 Cab from Napa is worth every penny, then you should note that it is a great price value. And if that $10 Cab isn't worth two cents, make a note so you remember not to buy a case for your next big bash.

**THE RINGER:** Did you guess which one was Merlot? Here's a hint: The Merlot should be noticeably lighter in color than the Cabs. The Merlot will also be lighter and softer on the palate.

**R**ed wine served with a big, juicy steak is definitely a match made in heaven. But Cabs can pair well with lots of different menu items. This month, we are trying to complement our big reds with full-bodied foods like ice cream, blue cheese, and pudding or custard. We are also introducing savory bites including roasted garlic, prosciutto, and feta cheese to create a contrast with a very fruit-forward wine. Many of this month's ingredients play off the aromas of the wine, like mint and chocolate.

Note, too, that these recipes are full of aphrodisiacs like peaches and bananas. This month if your wine club gathering is a meeting of the lonely-hearts club, I can't be held responsible for any hanky-panky. You've been warned.

* * * * * * * * * * * * * * * * * * * * *

# BLUE CHEESE GRAPES
### and Peaches

*This simple assembly is a beautiful presentation and a perfect bite to pair with Cabernet. On their own, the blue cheese and these juicy fruits are a great contrast. When paired with the Cab, the blue cheese stands up to the full body, and the sweetness of the grapes and peaches creates a perfect balance with the fruit-forward wine.*

| | |
|---|---|
| 12 | ounces blue cheese (room temperature) |
| 1 | large bunch seedless black grapes (40 to 60 grapes) |
| ¾ | pound walnuts, finely chopped |
| 4 | peaches, pitted and cut into thin wedges (8 wedges per peach) |
| ¼ | pound almonds, finely chopped |
| 16 | slices prosciutto, cut in half lengthwise |
| | Freshly ground black pepper |

1. Press a little of the blue cheese around each grape (use a total of 5 ounces of the cheese for this). Wear disposable plastic gloves if you like. Roll grapes in the walnuts. (If blue cheese is not soft enough to press around the grapes, place it in a food processor. Cover and pulse until soft. Or mash the cheese against the sides of a bowl with a wooden spoon.)

2. Spread the remaining 7 ounces blue cheese onto peach wedges with a knife. (Or place a thin slice on each peach wedge.) Roll peach wedges in almonds. Wrap each peach wedge in a piece of prosciutto. Sprinkle peaches with pepper. Cover and chill grapes and peaches for 30 to 60 minutes.

**Makes 40 to 60 grapes (depending on size) and 32 peach wedges**

# BASIL ICE CREAM

*I include a recipe from scratch for those of you with a little time, as well as a quick fix for those on the run. Basil may sound strange in ice cream, but trust me—it is an interesting as well as delicious alternative to mint. Use a very sharp knife to chop your fresh herbs or you will bruise the leaves and end up with brown polka dots!*

| | |
|---|---|
| 2 | cups whipping cream |
| 1 | cup half-and-half or light cream |
| 3/4 | cup sugar |
| 1/2 | of a vanilla bean, split lengthwise |
| 6 | beaten egg yolks |
| 1 | tablespoon chopped fresh basil or mint |

1. In a heavy saucepan combine cream, half-and-half, sugar, and vanilla bean. Bring just to a boil. Remove from heat.

2. Stir a small amount of the hot mixture into the egg yolks. Continue adding the hot mixture in small amounts until the egg mixture is hot. Return all to saucepan. Cook and stir for 1 minute. Strain through a mesh strainer into a metal bowl. Discard vanilla bean.

3. Place the metal bowl in a bowl of ice water to cool completely. (Or if you have the time, you can cool the mixture in the refrigerator. Just make sure the mixture is cold all the way through before you put it in your ice cream freezer.)

4. Put mixture in an ice cream freezer and freeze according to manufacturer's directions. The ice cream should still be soft after freezing. At this point, fold in the basil. If you like, scoop into small serving cups and place in the freezer until ready to serve.

**Makes 20 small scoops**

Quick-Fix Basil Ice Cream: In a chilled medium bowl stir 1 pint vanilla ice cream just enough to soften, using a wooden spoon to press ice cream against the sides of the bowl. (Do not stir the ice cream too much. It should look like soft-serve ice cream, not soup.) Quickly stir in 1 tablespoon chopped fresh basil or mint. Cover and freeze until firm.

# SPINACH, TOMATO,
## and Roasted Garlic Bouchée

*Bouchée is a fancy word for puff pastry that is formed into bite-size portions. The word* bouchée *actually translates to "little mouthful." I re-created this recipe from one my husband and I ate at a cafe in the Metropolitan Museum of Art one afternoon. It is so simple and so divine!*

1    cup ricotta cheese

24   frozen puff pastry shells

1    slightly beaten egg

1    tablespoon olive oil

2    large cloves garlic, minced

1    6-ounce bag fresh spinach, triple-washed, drained, and chopped

1    14½-ounce can diced tomatoes, drained

    Salt

    Black pepper

2    teaspoons roasted garlic paste

**1.** Drain ricotta cheese in cheesecloth or in a fine-mesh strainer. Set aside while you do the rest of the preparation.

**2.** Preheat oven to 400°F. Place pastry shells on a large baking sheet; brush with egg. Bake for 20 to 25 minutes or until golden brown. Cool completely on a wire rack.

**3.** In a large skillet heat olive oil. Add garlic; cook and stir about 30 seconds or until you can smell the aroma. Add spinach; toss in skillet until it is completely wilted. Add the tomatoes; cook for 5 minutes to reduce liquids. Season to taste with salt and pepper.

**4.** Combine ricotta cheese and garlic paste. Spoon some of the ricotta mixture into each pastry shell, filling about half full. Top with some of the spinach mixture. Keep warm in a 200°F oven until serving, or serve at room temperature.

**Makes 24 appetizers**

Serving tip: If you weren't serving these with red wine, you could add 1 teaspoon red pepper flakes to the ricotta for some heat.

**Homemade Roasted Garlic Paste:** You can buy roasted garlic paste at the grocery store or make your own. To make it yourself, trim the top off one head of garlic just enough to reveal the garlic cloves. Rub the entire head with olive oil. Wrap in foil and bake in a 400°F oven for 45 to 60 minutes. Cool completely. Squeeze out the garlic paste into a bowl.

# SUPER–SPICY HUMMUS

*It's important when adding a little heat to any dish to make sure you aren't covering the rest of its components. Taking a big bite of this and washing it down with a young Cab will produce the most heat and may leave you breaking a sweat—but the relationship between big reds and spicy food will be seared in your memory.*

1    14-ounce can garbanzo beans (chickpeas), drained

¼    cup fresh lemon juice (2 medium lemons)

2    tablespoons tahini (sesame seed paste)

1    tablespoon red curry paste

1    teaspoon garlic powder

½    teaspoon kosher salt

⅓    cup olive oil

    Pita Chips, recipe page 46

**1.** In a food processor or blender combine beans, lemon juice, tahini, red curry paste, garlic powder, and salt. Cover and process until almost smooth. With machine running, drizzle in the olive oil, processing until smooth. Serve with Pita Chips.

**Makes about 2 cups dip**

**✱ ✱ ✱ ✱ ✱ ✱ ✱ NO-COOK OPTIONS ✱ ✱ ✱ ✱ ✱ ✱ ✱**

★The basil or mint ice cream is easy to achieve with the quick-fix option that's listed directly after the homemade version. It's not quite as creamy as the real deal, but it will pass if you're in a hurry.

★The Blue Cheese Grapes and Peaches can be achieved by simply serving its parts. Just pick up a beautiful bunch of black seedless grapes, blue cheese, walnuts, almonds, peaches, and prosciutto. Wash and dry the entire bunch of grapes and lay in the center of the platter. Place the remaining accoutrements around the grapes to create a beautifully dramatic platter.

★Most grocery stores carry a spicy hummus, but if you can't find one, just add chili powder or chile flakes to regular hummus to get the desired heat effect. Be sure to take the hummus out of its plastic container and serve it in a nicer ramekin or glass bowl. Presentation counts! And if you don't have time to make pita chips, serve the hummus with crackers on the side.

★To achieve the contrast of the Cucumber-Feta Dip with the Cab, thinly slice two English cucumbers (also called seedless cucumbers) and serve with a packaged vegetable dip.

★This month, for fun purchase a big heart-shape candy box at the store and pass around the chocolates. Chocolate goes great with Cab—and besides, it's an aphrodisiac!

**✱ ✱ ✱ ✱ ✱ ✱ ✱ ✱ ✱ ✱ ✱ ✱ ✱ ✱ ✱ ✱ ✱ ✱ ✱ ✱ ✱ ✱**

# CUCUMBER–FETA DIP
## with Pita Chips

*When serving Cabs from different vintages, notice the younger wines have more heat in the palate and maybe the back of the throat. This dip is a great contrast to the fruit in the wine and the heat on the palate. As you sip and nibble, decide if the wine overpowers the dip, if the dip mutes the wine, or if this is a perfect pair.*

1   seedless (English) cucumber, thinly sliced

1   tablespoon salt

1   8-ounce package cream cheese, cut into small pieces

½   pound feta cheese, crumbled

½   teaspoon freshly ground black pepper

2   tablespoons fresh mint, sliced into thin strips (chiffonade)

1   12-ounce package pita bread rounds

    Olive oil

    Sesame seeds

    Freshly cracked black pepper

**1.** Sprinkle cucumber slices with salt; let stand for 30 minutes. Rinse well; press with paper towels to remove any excess liquid. Dice cucumber slices; set aside.

**2.** In a food processor combine cream cheese, feta cheese, and the ½ teaspoon ground pepper. Cover and process until combined. Transfer to a bowl; fold in cucumber and mint. Set dip aside.

**3.** Preheat oven to 350°F. For Pita Chips, brush one side of each pita bread round with olive oil; sprinkle with sesame seeds. Top with a little freshly cracked pepper. Cut each bread round into small wedges. Arrange on a large baking sheet. Bake for 20 to 25 minutes or until crispy. Serve dip with Pita Chips.

**Makes about 3 cups dip**

# BANANAS FOSTER TARTLETS

*I love banana pudding, banana bread, banana ice cream, caramelized bananas, banana smoothies, banana splits, banana cake … you get the idea. Bananas are considered an aphrodisiac and are a perfect match for the creamy-tart, tannic Cab and romance.*

| | |
|---|---|
| ¼ | cup butter |
| ½ | cup packed brown sugar |
| 3 | bananas, sliced |
| 2 | tablespoons bourbon or brandy |
| 1½ | cups homemade vanilla pudding |
| 24 | mini tartlet shells |

**1.** In a large skillet melt butter; stir in brown sugar until dissolved. Add bananas. Cook and gently stir about 2 minutes or until bananas just begin to soften.

**2.** Add bourbon. Use a long match or stick lighter to ignite the bourbon. Let the flame die out; remove skillet from heat. You don't want the bananas to turn to mush, so be very careful not to overcook.

**3.** Place pudding in a pastry bag with a large tip. (Or place pudding in a resealable plastic bag with a corner snipped off.) Pipe about 1 tablespoon pudding into each tarlet shell. Top each with a little bit of the banana mixture.

**Makes 24 appetizers**

**Homemade Mini Tartlet Shells:** If you can't find tartlet shells small enough, you can make your own by using a refrigerated unbaked piecrust. Preheat oven to 400°F. Roll pastry out to a 13-inch circle. Cut into twenty-four 2¼-inch rounds. Press rounds into 1¾-inch muffin cups. Using a fork, prick the bottom and sides of the dough in each muffin cup. Bake about 6 minutes or until golden.

# syrah
## *a spicy sip*

**On** *St. Paddy's Day, I like my green beer and Guinness as much as the next guy, but this March I insist you put down those pints! We're filling our glasses with something much, much better. Syrah (or Shiraz if you choose a bottle from our friends down under) is perfect for edging out winter and*

bringing on spring. It pairs well with winter comfort foods and is great when you get grilling. It also works great with pizza, of all things. Now that's my kind of wine!

No need to get all hot and bothered when you see some of the price tags on French and California Syrahs. You can find the juice under its sassier name, Shiraz, almost anywhere, and it's cheap, cheap, cheap! But for learning purposes, you need to keep the more expensive French and California

Syrahs in the mix for this month's tasting. You may spend a little more on the Syrah than Shiraz, but when you taste the Frenchies and the Aussies side by side, you'll see what this little grape is capable of on its own—and with some fantastic food.

### Getting to Know Syrah or Shiraz

Syrah and Shiraz are like identical twins separated at birth. They are exactly the same grape genetically but range dramatically in

the glass. What you taste depends on where these grapes are born and who raises them from the vine to the barrel. The Rhône region of France, especially the northern Rhône, is hailed for its awesome Syrah, although there are a few gems to be found farther south, like those in the Languedoc region. Shiraz is by far Australia's darling little grape. The Aussies' ability to showcase how delish this grape can be has brought their wine industry fame and fortune. California calls it Syrah. South Africa calls it Shiraz. So for this chapter when we talk about France and California, we'll call it Syrah; we'll call it Shiraz when the wine is from anywhere else.

Bear with me; you'll know the difference between the two once you start sniffing and sipping these stellar wines.

### Rhône 101

All the wines you'll be tasting this month are clearly labeled Syrah or Shiraz, except for the Frenchies. Because the French generally name their wines after where the grapes grow instead of by the grapes' names, before you head out to buy this stuff, you'll need a little Rhône 101 lesson. Don't worry—I'll be brief.

In general, wines from the Rhône region are called Côtes du Rhône. The Rhône region is split into two major growing areas, and it's the northern region we're after this month. While other grapes are grown in the northern Rhône region (namely, Viognier, which you'll savor in May), the black Syrah grape reigns over the area. But again, don't look for the word "Syrah"; the wines you're looking for will be labeled by the following winegrowing regions:

**Hermitage and Côte-Rôtie:** Wines from these regions are considered the big kids on the block—they develop big oak characteristics from the oak barrels they're stored in for aging; this translates to big tannins and high alcohol content. As you gleaned when drinking Cabs, these attributes make for a wine that's better after a few years in the bottle. When buying Hermitage and Côte-Rôtie, generally, I feel they taste better when they are at least

*A few grapes*

10 years old. You can uncork these when they are first released, but you'll miss out on the rich chocolate and tobacco characteristics that really blossom with age.

**Cornas, Saint Joseph, and Crozes Hermitage:** These are next in popularity, which suits me just fine. Less popular means more affordable, and that's right up my alley. These babies are full of flavor, at a price much more appealing to the consumer. Of the three categories, Syrah from Saint Joseph or Crozes Hermitage will be the most drinkable upon release.

### Heading South

While we're in the Rhône Valley, let's dip a little to the south—the wines from this region are definitely worth knowing. The southern Rhône Valley gives us highly renowned wines made from the Grenache grape as well as some terrific wines made from various blends. The best known of the blends is Châteauneuf-du-Pape, a sexy red wine made

from blending Syrah with many different red and white grape varietals—a total of 13 different grapes can be used.

Blending red and white grapes? You bet! This happens more often than you might have guessed. In fact, while those Syrahs from the northern Rhône Valley are made mostly from the Syrah grape, some are blended with small amounts of white grapes. Côte-Rôtie is a perfect example—it gets a special touch of *je ne sais quoi* from Viognier.

### Something Old, Something New ...

The Languedoc region, nestled in the sun-filled South of France, gives us some of France's best buys in wine. You may be hearing this name for the first time, but as a wine-growing region, Languedoc has been around as long as Bordeaux and Burgundy. However, until now mostly just the French have been enjoying its wine. About 80 percent of France's *vin de pays* (country wine) comes from the Languedoc. And though the region is known

* * * * * * * * * * * * * * * * * * * * * * * * * * * * * * * * * * * * *

### IF THE GLASS FITS ...

Riedel, the famous Austrian glassware company, actually makes a glass specifically for drinking Syrah (and every other varietal). This one has a wide bowl with a tapered rim, which is designed to direct the wine to the center of your palate. Riedel believes this is the best way to taste Syrah.

Seriously, even if you blindfolded yourself, I think you'd get the wine to the middle of your palate just fine—if not, you've already had too much to drink! Therefore, for this tasting in particular, I recommend the all-purpose red-wine glass. The larger bowl will allow you to aerate the wine more and let out all of those awesome aromas.

* * * * * * * * * * * * * * * * * * * * * * * * * * * * * * * * * * * * *

for the quantity of wines it produces, it's also pumping out quality juice. Because it's fun to go exploring, this month we'll include the good ol' Rhône wines, but we'll also jump into a Syrah from the Languedoc region.

### When Bad Things Happen to Good Wine

Wine doesn't always smell like roses, and Rhône Syrah can be one of those wines that bring a little funk to the table. If at first sniff you think you smell something offensive, don't keep it a secret. Discuss it with your fellow tasters—that's part of the fun of tasting with others. It is much harder to detect bad wine qualities in Syrah and other red wine than in white wine. That's because a lot of red wine aromas mask the flaws.

However, there are certain foul aromas that are deemed acceptable. In future chapters don't be surprised to see cat pee and barnyard as suitable sniffs in certain wines. For now let's call them acquired aromas. I'll bet you never thought burning rubber would be an aroma you'd want in your wine, but for Syrah … oh, you'll see.

Shiraz is a great place to really get up close and personal with the smells of wine because there's so much great stuff to take in. From the dark berries and plumlike, fruity aromas to more than a dash of spice, you're going to be intrigued. However, before we get to swirling and sniffing all those nice things, let's talk a little about some of the smells that aren't so nice: cork taint and that singular "cooked" aroma.

### ✶ ✶ ✶ THE MONA LISA ✶ ✶ ✶

Can there be two *Mona Lisas* in the world? Not in the world of painting—but in the world of wine, I know of two stunning Syrah/Shiraz wines that are equally worthy of your attention. From the Rhône, I recommend the Guigal, a Côte-Rôtie at $55 a bottle. Like the *Mona Lisa*, it is beautiful at first sip, but it also ages beautifully. You could save this bottle for 10 years (patience is a virtue) and then let the wine runneth over. When it's poured young you'll love its rich, full body, and when it's aged you'll be hypnotized by its decadent aromas.

As for the Aussies, the award goes to Penfold's Grange. Rich in history and luscious in flavor, this wine epitomizes the potential of Australia's soil and talent in winemaking. It consistently brings excellence to the table. As each vintage is poured you can be sure that its rich texture and concentrated fruits will deliver. At a steep—and I mean steep—$150 a bottle, this is truly the *Mona Lisa* of Australian Shiraz.

### ✶ ✶ ✶ SALVADOR DALÍ ✶ ✶ ✶

Woop Woop—yes, that's the name of this juicy pick from down under. Talk about starting a new tradition in wine! It's doubtful the French will ever name a bottle of wine Woop Woop, but leave it to the irreverent Aussies to bring a little fun to the table. At around $12 a bottle, this li'l darling earns a three-star rating from *The New York Times* and an all-star rating from me! I love its fruity taste and how well its lighter body makes for a great food and wine pairing.

**Cork Taint:** You may have heard the term "cork taint" or "corked" used to describe a wine. It does not mean that the cork broke and some of it ended up in the wine—that problem would be easily solved by simply straining the wine to remove the cork.

What the term does mean is that a faulty cork has allowed some TCA (a stinky chemical compound that comes from corks or the barrels where wine was aged or stored) to contaminate your wine. TCA isn't going to kill you—but it's a killjoy to wine.

Most of the time, TCA is present in such small amounts that it goes unnoticed. But sometimes, the wine will exude a musty, moldy smell (it reminds me of my brother's dirty socks, or the way our damp clothes smelled the day after we played in the snow). When you smell that, don't drink the wine. If you're in a restaurant, send it back; if you bought the bottle at a wine shop, ask for a refund. And take note: An alarming number of wine bottles are corked—between 5 and 15 percent, depending on whom you ask—so if you think your wine smells like sweaty socks, trust your judgment and open another bottle.

**Cooked Wine:** Another bad thing that happens to good wine is when it gets "cooked." The term means just what it says; somehow, after the wine was put in the bottle, it got too hot and sort of baked up a bit. The result is a thin wine without any oomph, with aromas that are more like stewed prunes than fresh fruit. And while a stewed prune aroma is acceptable in certain wines like ports, it is not what you should smell in Shiraz.

Chances are, you've tasted a cooked wine without even realizing it. If you remove the capsule (that metallic covering on the neck and mouth of the bottle) and the cork shows signs of leakage or the neck of the bottle gives you sticky fingers, the wine inside has most likely been cooked. Also, if you notice even before removing the capsule that the cork is poking through the foil, the wine has more than likely hit some high temps. Check out the cork in your bottle before you buy

* * **BANG FOR YOUR BUCK** * *

Penfold's Thomas Hyland Shiraz, Australia; $11 a bottle. Here you'll get to taste the juice from the same world-famous Australian winery that brings you this month's Mona Lisa, but in this case you won't have to empty your wallet. For what you're getting at this price, it's almost free—you'll want to buy a case.

it—the cork should be snug as a bug in the bottleneck and not poking out at all.

When it comes to cooked wine, there can be many culprits. A hot delivery truck will do it. Sometimes, distributors leave cases sitting outside in the heat; other times, stores don't have a proper cooling system in the summer months. Or you, my darling, may be the one to blame! I can't tell you how many times I've walked into friends' homes and caught them storing their wine on top of the refrigerator. People—that's WRONG, WRONG, WRONG!!! Usually your fridge is warm on top, or warm air blows from the motor in the back—not a good thing for

> To check out your wine's legs, swirl the wine in a glass. Then notice those little streams of wine that form as the wine begins to trail back into the bulb of the glass. These are the legs.

wine. If you don't have a wine cellar (how dare you?), a wine fridge, or a dry basement, keep your wine in the back of a cool, dark closet or cupboard. Your bottles can stay put there just fine for a while.

## Sulphur or Syrah?

Stick your schnoz in a glass of wine, inhale deeply, and take in those aromas of fruits and spices and freshly cracked black pepper and ... burning rubber? What you're smelling isn't the tire plant at the edge of town; it's sulphur dioxide. This is commonly used in the bottling process to help preserve wine; however, when your wine is given an overdose of the stuff, it will be more pungent. Count this as one of those not-so-good aromas.

That is, unless you're drinking Syrah from the northern Rhône. Then, believe it or not, that sulphur smell actually isn't from the addition of sulphur dioxide. Syrah that hasn't fully ripened can emit this burned rubber

smell, and certain parts of the Rhône region, like the Ardèche, are more likely to produce grapes that carry this stench. Some say this is a desired trait of the juice ... leave it to the French. I prefer my wine minus the funk. If I can swirl the glass and the aroma blows off after a minute or two, I'm cool with that. But I have no desire to drink stink. Remember this nugget when you are swirling and sniffing. If you find a hint of this aroma, you can bet it's a Rhône Syrah.

## Syrah's Got Legs

In the wine world, we often talk about a wine's legs (hmmmm, I wonder who first came up with that descriptor—a man or a woman?). To check out your wine's legs, swirl the wine in a glass. Then notice those little streams of wine that form as the wine begins to trail back into the bulb of the glass. These are the legs.

When the streams are thin, a wine is said to

* * * * * * * * * * * * *

### YOU'LL NEVER FORGET IT

This is going to be gross, but it's for your own good. One day before your tasting, take one bottle of wine (preferably one that you have also assigned someone to bring—this one should be an extra) and empty it into a saucepan. Heat it on the stove top. Don't boil it—just warm it through so that when you stick your finger in it, it feels hot but not burning.

Remove the wine from the heat and use a funnel to put it back into the original bottle. Cork it and keep in a cool, dark place until the tasting. Serve it alongside the other bottles, preferably wrapped in foil. Mix up the bottles so that even you don't know where it lands. Once you sip it, you'll never forget what a cooked bottle of wine tastes like.

* * * * * * * * * * * *          * * * * * * * * * * * *

have loose or thin legs, an indicator that the wine is light- to medium-bodied—Sauvignon Blanc generally has thin legs. Thicker legs signal a high alcohol content and can also indicate viscous, fuller-bodied wines like Cabernet and Syrah.

So swirl that Syrah and check out those legs. Its body will be revealed to you before you take a sip.

### Syrah/Shiraz Know-How

Syrah is a big, tannic red wine, best enjoyed at room temperature. That means you shouldn't put it in your fridge (too cold) or on top of your fridge (too hot). Of course, room temperature varies whether you're in a castle or in a hut, but for a reference point, when talking wine, room temperature is usually around 62 to 65 degrees.

If you're planning on cellaring a few bottles, you should keep them in a place that has a constant temperature and aim for around 55 degrees. For most of us this isn't realistic; just be logical and don't store them on a sunny windowsill or in a musty, moist basement. Go for a dry, dark area where they won't be disturbed. Later down the road if you really get gung ho on this wine thing, you can think about getting one of those fancy temperature-controlled wine storage units.

### Out, Damn Spot, Out I Say ...

Spring is upon us, and you may have the urge to start pulling out those white linen pants and tablecloths, but for your Syrah tasting, I forbid it. Inevitably, if I wear white to a wine tasting, I end up polka-dotted with purple by the end of it, so take my word for it: With Syrah, light-colored cloths—whether draped on your table or over your

### ✴ ✴ THE ART OF SPITTING ✴ ✴

It's recommended when tasting wines for learning purposes that you spit after you swish the wine around your palate. This way you aren't influenced by your alcohol intake. You should also cleanse the palate by drinking water before tasting each new wine. When tasting red wine, like Syrah, consider passing out individual opaque glasses or plastic cups (rather than using a spit bucket) so tasters can keep their spit to themselves.

body—are a very, very bad idea.

Some guidelines for keeping your red wine tastings spot free:

Use darker tablecloths or none at all for a red wine tasting. However, because guests will want to look at the color of the wine, pass out white sheets of paper so they can hold their glasses up to something white.

When you pour a bottle of wine (especially red), have a napkin in one hand to catch drips.

Turn the bottle slightly as you finish the pour. This will prevent dripping. If a drop does get loose, it usually runs down the bottle—that's why you have the napkin.

Normally you would get four to five full glasses from every bottle of wine; however, since this is a tasting, be sure to fill the glass with only enough wine to swirl, sniff, swish, and repeat. If you fill it fuller, your guests will end up swirling the wine right onto their clothes—or onto your rug.

Spit buckets are just about as dainty as they sound, so use individual cups (see "The Art of Spitting," page 55).

## March's Picks

This month we will taste Syrah from two regions of France—the Rhône region and the Languedoc region, as well as one from California. We'll also see what Australia brings to the table with its Shiraz.

These are my picks in each category:

**France's Rhône region:** Look for these regions on the label: Côtes du Rhône, Côte-Rôtie, Saint Joseph, or Croze Hermitage, starting at $15 a bottle.

**France's Languedoc region:** Look for a bottle in the $12 to $15 range.

**California:** In the $15 to $20 range.

**Australia:** In the $10 to $20 range.

**Ringer:** Let's jog your memory from last month's tasting by including a Napa Valley Cabernet as the ringer. Aim for a bottle priced between $10 and $15.

* * * * * * **WINE TREND** * * * * * *

French wines with labels we can all understand—now how's that for a trend? Traditionally, wines in France are labeled by growing region (often, the label doesn't even mention the grape), so how are you and I supposed to know that Hermitage is a Syrah? Of course, there is something to be said for tradition, but these days some French winemakers are changing their tune when it comes to non-user-friendly wine labels. Red Bicyclette is a French wine with a label that everyone will understand. If it's Syrah, it says Syrah. Merlot is called Merlot. Chardonnay goes by—you guessed it, Chardonnay. Now, was that so hard?

Oh, sure. Some purists will say that such labels are dumbing down the magic and mystique of French wines for the American public. But guess what? Sometimes even the French get confused. When I spoke to Red Bicyclette's winemaker, he said, "With hundreds of French winegrowing regions, even the French can be mystified by what's in the bottle." So the French aren't smarter than we are after all! And now that the cat's out of the bag about us all being in the same boat, more and more French table wines are available with lovable labels. *Sacré bleu!*

* * * * * * * * * * * * * * * * * *

# GET YOUR DRINK ON

*Syrah and Shiraz show off differently once poured. I'm a sucker for the beauty of this juice. You, too, may be entranced by its red-purple velvet visage. And more than any other, these wines emit an enormous variety of aromas. Some will deliver fruit first, while others will whop you with black pepper and spicy notes. And for your sensitive side, there are flowers and chocolate, too. This tasting will really test you. With so much going on in the glass, it may be hard to choose a favorite. But with Shiraz and Syrah side by side, you're sure to learn the distinction between the styles. Cheers!*

**COLOR:** Syrah and Shiraz have darker purple hues than the Cabs you tasted last month. Their color can vary from brownish red to a deep, dark blood red; the one with the brownish tinge is most likely the one from the Rhône. Syrah/Shiraz tends to have a dense, inky color.

**AROMA:** The spice most often attributed to Syrah/Shiraz is freshly cracked black pepper. If you have a pepper mill, crack some pepper right before the tasting starts and put a little ramekin out for your guests to sniff as they taste—it will help them perceive this aroma in the wines. You'll note that all Syrah/Shiraz tend to have black pepper and spice in the nose. While the Rhône wines may also exhibit plum and berry aromas, they're not generally as fruit forward (see "Wine Speak," page 55) as the Aussie Shiraz, which tends to show ripe fruit aromas first, after which come the layers of chocolate, black pepper, and sweeter spices. The California Syrah will also exhibit sweeter spices, like clove, and can bear floral aromas like violet. Continue swirling your Syrah/Shiraz and you may also notice dark chocolate, cocoa, mint, and licorice. And if that's not enough, this grape can also display aromas of smoked meats and wet rocks—again with those acquired aromas!

**TASTE:** In general, Syrah tastes like it smells; you'll get spice and earth and raisiny ripe fruits along with ripe berries. Shiraz will come through as a fruity red with pepper and chocolate notes. Syrah from the Rhône is a little more shy about expressing big, bold fruit, but it is definitely right in there with the spice.

**BODY:** Syrah/Shiraz tops the list for full-bodied wines. It's lush on the palate, with full tannins that usually linger, and it has a very rich mouth feel. Remember those legs I mentioned? Give this wine a good swirl and you're sure to see those lingering, voluptuous legs of Syrah/Shiraz clinging to the inside of your glass. It's a sure sign that there is more alcohol in this juice than one with loose legs. And that, my friends, equals a bigger-bodied sip.

**FINISH:** These big reds are often high in tannins, and if you get a very young Rhône Syrah, it can leave your mouth puckered for a kiss. It's not that they're sour; rather, it's the dryness of the tannins that draws your cheeks together. Well-made Syrah/Shiraz is a harmonious balance between fruit and tannins in the finish.

**RINGER:** If there's one in the bunch that seems a little lighter in hue, you're likely looking at the ringer. In the nose, the Cab will show black cherries, cassis, asparagus, bell pepper, and even vanilla. It may show some spice, but it won't be as prevalent as in your Syrah or Shiraz. Like Syrah or Shiraz, the ringer will have big tannins, but the mouth feel may not be as silky and rich.

## 🍃 LET'S EAT! FOOD AND WINE PAIRING 🍃

**P**eople often think you have to serve rich and creamy French food with red wine. I find that the simplest foods pair just as well. This month we are going to serve gourmet pizza. With a good crust carrying everything from wild mushrooms to pears and Gorgonzola, you are sure to find a food and wine pairing that will rock your palate. No need to worry about your skills in the kitchen. You don't have to go to culinary school to create these awesome bites.

\* \* \* \* \* \* \* \* \* \* \* \* \* \* \* \* \* \* \* \* \*

# PIZZA DOUGH

*To make a pizza, we start with the base: the crust. Making dough isn't my favorite, so I like to go to my baker, pizza shop, or grocery store and buy the raw dough. You just need to call ahead and find out what time they bake it off so you don't miss your chance. You can also try the pizza toppings on tortillas, pita bread, or plain foccacia.*

1    pound raw pizza dough

Cornmeal

1    recipe Garlic Olive Oil, page 59

1. If your pizza dough is frozen, thaw it at room temperature for about 2 hours or in the refrigerator overnight. (Keep dough refrigerated until ready to use.)

2. Stretch your dough by hand in a circular motion, working from the center of the ball to the edges to get an even rectangular shape. (One pound of dough will stretch into about an 8×12-inch rectangle.)

3. Generously sprinkle a pizza peel or an inverted cookie sheet with cornmeal. Place the stretched dough on the pizza peel or cookie sheet so it will slide easily onto your preheated pizza stone after you have added the toppings. Brush stretched dough with Garlic Olive Oil as directed in recipes.

**Makes 1 pizza crust**

# CAPRESE PIZZA

*You may know this as a simple salad, but it makes for a tasty pie as well. I love to serve this in the summertime when the tomatoes are ripe and juicy and the basil in my garden is intoxicating. With fresh in season ingredients this pizza is superb.*

1  pound raw stretched pizza dough

2  tablespoons Garlic Olive Oil, plus more for drizzling (see recipe, below)

5  roma tomatoes, sliced

3  2-ounce balls fresh mozzarella cheese, thinly sliced

2  tablespoons grated Parmesan cheese

12  fresh basil leaves, torn in half

1. Preheat a pizza stone in a 400°F oven. (If you don't have a pizza stone, line a large cookie sheet with parchment paper but do not preheat in oven.)

2. Brush the stretched pizza dough with Garlic Olive Oil. Shingle tomato and and mozzarella slices over dough (shingle tightly to get as much on as possible—the tomatoes shrink when cooked and the dough expands as it cooks). Sprinkle dough edges with Parmesan cheese.

3. Slide pizza onto preheated pizza stone or prepared cookie sheet. Bake for 20 to 25 minutes or until crust is golden brown. (Don't try to speed up the process by raising the oven temperature—you'll just end up with a burned crust.)

4. Cool pizza slightly; drizzle lightly with additional Garlic Olive Oil. Sprinkle with basil. Cut into twenty-four 2-inch squares.

**Makes 24 pieces**

# GARLIC OLIVE OIL

1  cup extra-virgin olive oil

3  cloves garlic, crushed

1. Combine oil and garlic in a small bowl. Use enough to lightly coat the pizza crust. You may brush again once the pizza is removed from the oven. And you may use this to lightly drizzle across the pizza once it has been cooked. Do not drizzle this on the sauced pizzas or the Pear and Gorgonzola Pizza.

**Makes 1 cup garlic oil**

# GREEK PIZZA

*The tang of the feta cheese makes this pizza. The veggies give it a great fresh crunch, and when you pair it with a sip of Shiraz, you get juicy, fruity spiciness all wrapped up in one bite! This is always a wine club fave!*

| | |
|---|---|
| 1 | pound raw, stretched pizza dough |
| 2 | tablespoons Garlic Olive Oil, plus more for drizzling (see recipe, page 59) |
| ½ | cup chopped tomato |
| ½ | cup chopped green sweet pepper |
| ½ | cup crumbled feta cheese |
| ¼ | cup diced onion |
| ¼ | cup kalamata olives, pitted and sliced |
| 2 | tablespoons grated Parmesan cheese |
| 1 | tablespoon chopped fresh oregano |

1. Preheat a pizza stone in a 400°F oven. (If you don't have a pizza stone, line a large cookie sheet with parchment paper but do not preheat in oven.)

2. Brush the stretched pizza dough with Garlic Olive Oil. Top evenly with tomato, sweet pepper, feta cheese, onion, and olives. Sprinkle dough edges with Parmesan cheese.

3. Slide pizza onto preheated pizza stone or prepared cookie sheet. Bake for 20 to 25 minutes or until crust is golden brown. (Don't try to speed up the process by raising the oven temperature—you'll just end up with a burned crust.)

4. Cool the pizza slightly and drizzle lightly with additional Garlic Olive Oil. Sprinkle with oregano. Cut into twenty-four 2-inch squares.

**Makes 24 pieces**

# BLACK OLIVE–SALAMI PIZZA

*Both of these main ingredients—black olives and cured meat—are often aromas and flavors found in Syrah. Paired with the black pepper essence of the wine, this is a dynamite bite. Yummy!*

1   pound raw stretched pizza dough

2   tablespoons Garlic Olive Oil (see recipe, page 59)

½   cup marinara sauce

16   thin slices hard salami

1   cup shredded mozzarella cheese

3   ounces pitted black olives, sliced

2   tablespoons grated Parmesan cheese

1. Preheat a pizza stone in a 400°F oven. (If you don't have a pizza stone, line a large cookie sheet with parchment paper but do not preheat in oven.)

2. Brush the stretched pizza dough with Garlic Olive Oil. Spread the marinara sauce evenly over the dough. Shingle 8 of the salami slices over dough; top with ½ cup of the mozzarella cheese. Shingle the remaining 8 slices of salami; top with the remaining ½ cup mozzarella cheese. Sprinkle olives over the mozzarella. Sprinkle dough edges with Parmesan cheese.

3. Slide pizza onto preheated pizza stone or prepared cookie sheet. Bake for 20 to 25 minutes or until crust is golden brown. (Don't try to speed up the process by raising the oven temperature—you'll just end up with a burned crust.)

4. Cool the pizza slightly and cut into twenty-four 2-inch squares.

**Makes 24 pieces**

# ITALIAN SAUSAGE, WILD MUSHROOM,
## and Asiago Pizza

*This pizza is awesome with the earthy mushrooms, the meat lover's sausage, and the sharp Asiago cheese, all piled high. It's a very rustic-style pie that plays well on the palate with Syrah. But don't overdo it on this one; remember, there are plenty more pizzas to tempt you!*

¾  pound uncooked mild Italian sausage links (remove casings)

1  pound raw stretched pizza dough

2  tablespoons Garlic Olive Oil (see recipe, page 59)

½  cup marinara sauce

4  ounces fresh cremini, shiitake, and/or oyster mushrooms, thinly sliced

3  ounces Asiago cheese, shaved

2  tablespoons grated Parmesan cheese

**1.** Preheat a pizza stone in a 400°F oven. (If you don't have a pizza stone, line a large cookie sheet with parchment paper but do not preheat in oven.)

**2.** Meanwhile, in a large skillet cook sausage over medium heat until brown. Use a wooden spoon to break up the sausage as you cook it. Drain off fat.

**3.** Brush the stretched pizza dough with Garlic Olive Oil. Spread marinara sauce evenly over dough. Top with the sausage, mushrooms, and half of the Asiago cheese. Sprinkle dough edges with Parmesan cheese.

**4.** Slide pizza onto preheated pizza stone or prepared cookie sheet. Bake for 20 to 25 minutes or until crust is golden brown. (Don't try to speed up the process by raising the oven temperature—you'll just end up with a burned crust.) Top with the remaining Asiago cheese.

**5.** Cool the pizza slightly and cut into twenty-four 2-inch squares.

**Makes 24 pieces**

Note: If you prefer a little more spice, you can use spicy Italian sausage in place of the mild Italian sausage. Also, the mixture of mushrooms does not have to be these exact types, but you should stick with wild mushrooms, not white button mushrooms, to get that real earthy flavor.

# CARAMELIZED ONION, PANCETTA,
## and Red Chile Pizza

*This is my favorite pie. I love the way the sweetness of the onions melts into the salty pancetta, and then you kick it up with the heat of the chile flakes. It's the perfect amount of spice to complement a sassy Shiraz.*

| | |
|---|---|
| 6 | medium red onions, thinly sliced |
| ¼ | cup olive oil |
| 1 | pound raw stretched pizza dough |
| 2 | tablespoons Garlic Olive Oil, plus more for drizzling (see recipe, page 59) |
| ¼ | pound thinly sliced pancetta, cut into 2-inch pieces |
| 1 | teaspoon red chile pepper flakes |
| 2 | tablespoons grated Parmesan cheese |

**1.** In a large skillet cook onions in hot olive oil over low heat for 40 to 45 minutes or until onions are caramelized, stirring occasionally.

**2.** Preheat a pizza stone in a 400°F oven. (If you don't have a pizza stone, line a large cookie sheet with parchment paper but do not preheat in oven.)

**3.** Brush the stretched pizza dough with Garlic Olive Oil. Spread the caramelized onions evenly over the dough. Top with pancetta; sprinkle with red chile pepper flakes. Sprinkle dough edges with Parmesan cheese.

**4.** Slide pizza onto preheated pizza stone or prepared cookie sheet. Bake for 20 to 25 minutes or until crust is golden brown. (Don't try to speed up the process by raising the oven temperature—you'll just end up with a burned crust.)

**5.** Cool the pizza slightly and drizzle lightly with additional Garlic Olive Oil. Cut into twenty-four 2 inch squares.

**Makes 24 pieces**

# PEAR AND GORGONZOLA PIZZA

*According to the originator of my first book/wine club, Sarah, "You must have a little sweet with your salty." This pizza is the perfect balance of sweet and savory. If you're strictly a red sauce-and-cheese kind of person, be brave and branch out! I promise you'll love this with a li'l Syrah.*

1   **pound raw stretched pizza dough**

    **Olive oil**

2   **ripe Bartlett pears, cored and thinly sliced (about 3 cups)**

5   **ounces Gorgonzola cheese, crumbled**

1. Preheat a pizza stone in a 400°F oven. (If you don't have a pizza stone, line a large cookie sheet with parchment paper but do not preheat in oven.)

2. Brush the stretched dough with olive oil. Shingle pear slices over dough, sprinkling Gorgonzola cheese between the pear slices.

3. Slide pizza onto preheated pizza stone or prepared cookie sheet. Bake for 20 to 25 minutes or until crust is golden brown. (Don't try to speed up the process by raising the oven temperature—you'll just end up with a burned crust.)

4. Cool pizza slightly and cut into twenty-four 2-inch pieces.

**Makes 24 pieces**

* * * * * * * **NO-COOK OPTIONS** * * * * * * *

The aromas in Syrah/Shiraz run the gamut, and the flavors are all over the board, so I chose this month's no-cook options to complement and contrast all those varied and dynamic things happening in your glass. As you taste this month's eats, see if you can pick up on similarities between the food's aromas and flavors and those coming through in your wine.

A few no-cook suggestions:

★Order in a pizza or two, choosing the toppings recommended in the pizza recipes.

★Serve an antipasto platter of cured and smoked meats along with an assortment of cheeses, including fresh mozzarella, Parmesan, Asiago, feta, goat, and Gorgonzola.

★Serve dark chocolates like Hershey's Miniature Special Dark.

★Serve figs, raisins, and dried cherries.

★Put out an array of fresh herbs in glasses. Include basil, mint, and oregano. Encourage guests to sniff the herbs along with their wines to see if they can find any of the scents lingering in the wine. (A trick is to take a leaf of the fresh herb and rub it between your fingers to let out the smell.)

* * * * * * * * * * * * * * * * * * * * * * * *

# TOMATO PIZZA PIE

*When done well, tomato pie is anything but boring! They serve this at a little cafe around the corner from my apartment. When I bite into this, I tune out the blaring car alarms and sirens of New York City and daydream of lounging at an outdoor cafe in Rome's bustling Piazza Navona.*

| | |
|---|---|
| 4 | cloves garlic, thinly sliced |
| 1 | tablespoon olive oil |
| 1 | 28-ounce can crushed tomatoes, undrained |
| 1 | tablespoon tomato paste |
| 1 | teaspoon dried basil, crushed |
| 1 | teaspoon salt |
| ½ | teaspoon black pepper |
| 1 | teaspoon chopped fresh oregano |
| 1 | pound raw, stretched pizza dough |
| 2 | tablespoons grated Parmesan cheese |
| 1 | tablespoon chopped fresh oregano |

**1.** For sauce, in a saucepan cook garlic in oil over medium-low heat just until the garlic is fragrant. Do not brown. Whisk in tomatoes, tomato paste, and basil. Cook for 25 minutes, stirring occasionally. Add salt and pepper; cook 5 minutes more. Remove from heat; add the 1 teaspoon oregano.

**2.** Preheat a pizza stone in a 400°F oven. (If you don't have a pizza stone, line a large cookie sheet with parchment paper but do not preheat in oven.)

**3.** Spread ¾ to 1 cup of the sauce evenly over dough. Sprinkle dough edges with Parmesan cheese.

**4.** Slide pizza onto preheated pizza stone or prepared cookie sheet. Bake for 20 to 25 minutes or until crust is golden brown. (Don't try to speed up the process by raising the oven temperature—you'll just end up with a burned crust.)

**5.** Cool the pizza slightly and sprinkle with the 1 tablespoon oregano. Cut into twenty-four 2-inch squares. Serve with remaining sauce.

**Makes about 24 pieces**

# merlot
## my dear

**You've** *been a member of the wine club for more than three months. Once people get wind of this, you'll be considered their personal wine expert. The craziest question people ask me—and a question you are sure to hear soon—is, "What is your favorite wine?" That's like asking a mother*

which child is her favorite. It's pretty impossible to pick. But there are certain elements that indicate how I will respond. And you should ponder these, too, before blurting out an answer. First, what time of year is it? Second, what is the event? Is it a blustery winter night or a hot summer eve? Will you be having a casual dinner with friends or a power lunch with colleagues?

April usually means the warm spring winds are right around the corner (unless, like me,

you live in a place where it's likely you'll see more snow before the tulips begin to bloom). Merlot (mur-LOW) is ideal for April. I find it to be a transition wine. I crave big reds when it's chilly, and I love acidic whites when it's sweltering. So for this warming-up month, Merlot fits the bill, bringing a softer side of red to the table before we jump into a cool white wine next month.

Merlot tops the charts as America's favorite red wine ordered by the glass. If you've ever

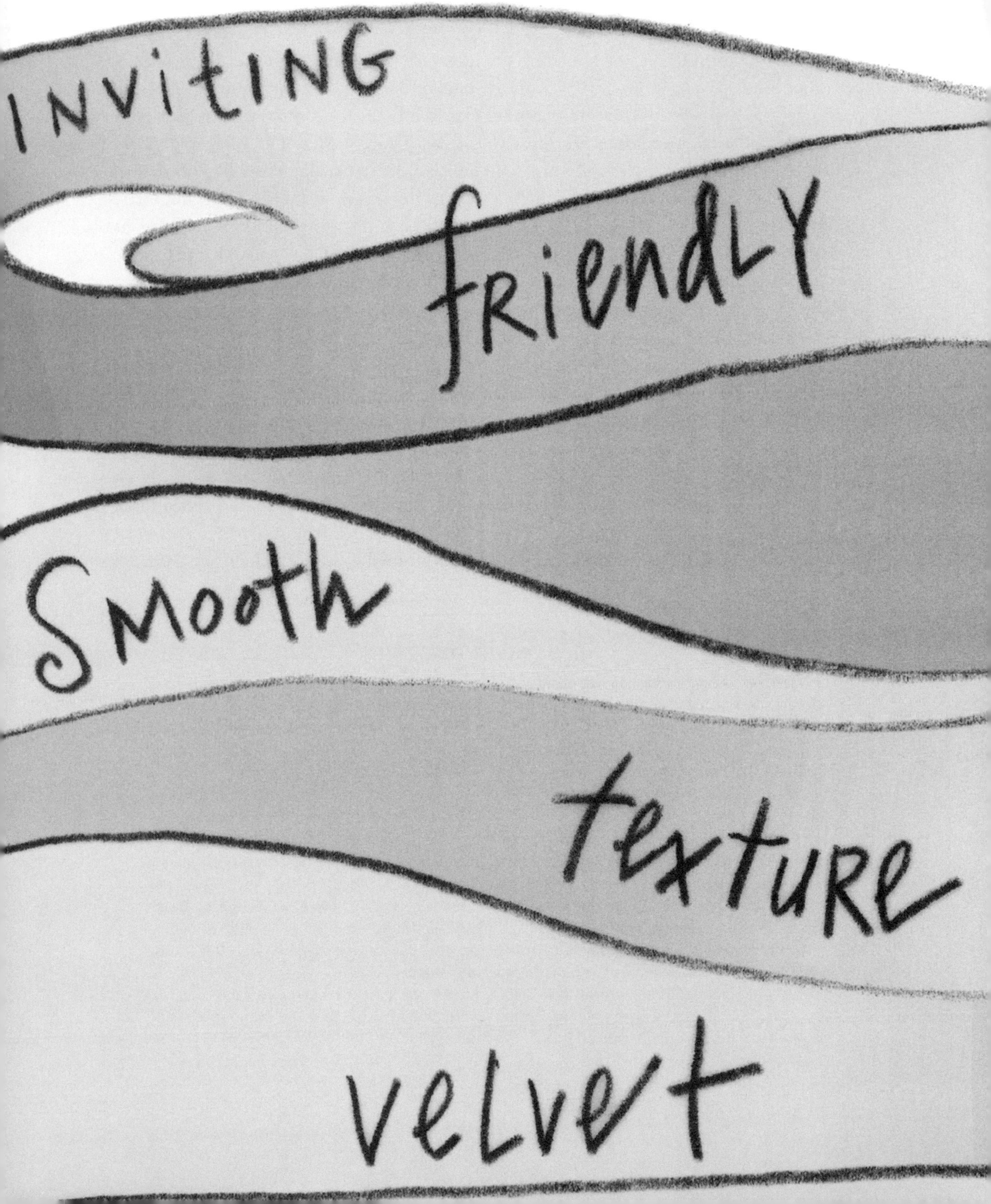

INVITING

friendly

Smooth

texture

velvet

tended bar or waited tables, you know this to be true. And if you've seen the movie *Sideways*—an homage to all wine geeks—you've heard the main character aggressively yell that he will not drink Merlot. (Although funny enough in the end he sips … well, I won't ruin it for you.) So while it's the most often poured red wine, it's not considered the fave in wine geekdom.

What gives? Merlot's got a reputation for being smooth, and that it is. It may be the only wine that has gotten so far on its texture and body. For this reason alone, lots of wine snobs see it as a simple wine, lacking complexity and character. Oh, please, get over yourselves already!

## Getting to Know Merlot

Merlot wins the popularity contest because it's so easy to approach and readily available. It blends well with other grapes, like Cab and Cab Franc. And it pairs pleasantly with plenty of foods. Merlot is shyer than Cab, but that doesn't make it any less of a wine. Jancis Robinson, a famed wine authority and Master of Wine, describes Merlot as "Cabernet without the pain." I don't know about you, but I'm all for less pain and more pleasure when it comes to my wine. In fact, I find it pleasing just to say the word Merlot. It rolls right off your tongue … Merlot, Merlot, Merlot. I'm positive you'll find its softer approach endearing after you've had such huge Cabs and Syrahs. Let's jump right into this juice!

The Bordeaux region's most planted black grape, Merlot is a mainstay of France's great wines from the Saint Emilion and Pomerol

* * * * * * * * * * * *
### YOU'LL NEVER FORGET IT

In March we talked about how wine can taste icky if it's been corked, cooked, or wrought with too much sulphur. Another nasty wine habit is oxidation. It sounds just like what it means: Oxidized wine is wine that has been exposed to too much oxygen. This is different from the aeration we're aiming for when swirling a wine. Overexposure to oxygen can happen during the winemaking process; it can also be caused by a faulty cork or if the wine has been open too long, which happens frequently in restaurants that serve wine by the glass.

With white wines, you may be able to notice oxidation before you even take a sip. Oxidized whites turn amber and then brownish in color, just like a cut apple turns brown when exposed to oxygen. Reds don't show it so much in the color, but one sip and you'll know—oxidized wine is LIFELESS!!! You won't get a pleasant fruity aroma or a nice full body. The wine will be flat and fruitless, and in extreme cases it tastes like vinegar.

So this month open a bottle of Merlot five days to a week before your wine club gathering. Pour yourself a glass and recork the bottle by gently pressing the cork back into the neck. Don't recork with a Vacu Vin or any other wine-saving device. Leave the bottle on the countertop until the wine club gathering. On the day of the tasting, put this bottle into the mix with the freshly opened wines. Taste it next to the new wines and you will never forget what oxidized wine smells and tastes like.

* * * * * * * * * * * *

regions. Both of these regions produce Merlot-based wines; however, staying true to the style of Bordeaux, they're not made from just the Merlot grape. Just as Cabs from Bordeaux are

Merlot wins the popularity contest because it's so easy to approach and readily available.

not straight-up Cabs, these Merlot-based wines are also blended, mostly with their big brother, Cabernet Sauvignon. Merlot is thinner-skinned than Cabernet, which means its juice is lighter in color and lacks that kick-you-in-the-teeth acid; it also doesn't mess with those austere tannins like Cab does.

Although wine "experts" give Cab credit more often than Merlot, Merlot is actually a much better-behaved grape in the vineyard and in the glass. In the vineyard, the grape ripens before Cab and more often has a successful growing season; in the glass it brings that smoothness that Cab can achieve only when blended or aged. Merlot vines pretty much grow all over the world, including France, Italy, Switzerland, Slovenia, Hungary, Romania, Bulgaria, Russia, California, Washington, New York, Argentina, Chile, Australia, New Zealand, and South Africa. Widely available translates to totally affordable. And pleasing price tags mean you can try many Merlots without going broke.

### Cabernet's Right-Hand Man

Cabernet and Merlot are similar in flavor

### ✶ ✶ ✶ THE MONA LISA ✶ ✶ ✶

Duckhorn Merlot, Napa, California; $40 to $50. There are plenty of California Merlots that fall into the everyday wine-drinking category, meaning there is nothing wrong with them, but nothing special about them either. But in all fairness, there are plenty that stand out. This month's *Mona* may be the most famed Merlot in America, but the best part is that its fame won't cost you a fortune. For under $50 a bottle, you get a full-bodied Merlot with that yummy blueberry pie à la mode aroma. The flavor follows through with ripe plum and full jammy effects accented by caramel and dark chocolate and a finish that will leave you wanting to get out of your chair and give it a standing ovation. This is the epitome of a New World Merlot.

### ✶ ✶ ✶ THE SALVADOR DALÍ ✶ ✶ ✶

Marilyn Merlot, Napa Valley, California; $25 to $40. You may have thought Marilyn Monroe gave her best on the big screen, but you'll be sure to find much of her lusciousness in a big glass of Marilyn Merlot. The 2002 vintage goes for about $25 a bottle, and the 2001 is priced around $40. Besides being a brilliant bottle suitable as a gift, this wine delivers a smooth Merlot with a fun flare. With the beautiful Marilyn right there on the label, you'll fall in love at first sight and then all over again once you've tasted the plush black-fruit flavors and inhaled the milk chocolate and toasty vanilla perfume.

Bordeaux-style glasses have a longer bulb with a tapered mouth, which allows Merlot's subtle aromas to build in the glass. That way, when you stick your schnoz in, you actually smell something.

profiles. Where they'll differ is in flavor intensity and body. Remember, Cab is a big-boy wine—big flavor, big alcohol, big tannins. Merlot—not so big. High alcohol provides viscosity, and we perceive this viscosity as body. Most often Cabs are higher in alcohol than Merlots; thus Cabs are fuller-bodied wines. Once again, this is the wine world we're talking about, so there are exceptions; for example, some more expensive Merlots from California and Washington can be just as high in alcohol as Cabs, making them much bigger wines on your palate.

While Cab and Merlot differ, they are more alike than a wine snob would admit. These two grapes are like two bees in a bonnet—or should we say vines in a vineyard? In France's famed Bordeaux wines, Cab and Merlot are blended to make the best of the best. Cab brings on the big guns, but when it is blended with Merlot, you get a wine with balance and character. In California, winemakers replicate this art of blending in what's called Meritage-style wine (see "Wine Speak," page 72). And America isn't the only player to make these Bordeaux-esque blends; winemakers the world over blend Cab, Merlot, and other traditional Bordeaux grapes for their own takes on Bordeaux-style wines.

And speaking of the world …

## Old World, New World

"Old World" and "New World" are terms that get tossed around a lot among wine geeks. Talking Old versus New World is a lot like when you're talking music and you get into that old school versus new school discussion. In music, jazz is old school, meaning it's been around awhile, it continues to get recognition throughout the decades, and it's considered a classic style of music. Rap and hip-hop are

**WINE SPEAK**

* * * * * * * * * * *

**Black grapes:** Grapes used to make red wines. Merlot, Cabernet Sauvignon, and Syrah are just some of the black grapes.
**Meritage:** Wines made in the United States in the style of Bordeaux wines. The typical blend for reds includes Cabernet Sauvignon, Merlot, and Cabernet Franc but may also include Petit Verdot and Malbec. There is also a white Meritage.

* * * * * * * * * * * *

**Earthy:** Describes wines with aromas and tastes reminiscent of wet rocks, minerals, or mushrooms.
**Château Petrus:** A famous wine from the Pomerol district of the Bordeaux region in France. Made with 95 percent Merlot, it costs close to a grand upon release; older vintages can get upward of $5,000 at auction.

* * * * * * * * * * * * * * * * * * * * * * * * * * * * * * * *

new school. Even though they have a few decades under their belts, they are anything but traditional and can get a little crazy at times. Same goes for the world of wine. The old Frenchies are Old World, and new wines from New Zealand are New World. To sum it up, Old World wines are from Europe and the Mediterranean, and New World wines are from everywhere else: California, Australia, and South America.

Old World, like old school, means steeped in tradition. New World vintners take advantage of science and

technology when planting vines and making wine. New World winemakers can and do change their style on a dime, whereas Old World winemakers aren't so interested in what's fashionable with wine.

Once they're in the bottle, there are two main differences between Old World and New World wines. First—and easiest to

> Inexpensive wine does not mean bad wine. It means there are more available. And these days, there are tons of great wines for under $15 a bottle.

grasp—is that New World wines are mostly made to be drunk immediately upon release, while some Old World wines are nasty when first released but with age gain grace and beauty. Second, Old World wineries depend on Mother Nature, whereas New World wineries can manipulate her. On that note, it's time to talk *terroir*.

## Terroir's Not So Terrifying ...

The word *terroir* (ter-wahr) is a little awkward to spit out, but the concept is important as we move forward and learn more about wine. Since there is no direct English translation, we use this fancy French word to describe all of the influences on a vine, including soil, climate, and wind. This is that Mother Nature thing. *Terroir* is attributed to Old World wines more often than New World wines; the thinking is that wines made from vines grown in a particular place will—year after year—show distinctive elements of its *terroir* in the glass. A Merlot from Pomerol will always be identifiable and different from a Merlot from the Languedoc region because of its *terroir*.

It's a bit abstract to grasp, but as you continue to taste and sniff, try to take note of what you smell. Is it earthy or fruit forward? If it's earthy in aroma, you're more than likely swirling an Old World wine, and if it's fruit forward you're probably sipping something from the New World.

## Price Value

My little sister, K. C., told me the way she knows if a wine is good is by looking at its price tag. If it's expensive she buys it. WRONG—there are two things that make a wine expensive. The first is availability; if limited bottles are available, the wine is more expensive. Second is name recognition. You've heard of Dom Perignon Champagne; so the makers can charge you $150 a pop (no pun intended). Translation: Inexpensive wine does not mean bad wine. It means there are more available. And these days, there are tons of great wines for under $15 a bottle. In most cases and certainly when it comes to wine, money isn't everything.

## April's Picks

I mentioned before that the Merlot grape

* * * * * * * * * * * * * **WINE TREND** * * * * * * * * * * * * *

You already know to steer clear of your favorite white sweater when tasting red wine. But if you must put out that white linen tablecloth, there are a few new gadgets you'll want on hand when hosting a red wine tasting.

**Wine Away:** This is a cleaning product that does just what it says. So if you are insistent on wearing that white shirt and you do indeed dribble a bit, spray this on and follow the bottle instructions for cleaning the wine away. Order it online or see if your wine merchant carries it.

**Vino Pour Disks:** Also called wine pour disks, these are oval, shiny Mylar disks that you insert into a bottle's opening. The disk will prevent dripping while pouring, thus saving your tablecloths and linens from stains. They average about $1 a disk and can be washed and reused. These can also be ordered online, or check with your local wine shop.

* * * * * * * * * * * * * * * * * * * * * * * * * * * *

grows all over the world, but for this tasting, we are going to focus on France (Old World) and a few picks from the New World. I recommend choosing two Merlots from California at different price points. This way you can see how a Merlot changes as the price goes up; you can also see if you agree with my little sister about price value. We'll also be for the first time tasting wine from Washington, a noteworthy wine region that produces delish Merlot. All of these sips should be an adventure. Remember to have fun and laugh a little—but not at the same time you're sipping!

**France:** Choose one from Pomerol (you're looking at anywhere from $30 to $50 a bottle) or Saint Emilion (you may find some between $20 and $30 a bottle, but most will be priced between $30 and $60 a bottle).

**California:** Choose one bottle priced from $10 to $15 and another priced from $20 to $30.

**Washington:** In the $18 to $30 range.

**Chile:** In the $6 to $15 range.

**Ringer:** Since Merlot is lighter than a Cab but bigger than a Pinot Noir, you could use either varietal for the ringer this month. But since we've sipped Cab already, and because it can be so similar to Merlot, I suggest you throw in something new, like an Oregon Pinot Noir.

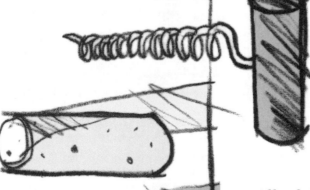

All of these sips should be an adventure. Remember to have fun and laugh a little—but not at the same time you're sipping!

# GET YOUR DRINK ON

*I was recently packing up wine for yet another move and left out only what I would need for tasting notes. My husband came home and we decided to unwind over a glass of red. Riffling through the unpacked lot, I realized I'd made a big boo-boo—I had left behind only Merlot; the rest were all whites. He doesn't like Merlot. So like a good wife, I opened a bottle, poured a glass, and told him it was a Cab. He first seemed skeptical, but I didn't make a peep. When he got up to pour a second glass, I knew he was converted. It just goes to show that if you think you don't like a varietal—like Merlot, for instance—you could be selling yourself short. You may be a Merlot lover after all.*

**COLOR:** Merlot should be a few shades lighter than Cab, but depending on who's making it, the color can be even deeper. French Merlot is more likely to be true to the varietal—a lighter, more ruby-toned wine. Lower-priced California Merlot should also seem lighter hued in the glass; however, California and Washington Merlot made to be in-your-face (usually more expensive) will have a deeper, darker hue of purplish red.

**AROMA:** Merlot shows juicy berries, like blueberries and blackberries, and the words *plummy* or *jammy* come to mind when sniffing. A California Merlot may show some of its alcohol when you sniff and tends to show riper fruits than those of the Old World style. A French Merlot will be on the softer side all the way around. Because French Merlot isn't usually created to show off, you may have to sniff a few times before you find something. With old school wines, you may have trouble finding the words to describe the aroma. That's that tricky *terroir*—try words like *earthy* and *mineral-like*. Merlot can present aromas of cocoa or milk chocolate; you may also smell vanilla and sweet spices like clove and cinnamon. When these scents are present in Merlot, it often reminds me of blueberry pie à la mode.

**TASTE:** Same as the aromas—the Frenchies will be softer on the palate. New World wine will be bigger on fruit. With either style, I'm sure you'll be pleased

how this smooth operator tickles your tummy. Oak might show itself in vanilla or spice when you sip, but again it will be very subtle. Everyday, inexpensive Merlot from Chile will be much softer than some of the big oaky guys from California.

**BODY:** Merlot is famous for its body. It is a soft, smooth, medium-bodied red wine. French Merlot will be lower in alcohol than California Merlot. Therefore, those from California will lean more toward being medium- to full-bodied. Merlot has medium tannins, also considered soft.

**FINISH:** French Merlot will not finish like a Cab or a Syrah but will have a shorter-term finish; notice the softer tannins and how your mouth isn't taken over by them. The general style of all Merlots should be suave with a soft finish. However, remember that the money you spend and where the wine comes from may dictate the wine's finish and finesse. I find French Merlot finishes with finesse, while expensive Merlot from California and Washington goes out swinging in the end, just like a big-boy Cab.

**RINGER:** In appearance, the Pinot Noir will be more translucent than Merlot. It will also be lighter in body and alcohol. When you sniff the ringer, think of red berries instead of the dark berries you're sniffing in Merlot. You should smell cherries and raspberries and taste them as well.

## LET'S EAT! FOOD AND WINE PAIRING

Since Merlot can range from a big fruit-forward wine to a soft and sensitive sip, I've chosen a variety of nibbles for this month. If you're full swing into warm weather, big Merlots pair nicely with grilled meats. But not everyone is up for grilling in a snowsuit so I've included a dynamite beef dish with horseradish sauce that's perfect paired with those big Merlots. On the softer side of the wine, we'll explore how Parmesan cheese, Spanish olives, dates, and cinnamon mingle with Merlot.

\* \* \* \* \* \* \* \* \* \* \* \* \* \* \* \* \* \* \* \*

# PARMESAN CHEESE STRAWS

*When I moved to Atlanta, I fell in love with red velvet cake, sweet tea, and cheese straws. These yummy staples of the South aren't the same without the sunshine. But if I close my eyes tight enough and nibble on these light and fluffy cheese straws, I swear I feel that southern sunshine!*

1  slightly beaten egg

1  teaspoon water

All-purpose flour

1  box (2 sheets) frozen puff pastry, thawed

½  cup shredded Parmesan cheese

**1.** Preheat oven to 400°F. Line two cookie sheets with parchment paper; set aside. Gently beat egg and water together with a fork; set aside.

**2.** Dust your work space lightly with flour. Unfold the puff pastry sheets; press seams together. Brush both pastry sheets with egg mixture; sprinkle each sheet with ¼ cup of the Parmesan cheese.

**3.** Using a pizza cutter, cut each pastry sheet crosswise into twenty ½-inch-wide strips or ten 1-inch-wide strips. (Don't worry if they seem too skinny—they will puff up.)

**4.** Twist ends of each strip in opposite directions several times. Place on prepared cookie sheets, pressing down ends of strips. Bake about 12 minutes or until golden brown.

**Makes forty ½-inch straws or twenty 1-inch straws**

Note: These are best the day they are made, but you can make them 1 day in advance. Store in an airtight container.

# DEEP-FRIED GREEN OLIVES

*I thank my husband, Michael, for these awesome olives every time I pop one in my mouth. He always talked about his friend's mom in Brooklyn who made amazing stuffed olives. So I did my best to re-create them—we were both drooling over the results.*

| | |
|---|---|
| 2 | slightly beaten eggs |
| 1 | tablespoon water |
| 40 | 1×¼-inch pieces mozzarella cheese (about 2 ounces) |
| 1 | 8½-ounce jar Santa Barbara Olive Company "Pitted Country" green olives or 40 large pitted green olives |
| 1 | cup Italian-seasoned fine dry bread crumbs |
| 4 | cups canola oil |

**1.** Gently beat eggs and water together with a fork; set aside. Stuff one piece of cheese snugly into each olive. Dip stuffed olives in the egg mixture; roll in bread crumbs.

**2.** In a large, deep saucepan or deep-fat fryer, heat oil to 375°F. Fry olives, about 10 at a time, for 30 to 45 seconds. Remove olives with a slotted spoon; drain on paper towels. Resist the temptation to pop one in your mouth until after they have cooled at least 5 minutes! Reheat the oil between batches (unless you are using a deep-fat fryer that maintains a constant temperature).

**Makes 40 fried olives**

# DATES
## with Goat Cheese, Almonds, and Prosciutto

*These are so easy and so delicious. The sweet date, the crunchy almond, the creamy cheese, and the salty prosciutto all mixed up create an explosion of flavor and texture in your mouth. When you see how simple these are to make and taste how superb they are, you'll want to make them for every party.*

| | |
|---|---|
| 12 | large whole dates, halved and pitted |
| 2 | ounces goat cheese |
| 24 | blanched whole almonds |
| 6 | thin slices prosciutto, cut into 4 strips each |
| 2 | to 3 tablespoons olive oil |

1. Fill each of the halved dates with ½ teaspoon goat cheese. Push one almond into the center of the goat cheese. Wrap one strip of prosciutto around each stuffed date.

2. Heat olive oil in a skillet. Cook wrapped dates about 1 minute on each side or until crisp. Remove the dates from skillet; drain on paper towels.

**Makes 24 stuffed dates**

**\* \* \* \* \* \* \* NO-COOK OPTIONS \* \* \* \* \* \* \* \***

Setting up an olive bar is a great no-cook option for nibbles this month. You can find a variety of olives in many grocery stores. In most deli sections, you can find mixed olives packed in herbs or packed with peppers for a spicy mix to see how well you feel Merlot pairs with a little heat. Here are a few types of olives I suggest you include:

**Kalamata:** Greek black olives, almond shape, deep purple in color, brine-cured with a rich, fruity flavor.
**Niçoise:** French black olives, small in size with a rich, nutty flavor; they're often packaged with herbs.
**Picholine:** French green olives with a lightly salty herbaceous flavor.
**Manzanilla:** Spanish green olives; these are big and great for stuffing.
**Gaeta:** Italian black olives, wrinkly in appearance; these are bitter but mild in flavor.

The only difference between green olives and black olives is ripeness when they are picked. After that they are cured, giving us that salty flavor.

You could also put out some fresh country bread and different styles of olive oil for dipping. This way you're partying with friends, enjoying the conversation, and learning about wine and food.

While you're at it, serve some store-bought cheese straws to see if you like cheese with these wines. You can also prepare a tray of the ingredients for the stuffed dates and serve these items separately: dates, almonds (I love the Spanish Marcona almonds), thin-sliced prosciutto, and goat cheese. Together or on their own, these all pair well with Merlot.

**\* \* \* \* \* \* \* \* \* \* \* \* \* \* \* \* \* \* \* \* \* \* \***

# CINNAMON-MERLOT ROASTED PEARS

*These easy, yet elegant pears are a great finale to an intimate dinner party. When you serve them in smaller portions like this, more guests can enjoy being spoiled. Bridging the Merlot in your glass with the Merlot in the recipe creates a refined touch for your tasting and makes for an excellent match.*

| | |
|---|---|
| 6 | large ripe Bosc pears |
| 1 | cup Merlot |
| 1 | cup cherry juice |
| 2 | cinnamon sticks |
| ¼ | cup sugar |
| ⅛ | teaspoon salt |
| ½ | cup mascarpone cheese |

**1.** Preheat oven to 375°F. Peel pears, leaving stems intact. Cut a thin slice from the bottom of each pear and insert an apple corer; twist and pull to remove cores.

**2.** Combine Merlot, cherry juice, and cinnamon sticks in an 8×8×2-inch baking dish. Add pears. Bake for 45 to 60 minutes or until pears are tender, spooning liquid over pears every 15 minutes.

**3.** Reduce oven temperature to 200°F. Remove pears from baking dish. Pour liquid into a saucepan; stir in sugar and salt. Gently boil liquid for 10 to 12 minutes or until reduced to a syrup. Return pears to baking dish and keep warm in oven until ready to serve.

**4.** To serve 12, cut each pear in half; to serve 24, cut each pear into quarters. Drizzle syrup over pears; dollop with mascarpone cheese.

**Makes 12 or 24 roasted pears**

# EGGPLANT PARMESAN BITES

*There are lots of foods I love, just not a heaping plateful. Eggplant parm is one of them. I find these treats to be the perfect serving size and an example of how a big Merlot can stand up to the big flavor and rich texture of tomato sauce and mozzarella cheese.*

2    Japanese eggplants (8 to 12 inches long)

2    slightly beaten eggs

1    tablespoon water

1    cup Italian-seasoned fine dry bread crumbs

2    tablespoons all-purpose flour

6    tablespoons cooking oil

    Salt

¾    to 1 cup tomato sauce

1    cup shredded mozzarella cheese

    Fresh basil, sliced into thin strips (chiffonade)

**1.** Cut eggplants crosswise into ¼-inch-thick slices (any thicker and you will end up with mushy bites, not crispy bites).

**2.** Gently beat eggs and water together with a fork. Stir together bread crumbs and flour.

**3.** Dip each eggplant slice in egg mixture, then in bread crumb mixture, turning to coat both sides.

**4.** In a large skillet heat 3 tablespoons of the oil over medium heat. Fry eggplant slices, half at a time, about 1 minute on each side or until golden. Place eggplant slices in a single layer on a wire rack inside a large baking sheet. Sprinkle eggplant slices with salt.

**5.** Wipe skillet with paper towels. Heat remaining 3 tablespoons oil; fry remaining eggplant slices.

**6.** Preheat broiler. Once all eggplant slices are fried, spoon about 1 teaspoon of the tomato sauce on top of each slice; sprinkle with mozzarella cheese. Broil about 2 minutes or until cheese is melted. Garnish with basil.

**Makes 32 to 48 bites**

Note: This recipe calls for the long, skinny eggplant, shaped kind of like a cucumber. It may be found in grocery stores under any of these names: Japanese, Italian, or Chinese.

# BEEF TENDERLOIN SKEWERS
## Au Jus with Horseradish Sauce

*Unless I'm painting a turkey to be photographed for a magazine, I don't use Kitchen Bouquet. In this recipe, it adds a touch of sweetness and makes a picture-perfect beef skewer. After all, people eat with their eyes. Once you've tasted these with Merlot, you'll see their success goes way beyond looks.*

| | |
|---|---|
| 2 | 8-ounce pieces beef tenderloin |
| | Salt |
| | Black pepper |
| 2 | tablespoons Kitchen Bouquet |
| 2 | cloves garlic, minced |
| ½ | cup dried mushrooms |
| 1 | cup diced onion |
| ½ | cup diced carrots |
| ½ | cup diced celery |
| 5 | sprigs fresh thyme |
| 2 | sprigs fresh rosemary |
| 1 | 14-ounce can beef broth |
| 1 | recipe Horseradish Sauce |
| ½ | cup red wine |
| 1 | bay leaf |

**1.** Season all sides of the beef tenderloin pieces with salt and pepper. Combine Kitchen Bouquet and garlic in a resealable plastic bag. Add meat to bag, turning bag to coat meat with marinade. Marinate in refrigerator for at least 4 hours or overnight.

**2.** Preheat oven to 425°F. Place mushrooms in a baking dish. Layer onion, carrots, celery, thyme, and rosemary on top of mushrooms. Pour ¼ cup of the beef broth over vegetables and herbs. Place meat on top. Bake for 20 to 25 minutes or until meat reaches 130°F. Remove meat from dish; cover and let stand.

**3.** Meanwhile, prepare Horseradish Sauce.

**4.** For jus, transfer vegetable mixture from baking dish to a large saucepan. Stir in the remaining beef broth, wine, and bay leaf. Cook over medium-high heat about 20 minutes or until the vegetables are soft and the sauce has thickened slightly. Season to taste with additional salt and pepper. Drain the liquid, pressing the vegetables to get out all the juice; discard the vegetables, thyme, rosemary, and bay leaf.

**5.** Cut each piece of meat into 12 to 15 very thin slices. Skewer slices and serve with au jus and Horseradish Sauce.

**Makes 24 to 30 skewers**

**Horseradish Sauce: In a bowl combine ½ cup dairy sour cream, ¼ cup mayonnaise, 2 tablespoons prepared horseradish, 1 tablespoon Dijon mustard, 1 tablespoon tarragon vinegar, ⅛ teaspoon salt, and ⅛ teaspoon cayenne pepper. Cover and chill until ready to serve.**

# *** Viognier

## *Chardonnay's sexy sister*

**You've** *heard how April showers bring May flowers, so this is the perfect month to explore a floral wine. For me, it's fascinating that a grape can smell like a flower; I don't know the science of it, but I do know that May's juice, Viognier (vee-oh-NYAY), will have you floating away on bouquets of*

gardenias, honeysuckle, and orange blossoms. Whether you're a romantic at heart or just in need of some pampering this spring, Viognier is the perfect pick.

Encouraging you to try Viognier is also my way of booting you out of the white wine rut by getting you to taste a wine that perhaps you've never sipped before. Viognier is a small taste of the many varieties in the wide world of white wine. If you're tired of ordering that same old house

white, or always picking up a bottle of Chardonnay, this month's tasting is sure to turn you on to trying new whites.

### Getting to Know Viognier

I call Viognier Chardonnay's sexy sister; actually, the two aren't really related, but if you put a glass of each side by side, they look like they could be sisters. And just like sisters they have a couple of things in common. They share traits of low acid and full

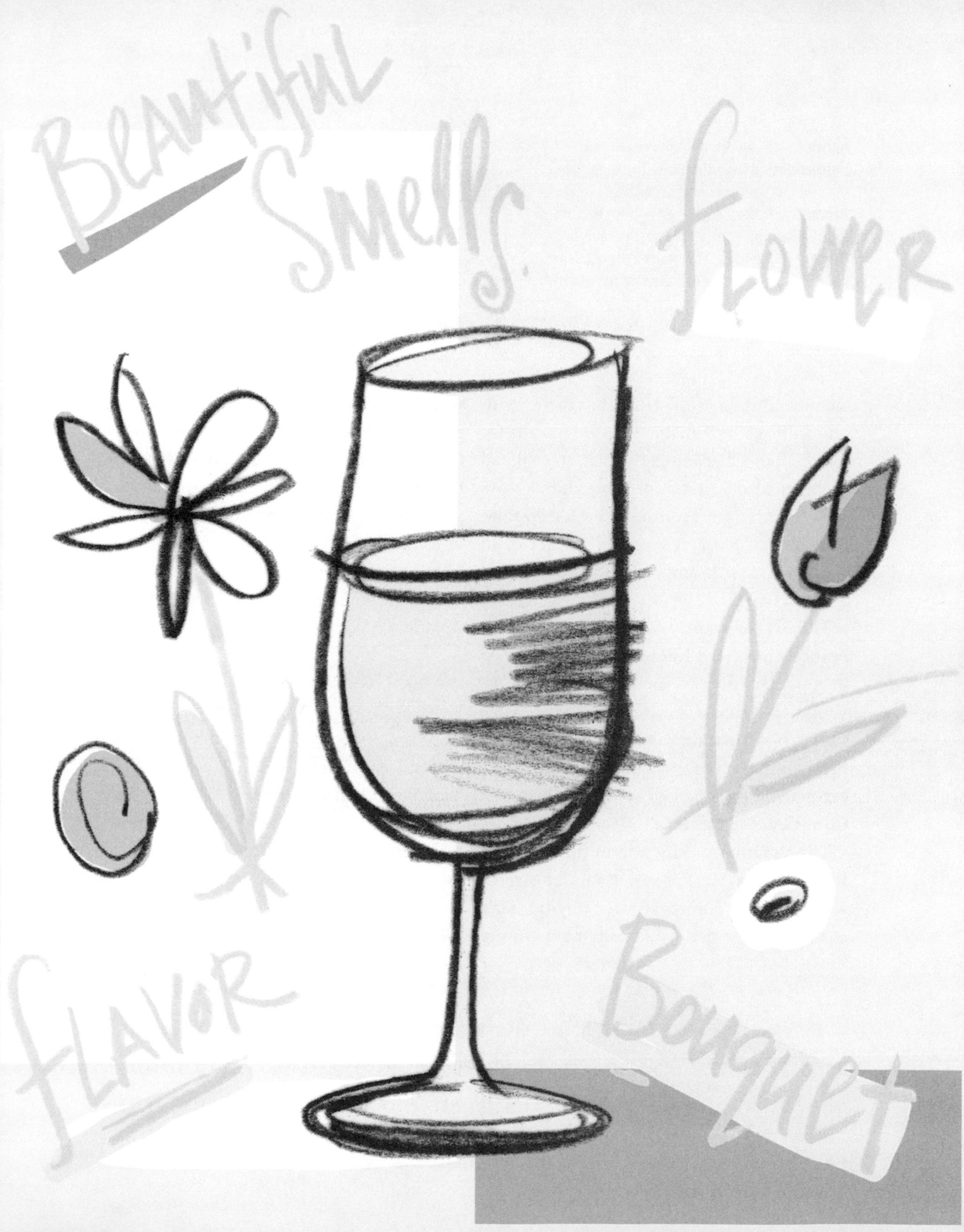
Beautiful
Smells.
Flower
Flavor
Bouquet

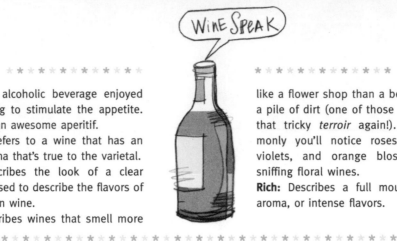
alcohol. But the similarities stop there. With one sniff it's undeniable that Viognier is far sexier than Chardonnay. Susie, an original member of my first book/wine club, always says, "If Marilyn Monroe is a Chardonnay, then Sharon Stone is Viognier—sexier in an exotic way, with ample sophistication and spice to boot."

This white grape, whose birthplace is in France's northern Rhône Valley, has gained in popularity over the years, and today, Viognier vines grow in places like California, Australia, and even Chile. That's pretty impressive for a grape that was nearly extinct not so long ago in its tiny home of Condrieu, France.

The Viognier production in the northern Rhône Valley is relatively small, and most wineries are family affairs. Buying land costs a pretty penny, so not many future winemakers are scrambling to pick up parcels—especially given the labor required to take care of the vines. Viognier is difficult to grow since it experiences rot and attracts pests easily. What the northern Rhône does offer, however, is its characteristic *terroir*. That's one of the reasons a Viognier from California will not taste like a Viognier from Australia or Chile.

### It's Good to Be …

Georges Vernay, a famed winemaker in Condrieu, believed in this fickle grape, and with his enthusiasm and tireless dedication Viognier began to thrive again, in the early 1990s. The vines of Condrieu are believed to be some of the oldest—if not *the* oldest—in France, and they grow on steep and rocky terraces. Growing and harvesting these grapes is the real definition of

Growing and harvesting these grapes is the real definition of backbreaking labor. But the results are worth it. If made well, as it is in Condrieu, a Viognier can be lusty, sexy, and musky, with hints of apricot and peach and exotic fruits.

backbreaking labor. But the results are worth it. If made well, like it is in Condrieu, a Viognier can be lusty, sexy, and musky, with hints of apricot and peach and exotic fruits. If made poorly, it can taste, well, flat and oh-so-boring.

The Rhône's other most famous white wine growing region is Château-Grillet, famed for its Viognier. While most Viognier should be drunk young, they say you can age Château-Grillet for up to 20 years. Honestly, I haven't the patience. If you fall in love with Viognier, you may like dreaming of this wine for 20 years. I'm positive you'll have sweet dreams, but I prefer to drink mine now.

## Syrah's Best Gal

I mentioned in February that this little white grape is blended with Syrah to produce the red wine Côte-Rôtie. It is rare for the French to allow a white grape to mingle with the likes of such a highly esteemed grape like Syrah. But in Côte-Rôtie, the addition of Viognier delicately softens the Syrah and adds depth to its aromatics. This goes to show that this little white grape is worthy of regal company.

## Viognier Challenge

Low production and finicky vines on steep slopes—that could mean only one thing to us: big bucks. Yep, Viognier wines from the northern Rhône aren't cheap, but they're definitely worth checking out if you can 1) find a bottle and 2) afford it.

Where the heck do you find a bottle, then? The two big guys, Condrieu and Château-Grillet, will be labeled just that. But if you want to sip some of what France has to offer before you invest big-time, head farther south in France. Viognier wines from the Languedoc region are less expensive and easier to find—and most often have labels that are easy to read, with the name Viognier right on the bottle for your buying pleasure! Just because down there they don't get the hype of Condrieu and Chateau-Grillet doesn't mean that they do bad Viognier. On the contrary, the juice from this region is lovely. And as I mentioned earlier, California, Chile, and Australia are producing Viognier well worth giving a try. So for this month's tasting do your best to include a bottle from each of these regions.

## It's All About Acid

Because Viognier is by nature low in acid, the wine is best consumed young (within one to three years). So if you're working on

> ### ✶ ✶ BANG FOR YOUR BUCK ✶ ✶
> Since Viognier in general may be harder to find in your stores, I'm going to recommend a couple. Both of these are widely available, so they should be easier to locate. Pepperwood Grove, California; around $9: A light gold Viognier with honey and pineapple in the nose and tons of fruit flavors. Rosenblum, California; around $12: This is an easy-drinking Viognier, with grapefruit, pear, and apricot aromas. It's crisp and clean and pairs well with food.

> Think about this when you're tasting Viognier: Are you getting apricot, peach, and hints of spice—or just oak?

building up your wine cellar, leave this one on the kitchen counter for quick consumption. What's acid got to do with aging? Generally, acid, tannins, and/or sugar are necessary for wines to age without going downhill. If you spot a Viognier that's been hanging around the shelves since '99, skip it, even if the "deep discount" is hard to resist. I think it's safe to say that you will be disappointed. Don't fret; there are still bargains to be had without sacrificing quality.

There are a few reasons why making a killer bottle of Viognier is no cakewalk. Viognier is picky about where it's planted. It likes a warm climate, so if a winemaker tries to grow vines in, say, Germany, the result will bear on the edge of nasty rather than sway to the side of tasty. Besides being so temperamental in the vineyard, the grape's low acidity makes it harder on a producer. If a winemaker isn't careful, a Viognier could end up blah, bleak.

Both the winemaker's and Mother Nature's hands are important. Some

### ✳✳✳ THE MONA LISA ✳✳✳

Miner Family Viognier, Simpson Vineyard, California; about $20. A lot of wine connoisseurs would balk at my choice here. They would say the best Viognier comes only from Condrieu or Château-Grillet in France. But my *Mona Lisa* may not be yours. Remember, wine, like art, is subjective. In this case I am biased. This was the bottle of Viognier that converted me to a die-hard fan of the juice. And without spending a fortune on one from France, you can see the beauty of this grape for around $20. It's drippingly sensual with all things Viognier. The star-bright straw color lures you to the glass, and at first sniff you are embraced by warm aromas of honeysuckle blossoms. These delicately delivered floral aromas are followed by luscious apricot and peachy flavors, and the wine feels creamy and dreamy on the palate. A refreshing finish brings a hint of mineral and a tangy twist that will leave your mouth watering for more.

### ✳✳✳ THE SALVADOR DALÍ ✳✳✳

Yalumba "Y" Series, South Australia; around $8 to $10. No matter how you pour it, this is an over-the-top Viognier. Viogniers from France and California tend to be more demure in their showing, whereas this little rock star goes big with flavor, aroma, and alcohol. If you're looking for a precious wine, this one isn't the choice—you're more likely to find a racy ride for your palate. This wine is definitely different. There's no mistaking this pick for anything but Viognier; it's plush with floral notes and honeysuckle and peach flavors. The lush, full-bodied mouth feel brings with it great acid—and we'd expect nothing less from a rock star.

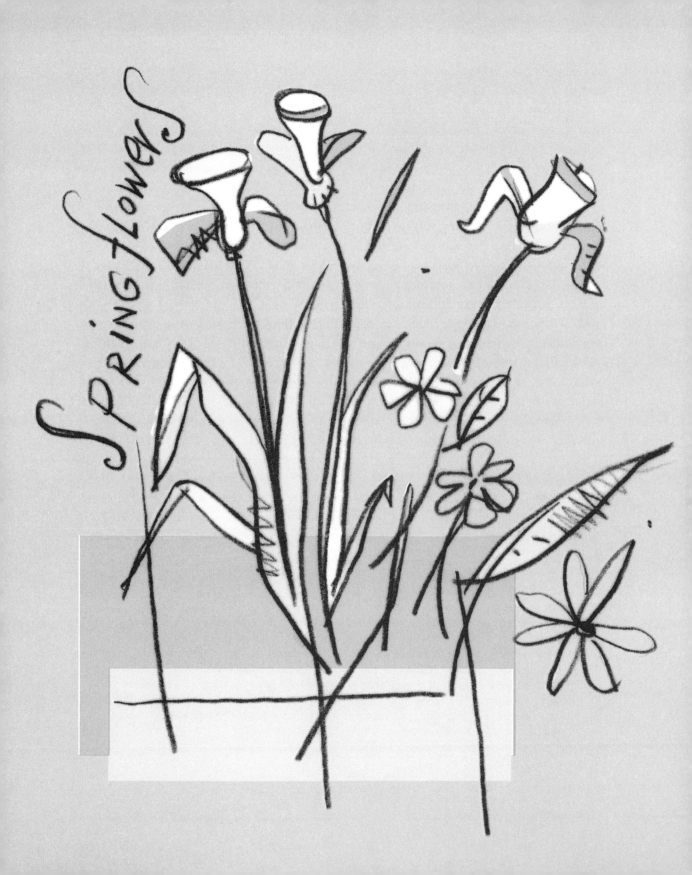

winemakers love aging their wines in oak, and in the case of Viognier, if there's too much, the wine loses its sensual qualities. Instead of being ravishingly beautiful, it will taste like the inside of an oak barrel. Some wine drinkers love their oak, but for this grape, it would be a sin to lose the seductive qualities Viognier has to offer. Think about this when you're tasting Viognier: Are you getting apricot, peach, and hints of spice—or just oak? If you're getting the latter, make a note and reach for another bottle the next go-round. If you think you are an oak lover, try to pair that oak-ridden Viognier with food and you'll quickly find that it just doesn't work. Overly oaked Viognier, or any wine for that matter, is like overly salty food. It makes me think the winemaker is trying to cover some mistake. Hmmmmm, think about it.

### Keeping Your Cool

I admire my sister Coleen for many reasons, but her food and wine savvy is not one of them. Inevitably, she calls every day with a cooking or wine query. She makes a stellar grilled cheese and tries on all the rest. Whether she knows it or not, her questions keep me on my toes, and sometimes she really throws me for a loop. For instance, recently she called me and asked, "Do you chill white wine?" At first I was speechless. I thought this highly educated, well-cultured 35-year-old woman surely must be joking. But she was serious. I recognized it was my folly, not hers, that led me to believe everyone knew that yes, indeed, you do chill white wine.

With that we began chatting about keeping wine cool and how wine benefits from being warmed to room temperature. I know this can be confusing, so hang in there. With all white wines, overly chilling a bottle will "lock up" the flavors in the wine, holding them hostage until it warms up to temperature. Traditionally wines are served at "cellar temperature," that is, about 55 degrees. But since we're against sticking thermometers in our wine, make sure the wine is chilled enough to be refreshing but

* * * * * * * * * * * *

## YOU'LL NEVER FORGET IT

If you're like me and despise being served a cold salad on a hot plate, remember that when you serve wine. All glassware should be room temperature. A warm glass is the wrong choice for a chilled white wine, and a cold glass is wrong for a full-bodied red. Never refrigerate or freeze wineglasses, especially champagne glasses; the moisture will dilute the wine. With the bubbly, you'll be missing the bubbles.

**Try this:** Pour one glass of Viognier in a room-temperature glass, another in a glass you have placed near the stove top to warm, and a third in a glass you have chilled in the freezer. Sip them side by side and you'll discover that the wine shows best in a room-temperature glass.

* * * * * * * * * * *

warm enough for you to detect those aromas and flavors. You'll know if it's too cold at first sniff. If you smell only alcohol, it needs a little warming up. If you find that's the case and the wine is too cold, take the bowl of the glass in your hands and swirl the glass around. The heat from your hands will warm the wineglass and, in turn, the

Traditionally, wines are served at "cellar temperature," that is, about 55 degrees.

wine. While this might not be "the" appropriate thing to do (according to wine snobs who insist you have a proper temperature-controlled wine storage unit), who cares? You're with friends, after all. And speaking of friends …

Because my friend Susie and I love to gab over a glass of Viognier, I must bring her back into the fold again for a story she told me of a near disaster in the kitchen. Her friend was upset recently because she had to use olive oil in a cake that called for vegetable oil. When the cake was baking, the smell of olive oil filled her apartment and she panicked. Taking the cake out of the oven, she smelled

* * * * * * * * * * **WINE TREND** * * * * * * * * * *

Viognier itself is a growing wine trend; with more vines popping up all over the world, it is gaining popularity. These days, wine lovers want more than just Chardonnay. In particular, a wine subculture called the ABCers (the ABC stands for Anything But Chardonnay) is desperate for a white wine that shows some character. Viognier is just the right juice to quash that desperation. In the wine world of yore, quaffers were loyal to their favorite Bordeaux or their best Burgundies. The biggest trend in wine is being adventurous. Too many to taste, too little time—but get sipping and you'll quickly find your faves.

* * * * * * * * * * * * * * * * * * * * * * * * * * *

olive oil. Tasting it hot—olive oil. She thought that the cake was a disaster until she let it cool down. Then, the cake was perfect.

Why? Food that is cooled will not release the aromas it did when hot. Think about that cake baking in the oven and all of the scents it released. Now think about your glass of arctic chilled wine. It's the exact opposite. We're back to the three bears here—too cold is not juuuust right. If you do prefer your wine ice cold, more power to you—tasting wine is all about personal preference, but let it warm up a touch just once and see what you think.

## May's Picks

While many grocery stores have extensive wine selections these days, Viognier might be difficult to locate outside of a wine merchant's shop. Since it's not as well-known as ever-present Chardonnay, many wine stores just don't carry it. So before driving all over town to find a bottle, pick up the phone. Call around and make sure that the retailer has a selection of Viognier before running yourself ragged. Small boutique wine shops are a good place to start the search. Don't be shy to ask for help—after all, that's what they are there for. And from my experiences, enthusiastic wine sellers are happy to help a curious customer.

This month we'll go globe-trotting with Viogniers and see how they differ from region to region, country to country.

**Chile:** There's not a lot of Chilean Viognier on the block, so any you find will work for this tasting. If you can find one from Valle del Maule or Casablanca Valley, pick it up; again, no worries if you can't.

**California:** Great California Viognier comes from any of these spots: Napa, Mendocino

> Don't be shy to ask for help—after all, that's what they are there for. And from my experiences, wine sellers are happy to help a curious customer.

County, and the Lodi Valley; look to spend between $15 and $22 a bottle.

**Australia:** Viogniers from South Australia and Victoria are the best. I especially like those from McLaren Vale and Barossa. You can find yummy bottles from $9 to $18.

**France:** No matter how you cut it, this is the most expensive category. Viognier from Condrieu starts at about $45 a bottle, whereas those from Château-Grillet are priced closer to $65 and up. Therefore, I recommend two or three guests chip in for this bottle. Don't skip it just because of the bucks. This will show the *terroir* of these distinguished regions. And you're worth every penny!

**Ringer:** I mentioned how similar Chardonnay and Viognier are in appearance, acid, and alcohol; however, because they have completely different aromas and taste profiles, Chardonnay is the perfect ringer for this month. Pick up a bottle of California Chardonnay priced between $12 and $20.

# GET YOUR DRINK ON

*I'll never forget the first time I sipped Viognier. After a long, hard day on my feet in the kitchen of Mumbo Jumbo restaurant, I couldn't wait to have a glass of wine. It was the first cold bottle I saw in the fridge, so I grabbed it, poured a glass, and melted into the couch. I took a sip and closed my eyes. My sore muscles and aching bones felt like they were slowly being massaged, and the room filled with the perfume of fresh flowers. I slowly opened my eyes to find that I was still in my same work clothes, on my same old couch, but with an empty glass in hand I was in a state of complete serenity. I read somewhere that actress Marisa Tomei said having a glass of wine is her beauty ritual. I'll bet she was talking about Viognier. But don't take my word for it—go ahead and start sipping.*

**COLOR:** The color of Viognier can range from clear to light golden. Viognier from France will be lighter in color, more like pale straw, whereas Viognier from California and Australia will be a deeper yellow color. No matter where the juice comes from, when you look at it, it should be bright (see "Wine Speak," page 84), not dull.

**AROMA:** Viognier is known for its powerful aroma. You'll find wisps of peach nectar and apricot when you sniff. Viognier shows pears; flowers like honeysuckle, gardenia, and orange blossoms; and sweet spices like cinnamon and clove. New World winemakers pull out the big guns with Viognier. When they say floral, they're not talking a slight touch of pansies, but rather bunches and bunches of gardenias blooming right under your nose. In addition to the in-your-face florals, New World Viognier brings more tropical fruit essences, like mango, passion fruit, and pineapple. The French Viognier is just as sexy but with a more subtle approach. It will show bits of earthiness and is musky in the nose. I swear the smell of this wine is designed to induce fanciful daydreaming.

**TASTE:** This wine may smell sweet, but it tastes dry. The French Viognier brings a more elegant palate of peaches and apricots, with hints of minerally *terrior*, whereas the California and other New World wines will taste more like tropical fruits. You may also detect vanilla flavors from the use of oak. Think of a pineapple sundae with all of that cream, vanilla, and tropical fruit toppings.

**BODY:** Viognier is a magic grape. Although it is medium- to full-bodied, it is low in tannins. If it shows tannins at all, they are soft tannins, and you'll notice them on the insides of your cheeks, rather than across your entire palate. This wine is low in acid, but there is still a nice hint of it. The body adds to Viognier's sex appeal, with a round mouth feel as rich as whipped cream.

**FINISH:** If ever a finish had finesse, it's Viognier's. A well-made Viognier, with that touch of acid, leaves a fresh and vibrant finish that lingers just long enough for you to crave another sip. A poorly made Viognier, however, can leave a bitter taste, and no matter how short the finish, it's too long for me.

**RINGER:** Chardonnay's aroma will be one of the fastest ways to pick it out of the lineup. Instead of the floral notes of Viognier, you are more likely to smell apples and vanilla. Also, those apples show up when you sip, making this sister a little more one-dimensional—compare the apple flavor to the variety of tropical fruits you may find in the Viognier.

##  LET'S EAT! FOOD AND WINE PAIRING

There are two schools of thought when pairing food with Viognier. Many people love Viognier paired with Asian delights, including spicy Thai treats. Others believe the simpler the food, the better to showcase the wine. This month, we'll have a mix of simple and spicy, and you can decide how you prefer to match your Viognier. When eating out, try a bottle with seafood, such as crab cakes or lobster (if you really want to be decadent!).

Viognier is an island. I like mine all by itself. Next time you're dining, instead of ordering a cocktail or a glass of bubbly, make yours a glass of Viognier for a fab-boo aperitif. In spring and summer, a glass of Viognier is a great way to start an alfresco dinner with friends or a picnic in the park with your honey. *Bon appétit!*

* * * * * * * * * * * * * * * * * * * *

# GOAT CHEESE SPREAD

*In Condrieu, Viognier is often paired with the region's famous goat cheese—slightly bitter (in a good way) with a great tang. Here, I've done my best to bring a bite of France stateside. As you put the two together, close your eyes and imagine you're completely relaxed with your feet up, gazing into the landscape of the French countryside.*

| | |
|---|---|
| 8 | ounces soft goat cheese |
| 1½ | tablespoons finely chopped fresh chives |
| 2 | teaspoons finely chopped fresh parsley |
| 2 | teaspoons grated fresh lemon peel |
| 2 | teaspoons fresh lemon juice |
| ½ | teaspoon freshly cracked black pepper |
| ⅛ | teaspoon salt (optional) |
| 1 | 8- to 10-ounce baguette-style French bread |
| | Cracked black pepper |

1. In a bowl soften goat cheese with the back of a wooden spoon. Add the chives, parsley, lemon peel, lemon juice, and pepper; stir until combined. If desired, stir in salt.

2. To serve, tear off pieces of the baguette and spread with goat cheese mixture. Serve with additional pepper.

**Makes 8 to 10 servings**

Note: If you prefer, toast the baguette in a 350°F oven for 5 to 10 minutes or until crisp and lightly browned. I like to just rip pieces from the untoasted baguette, but if you prefer your bread warm and toasty, go for it.

# PEAS AND PECORINO

*When we lived in Atlanta, every spring brought this dish to the menu at Oscar's, our favorite restaurant there. And we waited with salivating mouths. English peas at the height of their ripeness are so sweet, and when paired with pecorino cheese, the dish is a home run. This makes for an awesome salad or an adorable hors d'ouevre.*

2   medium ripe tomatoes

2   tablespoons diced shallot

2   tablespoons sherry vinegar

2   cups shelled peas or one 10-ounce package frozen peas, thawed

¼   cup diced pecorino Romano cheese

1   tablespoon finely chopped fresh mint

2   tablespoons extra-virgin olive oil

¼   to ½ teaspoon kosher salt

⅛   teaspoon freshly cracked black pepper

**1.** For tomato concassé, add the tomatoes to a small saucepan of boiling water for about 30 seconds to 1 minute. Remove tomatoes with a slotted spoon; place in ice water until cooled. With a small knife, remove core and peel off the loosened skin. Cut each tomato in quarters; remove seeds. Cut tomatoes into ¼-inch pieces; set aside.

**2.** In a bowl combine ⅔ cup of the tomato concassé, shallot, and sherry vinegar. Let stand for 10 minutes so the flavors can mingle. Add peas, cheese, and mint. Stir in olive oil, salt, and pepper. Serve in shot glasses as a miniature salad.

**Makes 10 to 12 servings (about 3 cups)**

# SALT AND PEPPER SHRIMP
## with Two Dipping Sauces

*Shrimp and Viognier make a nice match, but with these two dipping sauces you get to experience both sweet and spicy when sipping. The Mango Dipping Sauce brings out the tropical fruit flavors in the wine, and the Sweet Chile Sauce puts Viognier to the food and wine pairing test. I pass them both with flying colors!*

2   pounds large shrimp,
    peeled and deveined
    (about 26 to 30 per pound)

    Salt

    Black pepper

2   tablespoons vegetable oil

1   recipe Mango
    Dipping Sauce

1   recipe Sweet Chile
    Dipping Sauce

**1.** Season shrimp with salt and pepper. In a large skillet heat oil over medium-high heat. Add shrimp. (Do not crowd skillet—cook shrimp in batches.) Cook and stir about 3 minutes or until shrimp turn opaque. Remove shrimp from skillet. Serve with Mango Dipping Sauce or Sweet Chile Dipping Sauce.

**Makes about 50 pieces**

**Mango Dipping Sauce:** Place 3 to 4 cups diced mango in a food processor or blender. Cover and process until smooth. Transfer to a medium bowl. Add 1 small red sweet pepper, diced; 4 teaspoons fresh lime juice; 1 shallot, diced; 1 teaspoon kosher salt; and 1 fresh jalapeño chile pepper, diced. Season to taste with salt.

**Sweet Chile Dipping Sauce:** In a small saucepan combine 1 cup sugar, ½ cup water, and ½ cup rice wine vinegar. Bring to a boil. Remove saucepan from heat. Transfer to a heatproof container to cool. When completely cool, stir in 1 tablespoon Sriracha Garlic-Chile Sauce and ½ teaspoon crushed red chile pepper flakes.

# SEARED SCALLOP LOLLIPOPS

*When scallops are extremely fresh, the simplest preparation can be the most succulent. In this simple hors d'oeuvre, the subtle hints of ginger and cilantro are a perfect pair with a fruity Viognier. When you pop one in your mouth, notice how the rich texture of the scallop complements the body of the wine.*

| | |
|---|---|
| 24 | sea scallops |
| ½ | cup unsalted butter, softened |
| 1 | tablespoon grated fresh ginger |
| ¼ | cup chopped fresh cilantro |
| ¼ | teaspoon kosher salt |
| | Salt |
| | Black pepper |
| 24 | 4- to 6-inch wooden skewers |

1. Rinse scallops; pat dry. In a bowl combine butter, ginger, 1 tablespoon of the cilantro, and the ¼ teaspoon salt. Cover and chill.

2. Season scallops with salt and pepper. In a large nonstick skillet melt 1 tablespoon of the chilled butter mixture over medium-high heat. Sear half of the scallops for 2 to 4 minutes or until opaque, turning once. Remove scallops from skillet; repeat with remaining scallops.

3. Push each scallop onto a wooden skewer so they resemble lollipops. Arrange skewers on a serving platter. Place a small dab (about ½ teaspoon) of the remaining chilled butter mixture on each scallop; sprinkle with the remaining cilantro.

**Makes 24 servings**

### ✶ ✶ ✶ ✶ ✶ ✶ ✶ NO-COOK OPTIONS ✶ ✶ ✶ ✶ ✶ ✶ ✶

Why not go for Thai takeout for your club meeting? It's a great way to test food and wine pairings; try a bunch of different dishes and see what works best for you. Anything with lemongrass, cilantro, ginger, or mango would be delicious with a glass of Viognier. Do specify that you don't want the food too spicy; otherwise, you might as well just drink a cold beer.

On the simpler side you could buy some smoked salmon and crème fraîche to serve on bagels. This smoky dish will be a complete contrast to the wine, but it makes for a great culinary experience.

I often think of Viognier for brunch, so buy some scones and jams (especially apricot, peach, pear, and orange) to complement the wine's aromatics.

While you're at the bakery, you could pick up some fruit-and-cheese Danish. Viognier's rich body can stand up to sweets. But also buy some brownies or another chocolate item and see how quickly your Viognier gets crushed. Sweets that are too rich clash with the delicacy of the juice.

✶ ✶ ✶ ✶ ✶ ✶ ✶ ✶ ✶ ✶ ✶ ✶ ✶ ✶ ✶ ✶ ✶ ✶ ✶ ✶ ✶ ✶ ✶ ✶ ✶

# THAI LARB

*Now we're feeling the heat. This simple Thai stir-fry is jam-packed with tons of flavor and heat. You may make this dish as hot as you like, but I prefer to keep my brow dry and my taste buds intact. Thai food is fantastic with Viognier— now let's see if you agree.*

| | |
|---|---|
| 3 | tablespoons fish sauce |
| 2½ | tablespoons sugar |
| 2 | tablespoons fresh lime juice |
| 1½ | tablespoons Sriracha Garlic-Chile Sauce |
| 1 | pound ground raw turkey or chicken |
| 2 | tablespoons vegetable or peanut oil |
| ¼ | cup chopped green onions |
| 2 | tablespoons chopped fresh cilantro |
| 2 | tablespoons chopped fresh mint |
| 2 | tablespoons chopped fresh basil |
| 1½ | teaspoons grated fresh ginger |
| 1½ | teaspoons minced fresh jalapeño chile pepper* |
| 25 | small Boston or Bibb lettuce leaves |

1. In a large bowl combine fish sauce, sugar, lime juice, and garlic-chile sauce, stirring until sugar dissolves. Add ground turkey; mix well.

2. In a large nonstick skillet heat oil over medium-high heat. Add turkey mixture. Use a wooden spoon to break up any chunks of turkey. Cook until turkey is no longer pink. Remove from heat; drain off fat. Let cool.

3. When turkey mixture is cool, add green onions, cilantro, mint, basil, ginger, and jalepeño pepper; mix well. Let turkey mixture stand while you rinse and pat the lettuce leaves dry.

4. To serve, pile a small amount of the turkey mixture onto each lettuce leaf.

**Makes 25 pieces**

*Note: Because hot chile peppers, such as jalapeños, contain volatile oils that can burn your skin and eyes, avoid direct contact with chiles as much as possible. When working with chile peppers, wear plastic or rubber gloves. If your bare hands do touch the chile peppers, wash your hands well with soap and water.

# TOASTY COCONUT CRÈME BRÛLÉE

*This is to die for. Crème brûlée is always a special treat, but this one's toasty coconut makes every spoonful sinful. Coconut is a perfect flavor component to pair with Viognier, but too much will hide the delicacies of the wine. You'll see this dessert isn't too sweet, and the soft, toasty coconut flavors fit right in with the wine's subtle sex appeal.*

| | |
|---|---|
| 2 | vanilla beans |
| ¾ | cup flaked coconut |
| 4 | cups whipping cream |
| 2 | teaspoons coconut extract |
| 4 | cinnamon sticks, broken in half |
| 4 | whole star anise |
| 16 | slightly beaten egg yolks |
| 1¾ | cups sugar |

**1.** Preheat oven to 325°F. Using a small knife, cut vanilla beans lengthwise; scrape out seeds. Set beans and seeds aside. In a medium skillet cook and stir the coconut over low heat until toasted. Remove from heat; set aside.

**2.** In a medium saucepan combine cream, coconut extract, cinnamon sticks, star anise, vanilla beans and seeds, and toasted coconut. Bring to a simmer over medium heat. Remove from heat. Cover; let stand for 10 minutes.

**3.** For custard, in a medium bowl whisk together egg yolks and ½ cup of the sugar. Gradually stir about 1 cup of the hot cream mixture into the egg yolk mixture. Add egg yolk mixture to cream mixture in saucepan; whisk to combine. Strain the custard through a fine-mesh sieve. Discard coconut and spices.

**4.** Place ten 6-ounce ramekins or custard cups in a large baking dish (allow at least 1 inch between ramekins). Divide custard evenly among ramekins (this is easily done by using a small pitcher or large measuring cup). Place baking dish on oven rack. Pour enough hot water into the baking dish to reach halfway up sides of ramekins (the custards will bake more evenly and completely in a water bath and may curdle without one).

**5.** Bake about 35 minutes, until almost set. When removed from oven, custards will still appear slightly loose when shaken; they will set up completely as they cool. Remove ramekins from water bath; cool on a wire rack. Cover and chill overnight.

**6.** Just before serving, remove custards from refrigerator. Sprinkle 2 tablespoons of the remaining sugar over the top of each custard. Caramelize sugar with the flame of a brûlée torch. Serve.
**Makes 10 servings**

**Note: If you don't have a brûlée torch, place ⅓ cup sugar in a heavy skillet. Heat sugar over medium-high heat until it begins to melt, shaking skillet occasionally to heat sugar evenly. Do not stir. Once sugar starts to melt, reduce heat to low and cook about 5 minutes more or until all the sugar is melted and golden, stirring as needed with a wooden spoon. Quickly drizzle the caramelized sugar over custards.**

# riesling
## picnics and porch swingin'

**The** *stormy days of spring have passed, and the dog days of summer are yet to come. Yup, it's June, the ultimate picnic month and a divine time to dig into Riesling, the ultimate picnic wine. I'd always heard that Riesling tastes great when sipped atop a picnic blanket, but I had to find out for*

myself. Recently I put the theory to the test. I held a tasting, pitting Riesling against two other major picnic-wine contenders— sparkling wine and Pinot Grigio. We tasted all three in the great outdoors alongside typical picnic fare.

Sure enough, Riesling emerged as the champ—it just went so well with everything, from sandwiches and salads to pâté and pickles. My friend and book/wine club member, Susie, had told me this would be the case, but I

had to do it myself to believe it. I had always bet on bubbly being the winner. But this time I was dead wrong. I didn't quite mind because I had the perfect excuse to knock off and spend the day sipping Riesling. I knew I loved Riesling in summer because it is relatively low in alcohol (as low as 8 percent), which makes it a great wine to drink when you're so darn hot you think your head is going to explode. But after the picnic trials it has now made its way into my spring and fall lineups as well.

This month I say move your wine club outdoors. Spread a patchwork of picnic blankets under a tree or settle onto the front porch or backyard deck. You're about to discover why fresh, bright, and breezy June is the month to fall in love with this whimsical wine.

### Getting to Know Riesling

If Chardonnay is the Queen of Whites—beautiful, bold, powerful, and strong—and Viognier is Chard's sexy sister, then Riesling is another kind of charmer at the royal court. She's the ethereal beauty who needs no make-up, jewels, or glittering finery. She's stunning in her simplicity; her elegance is pure.

Too bad she's also so misunderstood. Somewhere along the line, Americans got the idea that Riesling was somehow unsophisticated and sweet as cotton candy—a

> The combo of pure fruit flavor zipped up with a crisp zing can be a beautiful thing indeed.

training-wheel wine on the level of wine coolers or Riunite on ice.

Maybe wine drinkers in this country are still suffering from a collective hangover after having imbibed too much Liebfraumilch in the '70s and '80s. Back in the day, this supersweet wine imported from Germany (but rarely drunk there) was incredibly popular in America. Then, when American wine drinkers started to get more serious about wine, moving from the supersweet Blue Nun to something else, everyone suddenly started dissing German wines,

### ✱ ✱ ✱ THE MONA LISA ✱ ✱ ✱

Trimbach Riesling, Alsace; $14. I worked in restaurants for a long time, and I never saw an entire waitstaff order the same shift drink (that's what you call a drink on the house after you've finished working your shift). That is, until we put Trimbach Riesling on the menu. It is like getting a little present wrapped in gold with green trim. You'll be pampered with aromas of minerals, lemon, and peaches. It's got refreshing acidity and a crisp, clean finish and is the perfect baby sip into the world of Alsatian Riesling.

### ✱ ✱ ✱ THE SALVADOR DALÍ ✱ ✱ ✱

Dr. Konstantin Frank, Johannisberg Riesling Dry; $17. This wine makes the Dalí list because it's a world-class wine from New York! The Finger Lakes region of New York is considered the Napa Valley of the East Coast, and Dr. Konstantin Frank is responsible for it. The doc knew the *terroir* was perfect for grapes like Riesling and Pinot Noir. This dry Riesling is dripping in apricot, lime peel, apple blossom, and that smoky, wet-slate aroma that's particular to the Finger Lakes region. It's got the fruit, minerals, and acid that make Finger Lakes wines more than memorable. It's got the status and the juice to back it up!

## IF THE GLASS FITS ...

Riedel, of course, makes wineglasses specifically for Rieslings—no surprise here. However, at this point in your wine-loving life, I recommend an all-purpose, practical white-wine glass. And by the way, avoid the traditional Mosel glasses—the ones with the short, squat lime green stems. While the stems are a pretty color, they are pretty useless as wineglasses. Their old-school design with the wide mouth lets the aromas blow off too quickly, plus when you try to swirl, the wine ends up on your rug (your shirt, your couch, your dog, etc.).

assuming all were as saccharine sweet or boring as the worst kinds of Liebfraumilch.

Even these days, you've likely been in the company of some wannabe wine snob who furrows his or her brow at the mention of Riesling and says, "Well, I just don't like sweet wines." It kills me when they say this—as if all Rieslings are sweet and as if not liking sweet wines is some sort of badge of honor!

Not only are such Riesling bashers misinformed, they're also missing out. Rieslings range from sweet to quite dry; plus, there's nothing wrong with sweetness in your wine—the best Rieslings balance their sweetness with a piercing acidity. It's a clean kind of sweetness that's never cloying in your mouth. The combo of pure fruit flavor zipped up with a crisp zing can be a beautiful thing indeed. Think of Audrey Hepburn in *Roman Holiday*—the charming, elegant princess who definitely has a racy side.

While the charms of Riesling are slowly being discovered by Americans, a lot of people here still don't quite get it. That's just fine with me—until Rieslings become wildly popular, they'll remain a good value. There are still some awesome finds to be had at around $10 to $15.

### The Cool Beauty

Don't go hunting for Rieslings in Spain, Italy, or the South of France; the finest Rieslings are produced from grapes grown in colder climates because the grape needs to ripen through a long, cool season and hang on the vine until autumn. While it's

### ★ ★ BANG FOR YOUR BUCK ★ ★

Pacific Rim Riesling, Bonny Doon Vineyard, California; $10. This bottle, screw cap and all, is an incredible buy. The Pac Rim Riesling is rich and tropical, with tingling peach and apricot flavors. It's got a great tartness and is a match made for sushi. Just look at the label and you'll see the beautiful woman dreaming of sashimi. This wine has style, flair, funk, and fantastic flavor to boot.

true you'll find Rieslings in Australia and California, these will be much more full-bodied, without that racy acidity you'll taste in wines from grapes grown in cooler climates like northern Germany and Alsace. And if Riesling is planted in a region that's too hot, the grapes will ripen too quickly. The wine will come out tasting flat, with no acidity—yuk!

When looking for Riesling, reach for those from these relatively northern regions of winegrowing countries.

**Mosel-Saar-Ruwer:** Located in the north of Germany, this is one of the country's finest

Riesling dominates its supersteep slopes, where the grape truly shines—the wines from this area are exquisite and nuanced, with a touch of sweetness.

winegrowing regions. Riesling dominates its supersteep slopes, where the grape truly shines—the wines from this area are exquisite and nuanced, with a touch of sweetness. For your tasting, a bottle of wine from this region is a must so that you can see just how elegant this grape can be.

**Alsace, France:** While other grapes are grown here, Riesling is the grape of Alsace—

the most prestigious and widely planted in the region. Though Alsace is right next door to Germany (and, in fact, used to be part of Germany), the Rieslings from this area are completely different from those from the Mosel-Saar-Ruwer. Alsatian Rieslings are known for their amazing acid and fruit balance and their steely, mineraly characteristics. Well-made Rieslings from this area become more refined as they age; when they are young, they're somewhat closed up. In general, I look for bottles that are at least three years old. If you want to drink them young, my friend, Ed McCarthy, author of *Wine for Dummies*, says to reach for the least expensive bottle you can find, because

**A.O.C.:** Appellation d'Origine Contrôllée: A formal designation conferred by the French government for wines grown and produced in the region of their origin using traditional processes.

**Trocken, Classic, Selection, Kabinett:** Think "dry." *Trocken* literally means "dry" in German; the other terms are various designations found on labels of German wines. All indicate a drier style of wine.

**Halbtrocken/Spätlese:** Think "kinda dry/kinda sweet."

*Halbtrocken* is German for "half-dry" and refers to a wine that's a little bit sweeter than Trocken wines. Spätlese refers to a particular category of wine that's also half-dry—or slightly sweet.

**Auslese, Beerenauslese, Eiswein, Trockenbeerenauslese:** Think "sweet." These are categories of sweeter German wines, listed from sweet to sweetest.

**Racy:** A term often used for that pleasing zippy quality that comes from the acidity in white wines.

---

these are usually the lightest in style and more ready to drink. He's a smart guy, so take his advice. I do.

**Northern Austria:** Although Austria and Germany are neighbors, their Rieslings are nothing alike. Austrian Rieslings are more full-bodied, powerful, and fruit forward than German Rieslings; they're often described as vibrant and lively, smelling of rose and peach.

### IN ALSACE IT'S CALLED RIESLING

Remember last month how you had to look for Condrieu or Château-Grillet if you wanted to find a French Viognier? Alsatian wines are much easier to decode because Alsace is the only winegrowing area in France where wines are named by grape, not region. If the wine inside is made from the Riesling grape, it's called Riesling. Gewürztraminer is simply called Gewürztraminer; Pinot Blanc is Pinot Blanc. Doesn't that make life easy?

They may be difficult to find, so they're not required tasting for this month.

**Upstate New York—Finger Lakes:** Riesling is a major grape grown in New York State, and the styles here range from dry to off-dry, late harvest to ice wines (which we'll talk about in the Stickies chapter). For me, the best Rieslings in the United States come from this region—it's well worth seeking one out for your tasting.

While these are the most renowned regions for Riesling, the grape is also grown and produced in Washington State, Oregon, California, Australia, New Zealand, South Africa, and Canada. I'll be honest—some are awesome, some aren't. When starting out, I suggest focusing on the Rieslings from regions I've detailed above. You can taste the best and decide for yourself later if you like the rest. If you're headed to the Big Apple or are already sweltering in the city, a road trip to the Finger Lakes region is a must.

### Aah—Breathe In and Smell the ...

You're into month six of your wine club. So how's it going with the name-that-aroma game? Smelling that guava and quince yet? OK, maybe not. How about more general notes, like citrus, flowers, and berries? Or maybe to you, the wine in your glass still smells like, well, wine.

You'll find in your wine club that some people have supersensitive schnozes that really pick up on this stuff. So while you're all proud of yourself when you can detect a little citrusy aroma, suddenly some supersmeller smarty-pants takes it a step further. Not only can he or she smell grapefruit—it's pink grapefruit in the nose, for sure. It's not lime, it's Key lime, for heaven's sake.

Wherever you are on the smelling scale, don't be discouraged. It takes a lot of sniffs and sips before you really know how to talk about what's in your glass. Besides, it's all subjective. You might think a wine smells like pepperoni pizza; someone else might say it smells like cured meat. I used to sit on

> It takes a lot of sniffs and sips before you really know how to talk about what's in your glass. Besides, it's all subjective.

a tasting panel with a guy who said every other wine smelled like a cigar box. Frankly, I had no idea how a cigar box smelled any different from a cigar, but to him, there was a big difference.

Smelling wine is all about drawing from aromas you already recognize, so if you're having trouble nailing those papayas and persimmons, go with what you know (I imagine my fellow taster had smelled lots of cigar boxes—he seemed the type). Next time you're stumped, breathe in the aroma and don't try so hard to discern whether it's grapefruit or pink grapefruit, Persian lime versus Key lime, mango versus papaya. Think of what you know. When tasting Riesling, maybe a sniff suddenly takes you back to your grandmother's backyard after a spring rain, where a certain sweetness in the air mingled with that earthy smell of those wet stones you used to skim across the water as a kid. Another sniffer in your group might say, "The nose is all about pears and roses, with mineral undertones." What smells like apple blossoms and wet stones to you may smell like pears, roses, and damp earth to him.

You know what? You're both right. And if

> What smells like apple blossoms and wet stones to you may smell like pears, roses, and damp earth to him.

someone else insists what you're smelling is a rusty hammer and apricot pie, just smile—and keep on sniffing.

## June's Picks

I love doing tastings of Rieslings from a variety of winegrowing areas, because this wine shows off its *terroir* big time. We'll taste wines from the superstar regions of Alsace and Mosel-Saar-Ruwer, as well as a superior region in the United States for the grape, the Finger Lakes of upstate New York. I'm also throwing in a California Riesling.

**Mosel-Saar-Ruwer Kabinett:** Choose a bottle priced from $14 to $20.
**Mosel-Saar-Ruwer Halbtrocken or Spätlese:** Look to spend between $10 and $18.
**Alsace, France:** Priced from $13 to $20.
**Finger Lakes region, upstate New York:** Priced from $17 to $25.
**California:** Priced from $10 to $22.
**Ringer:** This month, throw in Gewürztraminer, another highly fragrant wine made from grapes that thrive in cool climates. Choose one from Alsace; that region is particularly renowned for its Gewürztraminer. Look to spend from $13 to $20 on a bottle.

### ✴ ✴ JOHANNISBERG RIESLING ✴ ✴
When poking around for this month's pick from the United States, you might spot something called Johannisberg Riesling. In United States winemaker speak, what they're trying to tell you is the wine was made from the true Riesling grape—the same grape used in the great Alsatian and German Rieslings.

# GET YOUR DRINK ON

*This is a great month to really get your schnoz into the glass and talk about what you smell as opposed to what you taste. With its seductive floral and fruity notes, this aromatic white will definitely play tricks on your nose, but after a few sips you'll understand once and for all that fruity is not always the same as sweet. And since we're getting into German wines, you may find a new tingle in your nose that reminds you of a gas station. That's right—diesel and petrol are words you may find flitting around the tasting table this month.*

**COLOR:** Most Rieslings range from pale yellow with a green tinge to slightly more golden. California Rieslings tend to be a little golden in comparison to the very pale wines from Germany, but they are very close in hue and often there is no notable color difference.

**AROMA:** Riesling is often described as crisp and refreshing even in the nose, yet it ranges to include floral aromas and riper fruits in its repertoire too. Aroma will be your first clue to where these wines come from. If you smell anything other than fruit, say something that reminds you of a gas station, you can rule out New World Riesling. Diesel fuel is an aroma that may pop up in German wines, but you may find that note lingering in the juice of Alsace as well; this quality is an earthiness that shows off the wine's *terroir*. Alsace and Germany will show citrus, especially grapefruit, along with apples, minerals, and a steely, clean nose. You'll find no oak in Alsatian and German Rieslings, and I hope none in the others in this tasting either, because Riesling is too delicate for the likes of wood. California, Alsace, and New York styles may show peach, apricot, and citrus in the nose. The German Spätlese or Halbtrocken is sure to show its sugar when you sniff.

**TASTE:** Riesling should have good acidity, so even though it may smell sweet, if balanced correctly it should still be totally tangy. Alsatian wines will range from bone dry to sweet, though the majority are dry and high in acid. New York Rieslings will be fresh with enticing fruit flavor and will have a smoky mineral quality that you won't find in California Rieslings. California's will have the fullest fruity flavors—peach and apricot, without the bite of the Alsatian styles. The German Kabinett will be lighter and more delicate with flavors of crisp apples; both German and Alsatian versions may also taste of citrus, especially lemon. You should be able to distinguish the sweeter German Spätlese or Halbtrocken immediately in comparison with the more austere Rieslings in this tasting.

**BODY:** Remember, high alcohol translates to bigger body. The New York Riesling will undoubtedly be higher in alcohol than the German and thus fuller-bodied. Another reason for big body in wine is the sugar content. Alsatian versions can range from light- to medium-bodied. The sweeter styles are fuller-bodied and thus feel richer in the mouth. The German Kabinetts are usually lower in alcohol than the Alsatian wines; your German Kabinett will likely be the lightest-bodied of all.

**FINISH:** Some Rieslings will go out with a powerful zing; others may linger longer with softer, riper fruit flavors. The finish should show the acid and leave your mouth watering for more.

**RINGER:** If you smell a little spice, along with full fruit and floral aromas like roses, you're most likely sniffing the ringer. As for the taste, your ringer may have a touch of sweetness and less acid.

Funny how people always order Chardonnay in restaurants—with its buttery and oaky qualities, it's a risky wine to pair with food. Riesling, especially those from Germany, Alsace, and New York State (the really cool climates), is a much easier all-purpose go-with. These wines have great acid, bringing an intense cleansing quality that sets you up for the next bite.

Riesling is one of Asian food's best friends, so this month we're sipping the wine with sushi—both have exotic, spicy flavors that complement each other well. In fact, they're such a dynamite pair that one California winemaker, Randall Graham, pictures sushi right on the bottle of his Pacific Rim Riesling.

For this gathering, I suggest you take a walk on the wild side and have guests "roll their own." No, nothing illicit here! I'm suggesting that the host set up a sushi station with all the ingredients and have guests assemble their own rolls. Riesling's light sweetness complements the sweet glazed Salmon Nigiri and provides balance for the hotter Spicy Tuna Sushi Rolls. Make sure there's plenty of pickled ginger and soy sauce to go round.

And Riesling is by no means a summer-only wine.

* * * * * * * * * * * * * * * * * * *

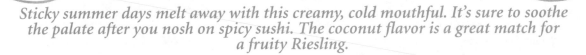

# COCONUT FROZEN YOGURT

*Sticky summer days melt away with this creamy, cold mouthful. It's sure to soothe the palate after you nosh on spicy sushi. The coconut flavor is a great match for a fruity Riesling.*

| | |
|---|---|
| 2 | cups fat-free coconut yogurt |
| 1 | 14-ounce can light coconut milk |
| ½ | cup light-colored corn syrup |

1. In a bowl combine yogurt, coconut milk, and corn syrup. Cover and chill for at least 2 hours or until the mixture is 40°F or below. (It is very important to chill the mixture before you put it in your ice cream freezer.)

2. Put mixture in an ice cream freezer and freeze according to manufacturer's directions. Transfer mixture to a freezer container; freeze for 2 to 4 hours before serving.

**Makes about 4 cups**

After freezing this mixture for a few hours, the texture is perfect—just like out of a soft-serve machine. After freezing overnight, it is very solid. Be sure to pull it out of the freezer and let stand before you scoop.

# SUSHI RICE

*The key to great sushi is the rice. Sushi chefs can spend up to seven years just mastering the rice. I promise it won't take you seven years. Your first go-round may not be perfectly sticky, but practice makes perfect, and with great rice you are one step closer to great sushi.*

| | |
|---|---|
| 3 | cups sushi rice (medium or short grain) |
| 3¼ | cups water |
| ⅓ | cup rice wine vinegar |
| 2 | tablespoons sugar |
| 1 | teaspoon salt |

1. Wash rice in a fine-mesh sieve under cold running water about 1 minute or until the water runs clear. In a large saucepan combine rinsed rice and water. Bring to a boil; reduce heat. Cover with a tight-fitting lid; simmer for 25 minutes. Remove from heat. Let stand, covered, for 5 minutes.

2. Meanwhile, combine vinegar, sugar, and salt in a microwave-safe dish. Microwave on 100 percent power (high) until sugar and salt dissolve, stirring every 30 seconds. Let stand until room temperature.

3. Place the cooked rice in a large bowl (a wooden bowl will help the rice cool down more quickly); sprinkle with the vinegar mixture. Stir just until combined. Do not overstir. Cover with a damp towel until ready to use.

**Makes about 6 cups**

## ★ ★ ★ ★ ★ ★ ★ NO-COOK OPTIONS ★ ★ ★ ★ ★ ★ ★

If the start of summer has made you a little lazy, take a load off and order take-out sushi, or go for some of these stay-out-of-the-kitchen alternatives:

★Muenster cheese and fresh-baked bread. Muenster cheese finds its home in Alsace. When you serve it with fresh-baked bread from your local bakery and some tangy mustard, you get a taste of food from the land where Riesling dominates.

★Apple or lemon pastries: Head to the corner bakery and pick up some sweets that will pair with the aromas and flavors of the wine that are sure to surface in this month's tasting.

★Coleslaw, deviled eggs, artichokes: Riesling clashes with these items, but to test your taste buds, put one or two of these out and see for yourself.

★Hot dogs and potato chips: OK, you'll actually have to heat the hot dogs, but they're no-brainers to throw on the grill. Because Riesling goes so well with the sausages of Alsace and Germany, hot dogs make perfect sense. Also, salt and acid are a great match, so salty potato chips and a zippy Riesling will be a good pair.

★Roast chicken and grilled peaches: Riesling is amazing with fruit-based dishes; a classic is pork with sautéed apples (remember that for fall). For summer, buy a roast chicken from the deli and cook up some peach halves on the grill.

★Peppered smoked salmon: Chop some onions and put out water crackers. The off-dry styles of Riesling pair nicely with this spicy item. The heat of the cracked pepper and the texture of the salmon go great with a nice, cool pour of Riesling.

★ ★ ★ ★ ★ ★ ★ ★ ★ ★ ★ ★ ★ ★ ★ ★ ★ ★ ★ ★ ★ ★ ★ ★

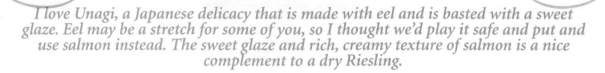

# SALMON NIGIRI

*I love Unagi, a Japanese delicacy that is made with eel and is basted with a sweet glaze. Eel may be a stretch for some of you, so I thought we'd play it safe and put and use salmon instead. The sweet glaze and rich, creamy texture of salmon is a nice complement to a dry Riesling.*

1½    cups Sushi Rice
(see recipe, page 109)

6    to 8 ounces salmon

½    cup Unagi Sauce, see
recipe below, or bottled
teriyaki marinade

   Daikon sprouts or
pea shoots

1    sheet of nori (seaweed)
(about 8 inches square),
cut into 20 to 24 strips
(4×½-inch)

   Soy sauce, wasabi paste,
and/or pickled ginger

1. With wet hands, shape about 1 tablespoon of the Sushi Rice into twenty to twenty-four 2-inch egg-shaped balls. Squeeze rice together tightly or balls will fall apart. (Keep a bowl of water on the counter to wet your hands before shaping each ball.)

2. Preheat broiler. Cut salmon into twenty to twenty-four pieces about 2 inches long and ⅛ inch thick. Dip each piece of salmon into the Unagi Sauce; place on a baking sheet. Broil for less than 1 minute or until salmon is cooked through.

3. Place one piece of salmon on top of each rice ball; brush salmon with additional Unagi Sauce. (The salmon will be delicate after it is cooked, so handle carefully.) Top each with daikon sprouts. Wrap a nori strip around each rice ball to hold salmon in place. Moisten nori strips with water to seal.

4. Serve sushi with soy sauce, wasabi paste, and/or pickled ginger.

**Makes 20 to 24 pieces**

Unagi Sauce: Peel and coarsely chop one 1-inch piece fresh ginger; set aside. Cut 1 green onion into 1-inch pieces; set aside. In a saucepan combine 1 cup soy sauce, 2 tablespoons sugar, 2 tablespoons honey, and 1 clove garlic, minced. Stir in ginger and green onion. Cook and stir over medium-high heat until sugar and honey dissolve. Bring to a boil; reduce heat. Simmer about 20 minutes or until thick. Strain sauce. Let cool.
Makes about ¾ cup

# SPICY TUNA SUSHI ROLLS

*This was, by far, the hardest thing for me to give up while I was pregnant—besides wine, of course! My husband and I were accustomed to devouring these on a weekly basis at our favorite Upper East Side sushi joint. Follow with a swig of Riesling for one of my top 10 favorite food and wine pairings.*

| | |
|---|---|
| 4 | ounces sushi-grade tuna, diced |
| 2 | tablespoons diced jicama or apple |
| 1 | tablespoon Sriracha Garlic-Chile Sauce |
| 3 | sheets nori (seaweed) (each about 8 inches square) |
| 1½ | cups Sushi Rice (see recipe, page 109) |
| | Soy sauce, wasabi paste, and/or pickled ginger |

**1.** Combine tuna, jicama, and garlic-chile sauce. Cover and chill until ready to use.

**2.** Cover a sushi rolling mat with plastic wrap. Place 1 sheet of nori, shiny side down, on plastic wrap. With wet fingers, spread ½ cup of the Sushi Rice onto nori. Place one-third of the tuna mixture just above the center of the edge closest to you.

**3.** Using the mat and plastic wrap as a guide, roll up nori into a tight spiral, rolling around the filling. Repeat with remaining nori and other ingredients. Cover and chill up to 4 hours.

**4.** To serve, cut each sushi roll into eight 1-inch pieces. Serve with soy sauce, wasabi paste, and/or pickled ginger.

**Makes 24 pieces**

# CALIFORNIA SUSHI ROLLS

*This is a baby step into the world of sushi, but a delightful one. My first California roll had me hooked. I love the way your mouth feels so clean after you nibble one of these. Pair it with Riesling and you've got pure pleasure on the palate.*

3   sheets nori (seaweed) (each about 8 inches square)

1½   cups Sushi Rice (see recipe, page 109)

1   tablespoon sesame seeds

6   sticks leg-style imitation crabmeat (surimi)

1   ripe avocado, cut into thin slices

1   cucumber, seeded and cut into matchstick-size pieces (3 to 4 inches long)

  Soy sauce, wasabi paste, and/or pickled ginger

**1.** Cover a sushi rolling mat with plastic wrap. Place 1 sheet of nori, shiny side down, on plastic wrap.

**2.** With wet fingers, spread ½ cup of the Sushi Rice onto nori; sprinkle with 1 teaspoon of the sesame seeds. Arrange 2 sticks of the imitation crabmeat on rice in a line 1 inch from the edge of nori that is closest to you. Place one-third of the avocado slices and one-third of the cucumber sticks just above the center of the edge closest to you.

**3.** Using the mat and plastic wrap as a guide, roll up nori into a tight spiral, rolling around the filling. Repeat with remaining nori and other ingredients. Cover and chill up to 4 hours.

**4.** To serve, cut each sushi roll into eight 1-inch pieces. Serve with soy sauce, wasabi paste, and/or pickled ginger.

**Makes 24 pieces**

# VEGETABLE SUSHI ROLLS

*These rolls are full of fresh, crunchy veggies. You can't help feeling healthy as you eat them. A little Riesling for good measure and you'll be one happy camper. Add some pickled ginger and wasabi for zing and watch how Riesling handles the heat.*

| | |
|---|---|
| 3 | sheets nori (seaweed) (each about 8 inches square) |
| 1½ | cups Sushi Rice (see recipe, page 109) |
| 1 | cucumber, seeded and cut into matchstick-size pieces (3 to 4 inches long) |
| 1 | ripe avocado, cut into thin slices |
| 1 | cup matchstick-size carrot pieces (3 to 4 inches long) |
| 12 | to 15 Thai basil or plain basil leaves |
| | Soy sauce, wasabi paste, and/or pickled ginger |

1. Cover a sushi rolling mat with plastic wrap. Place 1 sheet of nori, shiny side down, on plastic wrap. With wet fingers, spread ½ cup Sushi Rice onto nori. Arrange one-third of the cucumber pieces on rice 1 inch from the edge closest to you. Arrange one-third of the avocado and carrots just above the center of the edge closest to you. Top with 4 to 5 basil leaves.

2. Using the mat and plastic wrap as a guide, roll up nori into a tight spiral, rolling around the filling. Repeat with remaining nori and other ingredients. Cover and chill up to 4 hours.

3. To serve, cut each sushi roll into eight 1-inch pieces. Serve with soy sauce, wasabi paste, and/or pickled ginger.

**Makes 24 pieces**

# Chardonnay
## the Queen of Whites

*Now* *that summer's in full swing, put on your drinking shoes—we'll be kicking up our heels with the queen of whites, Chardonnay. You may have noticed that since we're getting into warmer months, I've switched gears from reds to whites. I'm no weather girl, but I can predict that when the wind*

turns warm, whites are far more fun than big reds. I can also predict another pretty sure thing: Whether you're dancing on the deck of a cruise ship docked in Morocco or dancing around the grill in your own backyard this summer, there's sure to be Chardonnay. It is, after all, the most popular white-wine grape in the world.

Let's face it, Chardonnay (we'll call it "Chard" for short) has gotten a pretty bad rap lately. And for good reason. A few years back,

the American palate decided the bigger, more buttery, and oakier the Chardonnay, the better. So that's exactly what winemakers gave us. Now some of the stuff is just gross: overly oaky, leaving no evidence of the grape's true flavors to be found. *Some* being the operative word here.

With the soaring demand for overly oaky Chard, the market became so saturated with this mediocre style of wine, most people didn't even know what the grape really tastes

like. Many wine drinkers, maybe even you, decided they hated this type of white and wrote off the grape entirely.

But that's all over now. It's time to take another glance at this glamorous grape. This month you'll learn about another side of Chardonnay—the side that keeps thousands and thousands of wine lovers coming back for more. I'm positive you'll find she's all sorts of sassy. You'll see that this wine ranges dramatically in style, because I'm taking you well beyond the realm of those overly oaked monsters and into a world where exquisite Chardonnays thrive.

## Getting to Know Chardonnay

Some of you might recall that you've already sipped Chardonnay at a wine club meeting—the grape is cultivated in the Champagne region and around the world to be blended with Pinot Noir and Pinot Meunier for bubbly and is the starlet of those yummy blanc-de-blanc bubblies you "studied" in January.

Chardonnay is one of the noble grape vari-

* * **IF THE GLASS FITS ...** * *

There are white Burgundy wineglasses on the market; they tend to have a larger bowl for swirling and aerating the wines. You may prefer to drink this big white in an all-purpose red-wine glass, but an all-purpose white-wine glass is also appropriate for this juice.

eties that can stand alone without being blended. Because the grape is relatively easy to grow, it is a favorite of vineyard managers around the world. Today you can order a glass of Chard almost anywhere, but in the 1960s it was relatively unknown outside of France. Can you imagine such a time? Now it grows in Australia, California (Carneros and the southern central coast are cool regions where delish Chard can be found), Oregon, Argentina, South Africa, Washington State … well, Chard vines are practically everywhere because the grape is so adaptable, unlike Riesling or Sauvignon Blanc.

* * * * * * * * * * * * * *

## WINE TREND

Wine connoisseurs who scoffed at the screw cap are now likely keeling over at the sight of more and more quality wines in a box. But me? If the occasion fits, I'm big on the box!

Decent box wines range in price from $17 to $23 per box for the equivalent of four standard bottles; do the math, and that's about $4 to $6 a bottle. Some boxes are particularly cute and convenient, fitting in the fridge like a carton of milk. The vacuum-sealed bag inside the box keeps the wine fresh for weeks, so you no longer have to sweat the idea of opening a bottle for just one glass and having the rest go bad. Box wines are also perfect for parties and great for outdoor getaways. But my favorite part is there is no glass to accidentally break, and no corkscrew required!

* * * * * * * * * * *    * * * * * * * * * * * *

* * * * * * * * *

**Pouilly-Fuissé:** The most famous of the wines from the Mâconnais region of Burgundy and the fullest-bodied. Made from Chardonnay grapes, these wines are usually aged in oak and priced starting around $20 a bottle.

**Mâcon-Villages:** A popular wine from the Mâconnais region of Burgundy. These are almost always made without oak, giving you a crisp, delish sip for about $10 a bottle.

* * * * * * * * *

**Premier Cru:** "First Growth." Without getting too technical, this refers to Burgundy wines that are considered superior to wines with "villages" designations (such as Mâcon-Villages).

**Grand Cru:** A wine that's considered better than premier cru. In Burgundy this designation is given to the top 34 wineries. It literally means "great growth" and translates to "open your wallet wider."

* * * * * * * * * * * * * * * * * * * * * * * * * * * *

### The Weathered Grape

Chardonnay will show dramatic differences depending on whether it grows in a cool climate or in a warmer one. The members of my wine club declared that the greatest Chardonnays come from cooler climates—we especially liked the way they paired with our favorite foods. But the flavors in the wine and its acid also played a part in our epiphany. Stick with me here.

When Chard grows in a cool climate like Chablis, France, for example, the acidity will be higher and the flavors will lean in the direction of crisp—like a crisp apple. In a warmer climate, such as the warmer regions of Australia, California, and South Africa, Chard will have more tropical flavors and generally more oak character. With their clean taste, those crisp Chardonnays from Chablis are more versatile in food and wine pairings than richer, fuller-bodied Chards from warm regions like California. And because we love to eat together as much as we like to share wine, we always reach for the bottles from cooler climates like Burgundy and Chablis first.

### Burgundy Brings It On

We've all been baffled by French wine labels because, generally, they don't tell you what grape was used to make the wine. But if the juice is from Burgundy, you can bet on the grape just by knowing if the wine is red or white: If it's red it's Pinot Noir and if it's white it's Chardonnay. These two grapes thrive there, and the Chardonnay from Burgundy rocks!

There are several subregions in Burgundy,

Chardonnay is one of the noble grape varieties that can stand alone without being blended. Because the grape is relatively easy to grow, it is a favorite of vineyard managers around the world.

When done well, the oak will impart a fuller body and flavors of vanilla, butter, and toasted nuts without masking the fruit.

but when it comes to Chardonnay, these are the ones to remember:

**Chablis:** Do not confuse this for a bland bulk wine. Although in the U.S. this name was slapped on many a jug to make a sale, this is in fact a phenomenal French wine-growing region. This is the northernmost region of Burgundy, close to Champagne. Here many of the Chards are aged in only stainless steel rather than oak, so the flavors are cleaner, with a crisp acidity and minerality; they typically smell of gunflint (this will be that smell you can't identify off the top of your head—at least I hope not!). Some winemakers do let their Chablis touch oak, but Chard from Chablis is

* * * * * * * * * * * * *

### YOU'LL NEVER FORGET IT

A very common flavor and aroma in Chardonnay is vanilla, a component that comes from the oak barrels in which the wine was aged. When you taste it, you can be sure you're sipping a Chard that hooked up with oak at some point previous to your pour.

This is a great exercise to help you learn if you prefer oak. First, pour two half-glasses of oak-free Chardonnay. Take a vanilla bean and scrape the seeds into one of the glasses. Can't find a vanilla bean? Use a teaspoon of vanilla extract. Sniff the two glasses side by side. Do you prefer the vanilla aromatics? Or do you think it covers the fruity nose? Now taste them side by side. Does that vanilla complement the wine? Or do you prefer the cleaner version sans vanilla? If you like it fruitier smelling and cleaner tasting, stick to buying white Burgundies. However, if you find that vanilla yummy, go for California Chards.

* * * * * * * * * * * *          * * * * * * * * * * * *

quickly overwhelmed by oak.

**Côte d'Or:** This region is where the majority of Burgundy's great wines come from and is considered Chardonnay's true home—some say its spiritual dwelling. *Côte d'or* literally means "golden slope." And the Chard coming from this soil is definitely worth its weight in gold. The Côte d'Or comprises two sections, the Côte de Nuits—mostly known for its reds—and, farther south, the Côte de Beaune, which also produces reds but is especially celebrated for its whites. Within the region, the winemakers have such different techniques that their wines are quite diverse; pinning a defined style to this region is nearly impossible. Puligny-Montrachet, Chassagne-Montrachet, and Meursault are villages in the Côte d'Or that are especially renowned for their whites.

**Côte Chalonnaise and Côte Mâconnais:** These two regions make great Chard at much lower price points. While the everyday drinking wines are considered the plain Janes of white Burgundies, I love how they still maintain the character of the grape, and I find they're awesome on a warm summer day.

### Where Does That Butter Come From?

This is a li'l wine science—but don't worry, it's worth it. The buttery taste in many Chardonnays comes from a winemaking process called malolactic fermentation, where crisp, tart acids are converted into softer acid. Think green apple versus the acid found in milk—the process produces a compound that reduces the acidity and makes the wine rounder, creamier, and what we call buttery in character. Wines like Riesling and Sauvignon Blanc most likely won't undergo malolactic fermentation, because acid is a quality that winemakers strive to keep in those particular wines.

### Easy on the Oak

Wood and wine sounds like a gross combo, but barrel-aging Chardonnay lends flavors and color that make this wine unique. Most everywhere, Chardonnay is fermented

#### * * BANG FOR YOUR BUCK * *

Louis Jadot Chardonnay, Burgundy, around $9 a bottle. If you don't want a big oaky, buttery Chardonnay, this little white love is for you. Made of a blend of Chardonnay grapes from the Côte Mâconnais, Côte Chalonnaise, and Hautes-Côtes de Beaune, it's the perfect kick-off to a summer soiree. Look for a clean, fresh taste with citrus and peach flavors; you'll also find a delicate balance of acid and a refreshing, crisp finish. It's medium-bodied with excellent fruit and a smooth, round mouth feel. There's a little vanilla from the little bit of oak contact but nothing offensive. For the price it's hard to find a better buy in this style of Chardonnay, and I love the way I can find a bottle of it at almost any wine shop I walk into.

(that's when the juice turns into alcohol) and aged (that's when the wine then gets to rest and round out) in oak barrels. When playing with oak, the winemaker really determines the fate of the wine. If the wine is left too long in oak, it will taste like, well, oak and not fruit. When done well, the oak will impart a fuller body and flavors of vanilla, butter, and toasted nuts without masking the fruit. In some big operations, winemakers will take the easy route and impart that oaky flavor by using oak chips. Internationally renowned British wine writer and educator Michael Broadbent likens this practice to using poor-quality tea bags to make tea. It's like steeping the oak chips in the wine. Yuk! You should not be hit in the face with the taste of oak. It should be a part of the wine's character, not the defining characteristic, as is often the case.

Most often, American Chard is aged in oak—you know, those wine barrels you see the geeky winemaker leaning on holding a glass of wine for his cover shot in *Wine Spectator*? Some of the most popular types of oak used in these barrels are Hungarian, American, and French oak. Each oak lends its own attribute to the juice. For example, American oak is known for the vanilla flavor it imparts, and Hungarian oak can lend a note of spice to the finished wine. And these oak attributes can completely change the taste and mouth feel of any grape.

You may often hear that a wine is aged in new oak. That means that the wine will have stronger oak characteristics, whereas Chard aged in used oak barrels will show the subtleties of the wood. The best Côte d'Or producers barrel-ferment the juice, using at least a percentage of new oak. I find that these wines have just the right balance of the wood and the wine. However much oak mingles with your wine is completely up to the winemaker, but in general you'll find more oak in

### ✳ ✳ ✳ THE MONA LISA ✳ ✳ ✳

Chateau Montelena, 2002, California; $33. Sometimes there's more to great wine than just what's in the glass. At the far north end of the Napa Valley sits this grand French-style chateau. With its Japanese-influenced garden lake, this landscape fusion creates a storybook setting, perfect for an afternoon stroll. There are many grand homes that polka-dot the valley, but its enchanted lake setting renders Chateau Montelena the most romantic place to watch the sunset or steal a kiss. And the wine is, well, awesome. The 2002 Chardonnay hit a home run, boasting all the best the grape has to offer. A bright yellow-gold color and aromas of green apple, lime, and minerals are backed up by a big mouthful of lime, apple, and kiwi. It lingered on oak to give us a full but still soft texture, and the finish leaves your mouth full of apple flavors. It's a great showing for the queen, and every sip is delish.

### ✳ ✳ ✳ THE SALVADOR DALÍ ✳ ✳ ✳

Feudo Arancio Chardonnay, Sicily; $9 to $11. When you mention Sicily, people are more likely to think of Marsala than Chardonnay. But this little white wine is hot stuff. We sipped it every day we spent touring Sicily and never tired of its fresh, lemony aroma, well-balanced structure, fruit and mineral flavors, and tart finish. And this is just a taste of what Sicily has to offer—keep your eyes open for other wine steals from this island.

You can drink Chard any time of the year, depending on the style of the wine. But because it is high in alcohol and often low in acid, it's best to avoid on a scorching-hot day.

California Chard than you will in any of those from France.

## When to Drink These Whites

Like most wines from the New World, Chardonnay is made to drink young, except for the premier and grand crus of Burgundy (See "Wine Speak," page 117), so don't hold on to them for too long. A few hints to when these French whites are in their glory:

**Grand cru Chablis:** These Frenchies are best eight to ten years after bottling.

**Premier cru Chablis:** These beauties shine five years after they've been bottled but can hang out in the cellar for up to ten.

**Côte Chalonnaise, Mâconnais, and Pouilly-Fuissé:** These are best when they are young.

No matter when you pull the cork, Chardonnay should not be served too cold. I like mine a little warmer than Sauvignon Blanc or Riesling. Oaked Chards definitely taste even more oaky when served too chilly. I suggest you pull the bottles from your fridge about 15 minutes before pouring.

## Shall We Sip in the Summer or the Winter?

You can drink Chard any time of the year, depending on the style of the wine. Because it is high in alcohol and often low in acid, it's best to avoid on a scorching-hot day. For warm summer nights and crisp fall evenings, big Chards are delightful. Overall I find a steely clean Chard from Chablis best suits the warmer months, and rich and buttery Chards from California make for good sipping all winter long.

## Ordering Wine Out: Leave Your Thinking Cap at Home

Ever settle into a hot date or a lively dinner with friends only to have the fun hit a major speed bump when that phone-book-size wine list is plunked down in front of you? Don't feel bad—in my guestimation about 1 percent of diners know everything in there. The other 99 percent of us are left feeling intimidated. I say you have two options.

The first is not to even open it. You're here to enjoy the people you're with, not spend precious party (or romance) time studying a wine list. Just ask your server for something you already know you like. Of course, a lot of people do this—which may explain why easy-to-love Chard and Merlot remain on the best-seller list.

But when you want to branch out, the best option is to rely on the experts. If the restaurant has a wine list as thick as the Bible, it should have someone on staff to decode it. That someone is the sommelier (saw-mul-yay)—a Frenched-up way to say wine steward. Listen to what this person has to say, because no matter how much you know about wine in general, the sommelier will know the restaurant's wine list in particular.

For the sommelier to bring you something

you'll love, he or she needs to know a little bit about you. Talk to the sommelier. Engage in a little back-and-forth to offer some knowledge of your taste buds. For example, do you like big, tannin-packed wines or soft, mellow wines? Sweet or dry? Zippy or smooth? If you're normally hooked on Cabernet Sauvignon but a spicy Shiraz is catching your eye, talk about it—what you like about what you normally drink, though you're looking to try something new. Tell the sommelier, too, what you'll be eating, because he or she should have a deep understanding of how the wines on the list match the restaurant's cuisine.

It's also very important to indicate how much you want to spend. The sommelier will have no idea how much dough you're looking to dish out, so give a range that seems compatible with the list. A good sommelier will work with this range and never try to force a $500 bottle on you.

### July's Picks

This month we'll taste Chard from California, Argentina, Australia, and two places in France (one's considered everyday drinking wine, while the other's considered elite—you decide which one is better). By sipping Chards from cooler regions alongside Chards from hot spots, you'll get to taste the effect of climate on this grape.

Here are my picks:

**California:** Choose a bottle of Chard in the $12 to $30 range.

**Argentina:** In the $6 to $14 range.

**Australia:** In the $8 to $12 range.

**France: Côte Chalonnaise:** Choose a bottle in the $15 to $30 range.

**France:** Find a premier cru from the Côte d' Or. You'll need to spend from $25 to $45.

**Ringer:** For this tasting, I suggest including both stainless steel–fermented and barrel-aged Chardonnay in the mix so you can decide firsthand whether you prefer oak on your Chard. So when buying the California pick, above, choose a bottle that's been aged in oak. For the ringer, choose a California

> By sipping Chards from cooler regions alongside Chards from hot spots, you'll get to taste the effect of climate on this grape.

Chard that has had no oak contact. These can run anywhere from $25 to $45 a bottle—they're a little steeper in price because there just aren't that many of them. Fortunately, some Cali winemakers are jumping on the "non-oaky" Chard bandwagon. For one, Trefethen Chardonnay has never had oak exposure. A few others to look for are Chalk Hill, Shafer, and Grgich Hills.

How can you tell if it's oaked? California Chardonnay usually says right on the back label whether it's hit oak, so turn it around and give the back label a once-over before buying. If the label doesn't specify whether the wine has been aged in steel or oak, just ask someone working at the wine shop. (Don't be shy—when you're at the grocery store and you can't find the peanut butter, you ask for it, right?)

# GET YOUR DRINK ON

*This is a really fun tasting because without a doubt you have some preconceived notion of this famous white wine; however, when you taste them side by side, you may be surprised by which whites you favor. You may also realize that spending a bundle isn't necessarily the way to go in this category! Celebrating Chardonnay this month may or may not turn you into a loyal fan of this great grape, but there's only one way to find out. So get sipping!*

**COLOR:** Cali shows its Chard in shades of yellow to gold. It is noticeably darker than the Riesling we had last month. In general, the Chards from Burgundy will be lighter, more straw colored, than those from California. Some Chards from Burgundy may have a green tinge. The Aussie Chards will lean toward being darker gold in color. If you spot a Chard that appears to have a brownish tinge, as with any white that could be from age. But since we're not tasting a vintage Chard this month, it's more likely to be a telltale sign that the wine is bad. This is just a friendly reminder that any bottle of wine can go south with improper storage or shipping. So I say dump that glass and take the bottle back to where you purchased it. You want this white to sparkle in the summer sunshine, and that means the word *brown* and anything even resembling it shouldn't be mentioned this month.

**AROMA:** The Burgundies will show the grape characteristics first, with apples and pears in the nose; these French Chards will also show their earthy character, with mineral and wet-rock aromas. The oaked California Chard will show its oak first, but it is also very fruit forward with citrus, green apple, and peach. And Cali Chard is known for that buttery aroma. There are a couple of California Chardonnays that don't have any oak, though, so don't be so hasty to guess the origin; you may be sniffing the ringer. Aussie Chard smells more like tropical fruits, such as pineapple, banana, and mango.

**TASTE:** Chard from Burgundy will show softer in the palate, with a light bite from the acid, and may show some of that *terroir*. Overall, it will be the most subtle of all the Chardonnay styles. Cali Chard will taste like the fruits you smell—lemon, orange, and green apples—along with that vanilla and butter as you continue sipping. The Chard from down under will show riper fruit flavors, like the ripe pineapple and mango you smell. Chardonnay aged in oak barrels can taste buttery, nutty, and spicy. Also see if you can detect the difference climate makes. Does one taste like green apple (typical of cooler climates) and the other like pineapple and tropical fruits (typical of warmer climates)?

**BODY:** Burgundy Chards are refreshing, with a crisp and more acidic style than those from the New World. California Chards are the richest and heaviest whites we'll taste (other than dessert wines). The use of oak in Cali is one of the reasons for that big body. An easy way for me to remember that California Chards show more body is to conjure the images of California: sun, sand, and those bikini-clad bodies. If you can remember that when sipping, you'll be reminded that the fuller, stronger-bodied Chards are sure to be from Cali. Cali gives us full-bodied Chard, whereas Burgundy will be a little lighter in the body.

**FINISH:** I find that the full fruit and oak flavors of New World wines definitely linger a little longer, whereas an Old World Chard shows its subtle grace as it leaves on a clean and crisp note. In general, the New World Chardonnays are bigger all the way around. So it follows suit that their finish is bolder and lengthier than that of the Frenchies.

For this month's food and wine pairing, we're putting this juice to the test. Since it's the middle of summer, we're going for a good ol'-fashioned barbecue, and we'll find out if America's favorite white wine can stand up to an all-American feast. We've got ribs, potato salad, skewers, and shortcakes, all with a "little" twist. That's right—we've miniaturized your favorite flavors of summer into one or two bites that will pair pleasantly with your Chard.

This month's BBQ aside, pairing Chardonnay with food can be tricky. If the wine is too oaky, it will take over the food. On the other hand, clean and acidic Chablis is a great complement to plain seafood (oysters in particular). However, if the seafood is served swimming in a butter sauce, or beurre blanc, a full-bodied and buttery Chardonnay would be the best companion. Indeed, pairing lobster in butter sauce and a full-bodied and rich Chardonnay is one of those unbelieveable matches. So when you're dining out think New World Chard to go with a buttery shrimp scampi or crab cakes with a citrus beurre blanc.

But for now, grab plenty of napkins—you're in for a taste of summer.

# BABY POTATO SALADS

*Potato salad is a must at any of our family gatherings, and my favorite way to serve it is as an hors d'oeuvre. Besides being adorable, these papas stand up to the creamy richness of a full-bodied Chardonnay.*

| | |
|---|---|
| 24 | to 30 small red potatoes (1½ to 2 inches in diameter) |
| ¼ | cup diced celery |
| ¼ | cup mayonnaise |
| 1 | teaspoon sherry vinegar |
| 1 | teaspoon Dijon mustard |
| ⅛ | teaspoon salt |
| ⅛ | teaspoon black pepper |
| 2 | slices bacon, crisp-cooked, drained, and crumbled |
| 1 | tablespoon chopped fresh chives |

1. In a large saucepan cover the potatoes with cool salted water. Bring to boiling. Cook, covered, for 20 to 25 minutes or until potatoes are fork tender (not mushy). Drain; rinse under cold water so you can handle them immediately.

2. Cut off ¼ inch from the top of each potato. Cut a very thin slice off the bottom of each potato so they will sit flat. Using a melon baller, scoop pulp out of the middle of each potato, leaving enough of a wall on the inside for the potatoes to be handled without being squished.

3. For potato salad, in a bowl combine potato pulp, celery, mayonnaise, vinegar, mustard, salt, and pepper. Use a fork to slightly smash potato chunks. Stir in bacon. Fill the potato shells with a heaping spoonful of potato salad. Cover and chill at least 30 minutes. Sprinkle each potato with chives.

**Makes 24 to 30 pieces**

Note: You can make these up to 2 days in advance. Cover and chill until ready to serve. Sprinkle with chives just before serving.

# SLOW-COOKED BABY BACK RIBS

*When we were kids, my mom made these every Christmas Eve. We really thought they were made by elves because they were especially tiny just for us. These saucy little ribs are still one of my faves and are so simple to prepare for a party.*

2   pounds pork loin back ribs (12 to 14 ribs), sawed in half by your butcher

1   teaspoon salt

1   teaspoon black pepper

1   red onion, thinly sliced

1   18-ounce bottle hickory-flavored barbecue sauce

**1.** Preheat broiler. Sprinkle both sides of ribs with the salt and pepper. Place ribs on a wire rack on a large baking sheet. Broil ribs, bone side down, for 15 minutes. Remove from broiler. Carefully cut ribs into single-rib portions (use tongs to hold them steady).

**2.** Place onion slices in the bottom of a 3½- to 4-quart slow cooker. Add ribs. Pour barbecue sauce over ribs. Cover and cook on low-heat setting for 4 hours or on high-heat setting for 2 hours. If desired, serve with onion slices.

**Makes 24 to 28 pieces**

* * * * * * * **NO-COOK OPTIONS** * * * * * * * *

With the abundance of food at most barbecues, you'd think it would take days to prepare for the feast. But it's easier than ever to throw together breezy summer bites. Head to your grocer or local deli and pick up some potato salad, coleslaw, and pasta salad. Go ahead and order some ribs and chicken from your favorite barbecue joint. Slice up a big bowl of fruit and pick up a pecan pie from the bakery. Now you're in full summer swing, and you haven't even turned on the grill!

* * * * * * * * * * * * * * * * * * * * * * * * *

# PECAN TURTLE BITES

*When I was brainstorming with my friend Vanessa about barbecue, she said pecan pie was a must. Seeing as how she's from Kentucky, I understood her plea. I thought mini pies would be too messy, and though this isn't exactly the same, we loved this mix between a pecan pie and those awesome turtle candies.*

| | |
|---|---|
| 10 | vanilla caramels, cut in half |
| 20 | Lorna Doone shortbread cookies |
| 20 | pecan halves |
| 6 | ounces dark chocolate, chopped |
| 2 | teaspoons canola oil |

1. Preheat oven to 300°F. Line a cookie sheet with parchment paper; set aside.

2. Place one caramel half on one corner of each cookie. Place one pecan half on top of each caramel. Arrange cookies on prepared cookie sheet. Bake for 5 to 8 minutes or until caramel is softened. Remove from oven; press each pecan half down into the softened caramel. Cool for 10 minutes.

3. Meanwhile, melt the chopped chocolate and oil in a double boiler; stir to combine.

4. Dip the caramel-pecan corner of each cookie in melted chocolate; let excess chocolate drip off. Return cookies to cookie sheet. Refrigerate for 35 to 45 minutes or until chocolate is set. Let stand at room temperature before serving.

**Makes 20 pieces**

# GRILLED BRIE

*We've all had grilled cheese before, but this is the ultimate. With a few simple steps you'll easily convince your guests you've been a culinary whiz for years!*

1     large round Brie cheese (8 inches in diameter), well chilled

1     loaf baguette-style French bread, cut into 20 to 24 slices

     Melted butter

**1.** Preheat your grill to medium heat.

**2.** Take Brie from the refrigerator and place on the grill. Grill about 6 minutes on each side. (If you like, turn the Brie 45 degrees after 3 minutes to make grill marks.)

**3.** Meanwhile, brush the baguette slices with melted butter. Grill bread about 2 minutes on each side or until toasted.

**4.** Place Brie on a platter; serve with toasted baguette slices. If you like, remove a small slice of the cheese so it begins to ooze onto the platter. The Brie is also great served with grilled fruits.

**Makes 20 to 24 pieces**

Note: For this recipe you can use any cheese that has a sturdy soft rind like Brie or Camembert. Stay away from cheese with a waxy rind or no rind at all.

# CHICKEN SAUSAGE, RED ONION,
## and Apple Skewers with Honey Mustard

*For all my friends in the Midwest who love brats at their barbecues, this one's for you. I love how the apples pick up the apple character of the Chard and the mustard lends a great tang to the smooth and creamy wine.*

| | |
|---|---|
| 32 | 6-inch wooden skewers |
| 2 | cups water |
| 4 | teaspoons fresh lemon juice |
| 1 | large Granny Smith apple, cored and cut into 1-inch pieces |
| 1 | tablespoon olive oil |
| 4 | uncooked chicken sausage links |
| 1 | medium red onion, cut into wedges |
| ½ | cup Dijon mustard |
| ½ | cup honey |

1. Soak wooden skewers in enough water to cover for 30 minutes.

2. In a bowl combine 2 cups water and lemon juice. Let apple pieces stand in water mixture to prevent browning.

3. In a skillet heat olive oil over medium heat; add sausage links. Cook for 7 to 9 minutes or until brown. Cut links into ½-inch pieces.

4. Preheat your grill to medium-high heat. Alternately thread sausage pieces, apple pieces, and onion wedges on wooden skewers, leaving ¼ inch space between pieces. Grill about 5 minutes on each side.

5. Meanwhile, in a small bowl combine mustard and honey; serve with skewers.

**Makes 32 skewers**

Note: To save time, you can buy prepared honey mustard in the grocery store. Look for it with the other mustards, not in the salad dressing section.

# GRILLED

*Miniature*
*Strawberry Shortcakes*

*These li'l grilled shortcakes bring a great outdoorsy flavor to sweet summer strawberries. You'll love how in one bite you get all the goods of the season. See if you like this with an oaked Chard or if you prefer the clean mouth feel of an unoaked version after you nibble this creamy treat.*

| | |
|---|---|
| 8 | refrigerated buttermilk biscuits |
| 1 | cup whipping cream |
| 1 | tablespoon pure vanilla extract |
| 1 | teaspoon confectioner's sugar |
| ¼ | cup butter, melted |
| 2 | cups fresh strawberries, sliced |
| ⅓ | cup strawberry jam |

**1.** Preheat oven to 350°F. Place biscuits on a baking sheet. Bake for 13 to 17 minutes or until golden brown. Cool slightly.

**2.** Meanwhile, chill a medium mixing bowl and the beaters of an electric mixer. In chilled bowl beat whipping cream, vanilla, and confectioner's sugar with an electric mixer on medium speed until soft peaks form. Cover and chill until you are ready to assemble shortcakes.

**3.** Preheat your grill to low heat. Separate each biscuit in half; brush biscuit halves with butter. Grill biscuit halves for 3 to 4 minutes or until toasted. Remove from grill; press each half down with a wide spatula (or the palm of your hand) to flatten slightly. Cut each biscuit half into quarters.

**4.** Place one or two strawberry slices on half of the biscuit quarters; dollop with whipped cream. Spread about ½ teaspoon strawberry jam on each remaining biscuit quarters. Place biscuit quarters, jam sides down, on top of whipped cream to make shortcakes.

**Makes 32 shortcakes**

# sauvignon blanc
## *get it while it's hot*

**This** *August we're all about acid. Not the Electric Kool-Aid kind—this ain't that kind of party. I'm talking about a different kind of acid: the one that makes your mouth water just thinking of it and makes your mind wander to thoughts of a chilled glass of Sauvignon Blanc. Go ahead—take a sip. Wait a minute.*

Can you feel your mouth watering?

That's the acid.

And it's so yummy!

Sauvignon Blanc rocks in the summertime because its acid makes it so refreshing. Think about that acidic zing in lemonade and you get the idea: Sauvignon Blanc does for wine lovers what lemonade does for kids and tee-totalers. On a hot, sunny day there is absolutely nothing I like to drink more than this sassy, high-spirited varietal.

This month, while swirling and sipping your Sauvignon Blanc, you'll learn other funky little features and flavors in wine that—like acid—are actually considered desirable. It's also time you learned about this whole appellation business—and drinking Sauvignon Blanc is a great way to let it all soak in.

### Getting to Know Sauvignon Blanc

First, let's learn how to pronounce this mamma jamma. The "Sauvignon" is

pronounced the same way as in Cabernet Sauvignon (that is: soh-vihn-yohn). That's easy—you've already been there. The "Blanc" part of it is easy too, but be sure to French it all up with a lot of "blaaaaah." Say it like "blahhhn-kuh" (with a hard k sound at the end). You won't sound snooty; that's the way everyone says it—not just wine snobs.

And while you're at it, learn to say it another way: Fumé Blanc. (That's FOO may blah-hhn-kuh). You see, once upon a time (in the 1970s) Robert Mondavi began calling his unpopular Sauvignon Blanc wines by the name Fumé Blanc. The "Fumé" part of the name was taken from Pouilly-Fumé, a Sauvingon Blanc wine produced in France's Loire Valley (Fumé is, after all, easier for Americans to say than Sauvignon!).

The name has stuck for some American and New Zealand wineries, but in the rest of the world, it's called Sauvignon Blanc. Well,

> The fact of the matter is that screw caps have been proven to preserve the integrity of wine far longer than corks.

except for in France, but that's another story—one I'm about to tell. Yes. You're ready.

## Appellation—Not Just a Mountain Range Out East

I've not made anyone jump into the appellation boat yet, because while understanding the whole idea of appellation is easy, trying to remember which grapes correspond to which appellation can make your head spin. But I think it's time for an overview of the concept.

We've discussed how most French wine

* * * * * * * * * * * * *

### WINE TREND

The screw cap—you've seen it; now let's talk about it. Old-school wine lovers hate the idea of not pulling cork. The fact of the matter is that screw caps have been proven to preserve the integrity of wine far longer than corks. I won't get into the science of it, but corks let air in and screw caps don't. These days, savvy winemakers have caught on to that fact, so you can no longer assume that every wine with a screw cap is of a lesser value. Great wines as well as crappy wines are now being packaged with screw tops. For example, there's a jug wine that you can buy at the grocery store that uses a screw cap; it happens to be my grandpop's favorite wine, but by my standards it's not so hot. And then there are Big House White and Bonny Doon

Riesling—fabulous wines with screw caps.

Although we don't see a lot of South African wines on the shelves in the United States, one winemaker from this up-and-coming region politely told me to "screw the cork" when I asked how he felt about the ongoing cork debate. There you have it: World-class wines can and do wear this shiny hat. As long as what's in the bottle is worth it, I don't care how you give it to me.

And just so you know, it takes 25 years for a cork tree to bear useful cork. After that the tree can only be stripped every nine years. Whether you have an environmental bone in your body or not, logically you can see why this may not be the best bet for bottling wine.

* * * * * * * * * * * *        * * * * * * * * * * * *

labels don't say what grape variety the wine was made with. That's because French wines are usually labeled with a geographical name; that is, instead of seeing "Chardonnay" or "Pinot Noir" on the label, you'll see "Chablis" or "Burgundy." You see, Chablis and Burgundy are both winegrowing regions—or "appellations."

That means you can look at a bottle of wine from France, then look at a map of France, and see where the wine was made.

Well, that's kind of cool, if you like maps, but

it won't tell the novice wine drinker (until he or she starts to learn these things) what grape the wine is made from. But you can break the code: In France (and Italy and other nations that use this system), wines from a designated appellation must be made from particular varieties of grapes. Chablis wines are always made from Chardonnay grapes. Burgundy wines are made from Pinot Noir. Bordeaux are made from a blend of five grapes (the blends vary by subregions). Condrieu is made from the Viognier grape; Beaujolais is from the Gamay grape—we could go on and on and on.

And on. It's easy to see why this can be overwhelming, because in Burgundy alone there are four levels of appellations and numerous appellations under each level. Where, oh where do we start?

Thankfully, to love wine you needn't ever memorize appellations and their corresponding grapes or grape blends. But what you might want to do is learn which Old World appellations correspond to varietals that you like at home. And vice versa. If you've always loved Chianti (named for a winegrowing region), remember that it's at least 75 percent Sangiovese—so go ahead and try a New World Sangiovese.

How do you learn which appellations correspond to the varietals you love? To get you started, see the list of popular varietals and their corresponding appellations on page 218. Also, most wine shop owners can point you in the right direction—they love to talk about this stuff. Just ask.

And if you love Sauvignon Blanc, check out wines from the following French appellations:

**Pouilly-Fumé:** Named for an area in France's Loire Valley region, these wines are made entirely of Sauvignon Blanc. *Fumé* is French for "smoke," and these wines possess a pleasant smoky or flintlike aroma. These wines are more full-bodied than those from Sancerre.

**Sancerre:** Also named for an area in France's Loire Valley region and also made entirely of Sauvignon Blanc grapes, this wine tends to be leaner or lighter-bodied than Pouilly-Fumé.

### Cheap Dates from the Southern Hemisphere

In the mid-'90s, U.S. imports of Australian wine increased by a whopping 50 percent, and imports from New Zealand, Chile, and Argentina rose sharply too. Sauvignon Blanc from these areas brought fun labels, playful flavor profiles, and good values to American wine lovers. In fact, you can often buy a variety of bottles for the price you'd pay for just one bottle from California.

Prices for Sauvignon Blanc from Australia and New Zealand have climbed above $10, so if you're looking for bargain-basement wines, check out those from Chile and

### ✳ ✳ ✳ THE MONA LISA ✳ ✳ ✳

Cloudy Bay, New Zealand; $25 to $35. Sometimes hard to find but well worth the search, this sassy wine is revered as one of the best examples of Sauvignon Blanc in the world and is considered THE BEST in the New World. For that reason alone it's definitely worth paying homage. Better yet, it lives up to its rep! Its style showcases the best attributes of the grape. It does have a li'l Sémillon for richness, and it does see oak before it sees you. Yet the result is not oaky or sweet. Instead you have a perfectly balanced wine with a clean finish and invigorating acidity.

### ✳ ✳ ✳ THE SALVADOR DALÍ ✳ ✳ ✳

Sauvignon Blanc from the Stellenbosch or Constantia region of South Africa; about $20. On a recent trip to South Africa, I fell in love with this country's Sauvignon Blanc. Unfortunately I found that almost all of what I was tasting was not available in the United States. I went to work filling my backpack with as many bottles as I could. After 24 hours of travel, the weight of the wine ripped my pack, but I was determined not to lose one drop. Fortunately, you don't have to travel to share in the fun. There are a few of these hanging around wine shops, and South African Sauvignon Blanc is sooo yummy, it's worth the hunt.

Argentina. Many can still be found for under $10. And don't feel bad about buying cheap wine! Cheap wine is great, as long as you like the way it tastes. I mention cheap wine when it comes to Sauvignon Blanc from Chile and Argentina because there are so darn many!

Of course, once these inexpensive wines are discovered to be delicious, you can bet their reputations will spread like wildfire and the blue-light special will be over, Kmart shoppers! So be sure to get in on the action and sip these Sauvignon Blancs while they're still a steal.

### A Summer Romance

Each summer my affair with Sauvignon Blanc from Australia and New Zealand grows deeper for every degree the temperature outside rises over 85. And one of my all-time favorite regions for Sauvignon Blanc is Marlborough, New Zealand. This hot spot blossomed into a wine lover's mecca when

Don't feel bad about buying cheap wine! Cheap wine is great, as long as you like the way it tastes.

Sauvignon Blanc shot from its stony soil in the late 1970s; the region now grows two-thirds of the country's Sauvignon Blanc grapes. These wines provide a perfect introduction to the "citric attack" so loved by fans of Sauvignon Blanc. At least one New Zealand Sauvignon Blanc is a must for your tasting this month.

These saucy little gems from down under exude what the grape is all about: Aah— stick your nose in the glass and smell the grapefruit, grass, lemons, and …

## Cat Pee?

Yes, cat pee. Weirdly enough, this term is often used by wine pros to describe Sauvignon Blanc. If you have a naughty kitty, you know the smell. If you don't, consider yourself lucky. Although it sounds repulsive, this is not necessarily considered a bad attribute when it comes to wine. In fact, for many, it's not as bad as it sounds, though the combo of grassiness and herbs may strike some sniffers as offensive.

## Get Your Oak Off My …

Sauvignon Blanc. I mean it. A lot of wine benefits from being aged in oak, but I don't think this is one of them. In this case, I'm for stainless-steel fermentation all the way—and I'll tell you why.

Most California Sauvignon Blanc is made in the Bordeaux style, which means it sees oak in its lifetime and is usually blended with another white grape called Sémillon. For me the best parts of Sauvignon Blancs—the acidity and

* * * * * * * * * * * *

## YOU'LL NEVER FORGET IT

This month during those lazy days of summer, I'll save you the hassle of making a mistake you'll never forget. Instead, I'll show you a quick way to ice up a bottle of Sauvignon Blanc—without losing your wine and cutting your finger all in one silly move.

If you've ever been a waiter, you know all about side work—all those little jobs customers don't see servers do before and after they sit down to dine. In all my years of waiting tables, it wasn't the pretty napkin folds that stuck with me; no, the most valuable lesson I learned when doing side work was how to make an ice bucket for chilling wine.

It's not a matter of just putting ice in a bucket. If you try to slam a bottle of wine into a bucket filled only with ice, you may break the bottle, leaving a dangerous mix of ice, glass, and wine. You should assemble your bucket with two parts ice and one part cold water. This will chill your wine much faster than ice alone; in fact, it will take about 25 minutes to chill a room-temperature bottle to the suitable serving temp, compared with the two hours it takes in the fridge.

Filling the bucket with both water and ice allows you to move your bottle in and out of the ice bucket without any force. Drape a clean napkin over the ice bucket to wipe the bottle of any dripping water when you remove it.

While we're at it, when serving iced cocktails or drinks, never swoop an empty glass directly into an ice bucket to fill it with ice. Always use tongs, or you risk smashing a glass and leaving the next person with a crunchy cocktail.

* * * * * * * * * * * *       * * * * * * * * * * * *

## IF THE GLASS FITS …

There are specific wineglasses made for Sauvignon Blanc, but the difference is so slight that it's not necessary to blow the cash on them. An all-purpose white-wine glass is perfect for this juice.

I know in the beginning of the book, I said to always use glass, and this is still my first choice. However, in the summertime you have the option to use acrylic glassware (this does not mean plastic tumblers you normally use for drinking Coke—those can be porous and carry odd flavors from the dishwasher).

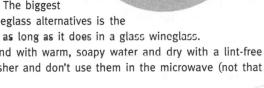

Acrylic glasses look sleek and are safer than glass if you're sipping poolside. Also, for a tasting, acrylic glasses make great stand-ins if you find yourself short on legit glasses. The biggest difference between glassware and these acrylic wineglass alternatives is the weight; I also find that my wine does not stay cool as long as it does in a glass wineglass.

As with stemware, it's best to wash them by hand with warm, soapy water and dry with a lint-free cloth or coffee filter. Don't put them in the dishwasher and don't use them in the microwave (not that you would ever want hot wine).

crispness—are softened when it spends time in oak, and that means a wimpy wine—wimpy in the acid department, at least.

If you're looking for that citrus rush and read on the back label that the Sauvignon Blanc in your hand has even brushed against an oak barrel, put it back on the shelf. Reach for something from New Zealand, Australia, or South Africa. On the other hand, you may find that you like the more elegant, rounded-out style achieved by the oak contact. Not sure what you like? Include a California Sauvignon Blanc that sat in oak for this tasting. Then you'll know.

### Time and Temp

Some say Sauvignon Blanc is best consumed within three to five years of the date on the bottle. I don't wait even that long. While some Sauvignon Blanc can be cellared (including California Sauvignon Blanc aged in oak and many wines from the Loire Valley), in general, when it comes to Sauvignon Blanc, I say drink this year's wine this year and next year's wine as soon as you can get the cork out.

Technically it is recommended this juice be served from 44 to 54 degrees. But there's no need to be sticking a thermometer in your wineglass. Most home refrigerators should be set between 38 and 42 degrees, so if you buy it cold, keep it cold. And if you buy it at room temperature, stick it in the fridge when you get home. After a few swirls on a hot summer day, your wine will warm up and the aromas will begin to show off—I'm pretty sure it won't stay in your glass long enough to get too warm.

If you are entertaining outside, keep the bottles of wine in a shady spot in ice buckets. But be sure to make your ice buckets correctly, or you'll learn a memorable lesson the hard way (see "You'll Never Forget It," page 136).

### August's Picks

With Sauvignon Blanc I'm like a kid in a candy store—there are so many great ones to choose from. In the heat of August this wine, cat pee and all, will tickle your tummy.

By tasting wines from France's Loire Valley, California, Australia, and New Zealand side by side, you'll be struck by the difference a birthplace can make.

**Pouilly-Fumé from France:** Priced $15 to $25.

**Sancerre from France:** Priced at $15 to $25.

**California Sauvignon Blanc:** In the $8 to $20 range.

Refreshing

✶ ✶ ✶ **GOOSEBERRIES?** ✶ ✶ ✶

Yep, I said it. I always thought "gooseberries" was one of those ridiculous terms wine snobs used to sound sophisticated. But in areas where gooseberries are part of the culture—in Great Britain, for example—using the term definitely makes sense. Even though many Americans have never seen, tasted, or smelled gooseberries, the term is worth mentioning because you are sure to see the term used to describe Sauvignon Blanc.

**Australian Sauvignon Blanc:** Priced from $7 to $17.

**New Zealand Sauvignon Blanc:** In the $10 to $15 range.

**Ringer:** Bring in a dry Vouvray from France, priced at $8 to $15. Like Sancerre and Pouilly-Fumé, Vouvray comes from the Loire Valley, but it's made from the Chenin Blanc grape. This is a good chance to learn the difference between the two grapes and get to know another varietal from this part of the world. Besides, Vouvray is simply a beautiful wine to sip in summer. Vouvray wines vary in style, depending on how long the growing season lasts. The longer the grapes dangle on the vine, the sweeter they become. I recommend buying one that says "sec" (dry) or "demi-sec" (off-dry) on the label.

In the heat of August this wine, cat pee and all, will tickle your tummy.

# GET YOUR DRINK ON

*Go ahead—take a sip. As soon as your mouth starts watering, you'll know why this wine is famous for its acid. You'll be sure to go back for another sip, and another, and another, and …*
*In the meantime, here's what else you may notice.*

**COLOR:** Sauvignon Blanc can be as clear as water; in fact, one giveaway that you're drinking Sauvignon Blanc is those loose legs hanging on the side of the glass. When it comes to color, a tinge is really all you will see, and a green tinge is a dead giveaway for this grape. It reminds me of the pale green of mint chocolate chip ice cream. It's very, very light and you can usually see it right around the rim of the wine. Other color-related words sometimes used to describe this wine include green-yellow, pale yellow, butter, straw, and golden. If it's toward the golden end of the spectrum, it's more than likely this juice has seen some oak. Whatever the color, the wine should be clear and free of sediment.

**AROMA:** Across the board, aromas will carry some of this wine's signature grapefruit characteristic and will be more citruslike overall than Chardonnay. You may find smoky hints in the Loire Valley's Pouilly-Fumé, due to the soil there. Lemon, lime, grass, hay, green fruit, tropical fruits, minerals, cat pee, herbs, asparagus, and gooseberries (see "Gooseberries?," opposite) are all common to this grape. Freshly cut grass, a signature of summer, is also a signature of this grape. Remember this when sniffing and swirling and you're sure to hear the word *grassy* slide off your tongue. Sauvignon Blanc from California may emit more banana, apricot, or melon smells. These wines are generally aged in oak and are often blended with Sémillon, a grape that adds body and cuts the acidity, usually with a touch of sweetness. Sauvignon Blancs from New Zealand, Australia, Chile, and South Africa will be much greener and grassier than those from France or California.

**TASTE:** As you taste the wines from the Loire Valley and New Zealand, your mouth will fill with a tart green apple flavor. Although you smell citrus, you will definitely taste green apple. Those Sauvignon Blancs from California will have you tasting ripe melon, citrus flavors, cantaloupe, and peaches. If you sense a taste of honey, that's most likely the Sémillon grape peeking out. Sauvignon Blanc will also taste dry in comparison with other whites because of its tangy acidity.

**BODY:** Most Sauvignon Blanc is medium-bodied. You'll notice that the ones you're tasting from the Loire Valley, New Zealand, and Australia will have a cleaner and crisper body than those from California. Remember that oak thing I told you about with those California wines? Aging in oak and blending the wine with some Sémillon grapes give them more body.

**FINISH:** The acid in this wine can result in a very long finish, but you be the judge. After you sip, if your mouth starts to water, the insides of your cheeks start to water, and your entire palate tingles—this could go on for more than 10 seconds—you've got a long finish. But if the wine feels more like water and washes over your tongue, disappearing down your throat without a trace, that is a very short finish.

**RINGER:** If you're paying attention, you will quickly notice that there's something not quite right; specifically, you'll likely notice one of the wines will seem sweet or off-dry. That's it! You've found the Vouvray! Whether you're testing sec or demi-sec, both will likely carry sweeter notes than the Sauvignon Blanc you're tasting.

# ❧ LET'S EAT! FOOD AND WINE PAIRING ❧

**G**reat wine makes great food better, and this is especially true with Sauvignon Blanc. While taking advantage of summer's fabulous produce, we'll highlight the multitalented acidity of Sauvignon Blanc. You'll feel it cut through creamy dishes and complement lemon meringue. We'll bridge the food and wine with dishes like the Li'l Juicy

Tomatoes soaked in Sauvignon Blanc and dipped in fleur de sel, a coarse, crunchy salt with a wallop of flavor. Ingredients like tarragon and lemon juice will complement the wine's flavors and aromas. And because it's usually hotter than heck in August, the nibbles I've chosen are simple and designed to keep you out of the kitchen.

\* \* \* \* \* \* \* \* \* \* \* \* \* \* \* \* \* \* \*

# CHILLED FRESH CORN SOUP

*The first time I heard of cold soup, I thought I was being punished. But when you taste this soup, you'll find it makes a perfect lunch on a hot summer day.*

| | |
|---|---|
| 10 | ears of fresh corn |
| 8 | cups water |
| 5 | sprigs fresh thyme |
| 2 | bay leaves |
| | Salt |
| 2 | tablespoons butter |
| 1 | cup diced onion |
| ½ | cup whipping cream |
| | Ground white pepper |
| | Ground anise or cayenne pepper |

**1.** Use a sharp knife to cut the kernels off of the corncobs; set corn aside. In a large pot combine corncobs, water, thyme, and bay leaves; sprinkle lightly with salt. Bring to a boil. Reduce heat and simmer for 45 minutes. Cool slightly. Strain; discard corncobs, thyme, and bay leaves.

**2.** Meanwhile, in a large skillet melt butter. Add corn and onion; cook and stir for 12 to 15 minutes or until soft.

**3.** Place half of the corn-onion mixture and half of the strained cooking liquid in a blender. Cover and blend until smooth. Strain. Place contents of blender in a large bowl. Repeat with remaining corn-onion mixture and cooking liquid. Strain. Add to bowl. Stir in cream.

**4.** Cover and chill 4 to 24 hours. Season to taste with additional salt and white pepper. Sprinkle each serving with anise.

**Makes about 5 cups (twenty 2-ounce servings)**

Note: You can make this soup up to 2 days in advance. Cover and chill until ready to serve; check seasoning. The shortcut version of this soup is on page 145.

# BLUEBERRY-GINGER SORBET

*Every summer as kids, we'd vacation at the Jersey shore. Along the way we'd stop for fresh blueberries and tomatoes from one of the many roadside stands. We loved the way the berries filled our mouths with sweet, juicy goodness and turned our teeth blue. This sorbet reminds me of those carefree days of summer.*

6    cups fresh or frozen blueberries

½    cup sugar

2    teaspoons ground ginger

2    tablespoons fresh lemon juice (1 medium lemon)

1. Stir together blueberries, sugar, and ginger. Cover and chill overnight.

2. Place blueberry mixture and lemon juice in a blender. Cover and blend until smooth. Strain. Discard blueberry skins.

3. Put mixture in an ice cream freezer and freeze according to manufacturer's directions.

**Makes about 3 cups (six ½-cup servings)**

Blueberry-Ginger Granité: If you do not have an ice cream freezer, you can pour the strained blueberry mixture into a baking pan. Cover and freeze until firm, scraping with a fork every hour.

* * * * * * * * * * * *

## BIG JUICY TOMATOES

If you have some big ripe summer tomatoes in the garden, let them star at this month's wine club meeting. If you don't, hit a roadside stand or a farmer's market for the freshest around. In the summer, the grocery store would be the last place I would buy tomatoes, but if that's all you've got, go for it. Make sure you are serving them in season. Winter tomatoes are watery and flavorless, so you're better off avoiding these dishes in the cooler months.

   A few suggestions:

★ Try serving them with crumbled blue cheese and a drizzle of olive oil.

★ Drizzle them with your favorite blue cheese dressing and top with a little freshly cracked black pepper.

★ Chop fresh mint and basil and sprinkle over sliced tomatoes layered with fresh mozzarella cheese. You can find fresh mozzarella in most grocery stores, either in the cheese section or in the deli case. Top with some kosher salt. Kosher salt can be found in every grocery store—please steer clear of iodized salt for this recipe.

**Note:** When you are cooking in the kitchen, go with your gut. If you like a little more blue cheese or a little less basil, be OK about making that decision. Trust yourself on amounts and substitutions.

* * * * * * * * * * * *      * * * * * * * * * *

# LEMON MERINGUE TARTLETS

*At summer picnics I am always in awe of the mom who brings a beautiful lemon meringue pie. The fresh lemon flavor of these baby meringues goes perfectly with our Sauvignon Blanc tasting, and the sweetness balances out the acid. With one bite you'll smile from ear to ear.*

| | |
|---|---|
| 3 | egg yolks |
| 1/8 | teaspoon salt |
| 3/4 | cup sugar |
| 2½ | tablespoons cornstarch |
| 3/4 | cup water |
| 1 | tablespoon unsalted butter, softened |
| 1½ | teaspoons grated fresh lemon peel |
| 1/4 | cup fresh lemon juice (2 medium lemons) |
| 2 | egg whites |
| ½ | cup confectioner's sugar |
| 24 | mini tartlet shells |

**1.** In a large bowl slightly beat egg yolks and salt together with a whisk or fork; set aside.

**2.** For filling, in a medium saucepan combine sugar and cornstarch. Stir in water. Bring to a boil over medium heat, stirring occasionally. Boil for 1 minute, stirring constantly. Remove from heat. The mixture will be very thick at this point.

**3.** Gradually stir a small amount of the hot filling into the egg yolk mixture. Slowly add the remaining filling to egg yolk mixture, stirring constantly. Return mixture to saucepan. Bring to a boil over medium heat. Boil for 30 seconds, stirring constantly. Remove from heat. Add butter; stir until melted. Stir in lemon peel and lemon juice. Cover and set aside while making meringue.

**4.** For meringue, in a large mixing bowl beat egg whites with an electric mixer until soft peaks form. Slowly add the confectioner's sugar, beating until firm peaks form.

**5.** Divide warm filling among tartlet shells. Place meringue in a pastry bag with a large star tip. Pipe meringue over warm filling on each tartlet. (Or dollop a tablespoon of meringue on top of each tartlet.)

**6.** Preheat oven to 400°F. Place the tartlets on a large baking sheet. Bake for 3 to 4 minutes or until the meringue is light brown. Cool on a wire rack for 1 hour. Cover and chill 3 to 6 hours. These are best if made the day of serving or no more than one day in advance. If you make them too far in advance, your tartlet shells will be soggy.

**Makes 24 tartlets**

Note: I make these with premade mini tartlet shells, which can be purchased at most grocery stores. If you cannot find these, see the recipe for Homemade Mini Tartlet Shells on page 47.

# GRILLED SHRIMP
## with Creamy Tarragon Dipping Sauce

*With fall looming you have to make the most of your grilling days. I know some of you are lucky enough to grill all year round. But with New York's winters, you won't find me bundled in snow gear out there flipping burgers. These shrimp on the bar-bee are perfect for that grilled summer goodness and a lovely match with the wine.*

24    to 30 large shrimp, peeled, deveined, tails left on

     Canola oil

     Kosher salt

     Freshly cracked black pepper

½    cup mayonnaise

2    tablespoons Dijon mustard

2    tablespoons chopped fresh tarragon

2    lemons, cut into wedges

1. Preheat your grill to medium-high heat or a stove-top grill pan over medium-high heat.

2. Place shrimp in a bowl; drizzle with a little oil. Toss to coat. Sprinkle shrimp with salt and pepper.

3. Grill shrimp about 1 minute on each side or until shrimp turn pink and begin to curl. Transfer shrimp to a serving platter.

4. For dipping sauce, in a small bowl combine mayonnaise, mustard, and tarragon. Serve shrimp with dipping sauce and lemon wedges.

**Makes 24 to 30 appetizers**

### * * * * * * * * LI'L JUICY TOMATOES * * * * * * * *

This little pick-me-up couldn't be easier to assemble or more fun to eat! My chef friend, Megan, showed me the hors d'oeuvre when I was visiting her in Paris; however, she made it with vodka. Next time you're having a cocktail party, feel free to prepare these Li'l Juicy Tomatoes with vodka; this month we'll be sticking with wine. I love serving cherry or grape tomatoes in an olive tray. You can pick up one at HomeGoods or in the home section of Marshalls or T.J. Maxx for under $20.

Here's how to serve Li'l Juicy Tomatoes:

★ Pour a little Sauvignon Blanc in the bottom of the olive tray and place a single row of tomatoes right on top.

★ Serve with toothpicks and a ramekin of fleur de sel. You may have to buy fleur de sel in a gourmet grocery shop or order it online.

★ Show your guests how they can prick a Sauvignon Blanc–soaked cherry tomato and then barely dip it into the ramekin of fleur de sel.

# SPICY CHICKEN
## and Chile Quesadillas

*It is often recommended to serve wine with the foods of the region where that wine grows best. This recipe includes fresh chiles, chili powder, and dried red chile pepper flakes if you need a little more heat. Much of Chile's cuisine is spicy, and it pairs perfectly with the country's luscious Sauvignon Blanc.*

1   pound chicken breast tenders, cut into bite-size pieces

2   tablespoons fresh lime juice (1 medium lime)

1   teaspoon salt

¼   teaspoon chili powder

¼   teaspoon ground cumin

    Olive oil

6   8-inch flour tortillas

2   cups shredded Monterey Jack or white cheddar cheese

¼   cup whole kernel corn

¼   cup diced scallions

¼   cup chopped fresh cilantro

3   fresh jalapeño peppers, seeded and diced*

    Red chile pepper flakes (optional)

    Dairy sour cream

    Lime wedges

**1.** In a large bowl toss chicken with lime juice. In a small bowl combine salt, chili powder, and cumin; sprinkle over chicken, tossing to coat.

**2.** Add enough olive oil to lightly coat a large skillet; heat over medium-high heat. Add chicken; cook and stir for 5 to 7 minutes or until no longer pink. Remove from heat.

**3.** Brush one side of each tortilla with olive oil. Layer chicken, cheese, corn, scallions, cilantro, and jalapeño peppers evenly on the unbrushed side of 3 of the tortillas. Top each with a tortilla, oiled side up. If desired, sprinkle one side of each quesadilla with red chile pepper flakes.

**4.** Preheat your grill to hot or a stove-top grill pan over medium-high heat. Grill quesadillas about 2 minutes on each side or until cheese melts.

**5.** Cut quesadillas into wedges. Serve with sour cream and lime wedges.

**Makes 24 to 30 quesadillas**

*\*Note: Because hot chile peppers, such as jalapeños, contain volatile oils that can burn your skin and eyes, avoid direct contact with chiles as much as possible. When working with chile peppers, wear plastic or rubber gloves. If your bare hands do touch the chile peppers, wash your hands well with soap and water.*

# CREAMY CORN and Potato Soup

*This version is a shortcut to the Chilled Fresh Corn Soup recipe. It also works if you can't find fresh sweet corn on the cob. I love this soup hot or cold, so try it in the middle of winter too!*

| | |
|---|---|
| 1 | to 2 tablespoons olive oil |
| 4 | shallots, diced |
| 2 | 10-ounce bags frozen whole kernel corn |
| 2 | Yukon gold potatoes, peeled and chopped |
| 6 | cups chicken stock |
| | Salt |
| | Cayenne pepper |

1. In a large pot heat olive oil. Add shallots; cook and stir until soft. Add corn; cook and stir to warm the corn. Add potatoes. Add enough chicken stock to cover the potatoes; reserve remaining chicken stock. Bring to a boil. Reduce heat and simmer for 30 minutes. Remove from heat; cool slightly.

2. Place half of the corn-potato mixture in a blender. Cover and blend until pureed. Strain. Discard corn kernels. Return strained mixture to pot. Add remaining chicken stock; heat through.

3. Season to taste with salt and cayenne pepper. Serve warm or cover and chill 4 to 24 hours.

**Makes about 5 cups (twenty 2-ounce servings)**

* * * * * * * * * * * * *

## NO-COOK OPTIONS

You'll notice that my recipes for Big Juicy Tomatoes and Li'l Juicy Tomatoes are easy to prepare without ever turning on the heat. Here are a few more simple-for-summer options:

★Lemon ice, lemon or lime Popsicles, and sliced fresh sweet, pink grapefruit are fun to serve with Sauvignon Blanc—they'll complement those acidic citrusy notes in the wine.

★You can buy precooked shrimp already peeled and deveined. Serve with dairy sour cream mixed with fresh chopped herbs (parsley, tarragon, basil, or mint) to get herbaceous flavors into the mix. Or look for bread with herbs or crackers with rosemary for that same effect. It's always good to have bread or crackers at a tasting.

★I also recommend you serve tortilla chips and purchased hot salsa to see how Sauvignon Blanc interacts with a little heat.

* * * * * * * * * * * *          * * * * * * * * * * *

# dessert *** wines

## (aka stickies)

*Can* *a wine truly be better than sex? The jury's out, but I must admit, I do feel a little naughty when I'm sipping dessert wines—those intense, sweet elixirs I like to refer to as "stickies." Sweet wines aren't just for beginners—they are sophisticated and can be as sublime as the most intense seduction.*

I promise this month you'll go home grinning and giggly!

Stickies have another kind of appeal, which my friend Wini summed up when she said, "Frankly, I like dessert wines because I'm not crazy about dessert, but I do like to hang out at the table and sip." Who doesn't like to linger a little longer when you're having fun? If nothing else, these wines give you even more reason to stick around the table and explore another drink. Dessert wines are great served before coffee and dessert, with dessert, or in place of dessert. Many of you are programmed to order that same ol' cup of coffee after dinner, but after this tasting you'll be asking for that wine list back!

### Getting to Know Dessert Wines

Not long ago, when I went off on a rant about how much I loved dessert wines, my mom thought I was making a big fuss for nothing.

"What's the big deal?" she asked. "Port's the only dessert wine, right?"

*Au contraire, ma mère!* There is a whole lot more to dessert wine than Port! This month a slew of styles and shades awaits your discovery, and we'll soon be sipping wines that are as different as apples and oranges.

In this chapter, I'm approaching wines differently from the months before. Because dessert wines are not made from the same grape or winemaking process, we don't expect too many similarities among them. So instead of our usual modus operandi, where I give you one overall tasting sheet that compares and contrasts the different styles of wine, I'll clue you in to the characteristics of each style separately as I discuss them. Let's get started with one of the most highly sought-after sips in this arena—Sauternes.

### Sauternes Sophisticate

You may have gone gaga for the acid in Sauvignon Blanc last month, but wait till you see what else this little grape is capable of!

Sauvignon Blanc is one of the grapes behind the great Sauternes wines of France; (Sémillon is the other; Sauternes can be made with SB, Sémillon, or a combo of both).

But get ready, because at the first sip you're

> Botrytis helps transform the grapes into a divine nectar draped in aromas of honey, dried pineapple, and nuts, with flavors ranging from apricot and peach to pineapple and vanilla.

going to taste that the Sauternes' take on Sauvignon Blanc brings something way different from those zingy darlings that zipped across your tongue last month!

As you know by now, France names its wines not for grapes but for the winegrowing region (that's right: the appellation— bonus points if you remembered that

* * * * * * * * * * * * **WINE TREND** * * * * * * * * * * * * *

Port has been long overdue for a makeover. Now, at last, the world-famous Sandeman Port has homed in on what it means to be modern—winemakers have stirred a little controversy into the world of Port with their new "Vau" Vintage Ruby. It's got a hot label with a sassy red "V" splashed across the bottle. Holding true to vintage dating, this wine is made only from the best grapes in the best vintage years—but that's all she wrote for the history books, because unlike the old-fogy Ports, this one's styled to be drunk young! Yes, that's right, drink it right now. Its luscious dark purple color is soaked in ripe plum, cherry, and spice flavors. After a few twirls in the glass, decadent dark chocolate aromas develop. Unlike the thick, syrupy, traditional Port wines, this wine is slightly more slender in body. You can do away with the decanter, because at 2 years old instead of 50, the sediment is negligible. And as far as the Port experience goes, this is fairly inexpensive. A half bottle will run you about $20, and for a full you'll be spending $35. Since its release there have been posers in the Port world, but remember, the only true Vau is Sandeman's. The time is now, the vintage is Vau, so go out and grab a bottle!

* * * * * * * * * * * * * * * * * * * * * * * * * * * * *

word!). While Sauternes may be made from Sauvignon Blanc, the difference between Sauvignon Blanc from last month and Sauternes this month is that the grape used for the latter has been bitten by botrytis (see "It Won't Kill You," page 150), that is, a healthy dose of rot.

Botrytis helps transform the grapes into a divine nectar draped in aromas of honey, dried pineapple, and nuts, with flavors ranging from apricot and peach to pineapple and vanilla. Often the flavor is trimmed with a whirl of burnt sugar, like a decadent crème brûlée. Another noteworthy attribute of sophisticated Sauternes is its roasted nutty notes, which develop as the wine ages.

When it comes to this Sticky, vintage matters, since a little weather can make or break the entire year's crop. The '90s were ripe for Sauternes because good vintages came four years in a row—1995, '96, '97, and '98 were all fine vines. Also, because this wine is a labor of love, it comes with a hefty price tag. The most famous French Sauternes is Château d'Yquem—it may take an entire vine to produce one glass, which is barrel-

aged for three and a half years before bottling. But even then, it should not be drunk for at least 20 years. For a good Château d'Yquem you're looking at spending well over $100. Fortunately there are less expensive Sauternes out there, but none are going to be what we'd call cheap.

A word of caution, my friends: When you're headed out to find this godlike wine,

## PASSING THE PORTO

Did you know that it's customary to pass a bottle of Port from the right to the left? This little quirk is steeped in history; in fact, the tradition is mentioned in Homer's *Iliad*, and mythology references mention the practice as one that brings good luck. So if you're superstitious—or if you just want to stick to tradition—pass that bottle from your right to your left.

On another note, if a bottle of Port has stopped being passed from one person to the next, the guilty party is called the "bishop." So unless you want to be known as holier than thou among your friends, be sure to pour and keep on passing the Porto.

beware of the "sauterne" without the "s" at the end. This usually refers to an inexpensive semisweet California wine that doesn't even come close to the real deal Sauternes.

## Ice, Ice, Baby

I'm a sucker for all sorts of dessert wines, but Ice Wine is my true Achilles' heel—I really can't ever turn down a chance to sip this stuff.

This style of winemaking was originally developed in the 18th century in Germany, where it's called Eiswein. These days it's produced in northern Germany, the northern United States, New Zealand, and Canada—all places that get their share of cold weather, a key element to making these beauties.

Most Ice Wines are made from Riesling grapes, except for those from parts of Canada, where they are made from Vidal, a thick-skinned hybrid grape. Whether Riesling or Vidal, the grapes are allowed to dangle on the vine until they shrivel into raisins. And there they stay until a cold winter's frost freezes them.

When harvest time arrives at last, the juice is pressed from the grapes before they get a chance to thaw. Shards of ice are removed, leaving behind the makings of an extremely sweet, intense, luscious wine. As you can imagine, this process is no walk in the park for winemakers, so be prepared to dish out some dough.

You'll be rewarded handsomely for your hard-earned cash. With Ice Wine you're in for a mouthful of thick, juicy sweet apricots, tropical fruit salad, butterscotch, honey, and an undeniable sharp acidity that will rock your world. The concentrated flavors in Ice Wine differ from those of a botrytis-affected wine, so it's fun to taste the two side by side.

## Fashionably Late

"Late-harvest" is an American term that refers to wine made from grapes picked at the end of the harvest season (in the U.S. that usually means later in the fall). Sometimes these grapes get the botrytis

* * **IT WON'T KILL YOU** * *

*Botrytis cinerea* sounds a little scary, but I promise it brings good things! The term refers to what's known as "noble rot" (also dubbed "noble botrytis"), and it boils down to one thing: divine wine. Basically, *Botrytis cinerea* is—catch this—a desirable mold. It forms on the plant and shrivels the grape, concentrating the sugars to make for lip-smackingly sweet wine. Botrytis-affected grapes yield special gifts from nature: a heavenly honey-flavored juice that, as it ages, turns from pale yellow to dark gold, maturing and concentrating the flavors even further. Deeeee-lish!

treatment (see "It Won't Kill You," above); however, even if not, the grapes get super-sweet simply by staying on the vine longer than most. White-wine grapes such as Riesling, Gewürztraminer, Sémillon, Sauvignon Blanc, or Chenin Blanc are used for late-harvest wines. France, northern Italy, New Zealand, California, Oregon, Washington State, and New York produce excellent late-harvest wines.

**Brix:** In the United States and other parts of the New World, this is the measurement of the degree of sugar content in the grape. The higher the Brix, the sweeter the wine.

**Cloying:** A descriptor that can refer to wines that are overly sweet and lacking acidity.

**Manzanilla:** The lightest, most delicate, and most pungent of the fino-style sherries, this straw-colored, dry wine is matured in casks near the sea, which can give it a slightly tangy, salty flavor. Because it is a type of fino sherry, it is subject to spoilage and should be handled like the fino.

**Amontillado:** Although a fino-style sherry, this is deeper amber in color and richer and nuttier (many people smell hazelnuts), with a pungent tang. True Amontillado costs about $20 to $35 a bottle.

**Amoroso, brown sherry, cream sherry, medium sherry, and East India sherry:** These are all dry sherries that have been heavily sweetened.

**Tokaji Aszú Essencia:** Aged five years with a sugar content of 8 ounces per liter, this is the rarest and most expensive of all Eastern European wines.

---

A good late-harvest wine will have the sweetness of tropical fruits and honey balanced by just the right amount of acidity so the sweetness isn't cloying. One of my faves is late-harvest Riesling. These wines have both the scent and taste of fresh lime, with soft fruits like ripe peach and apricot. There's often a gentle floral fringe in the aroma. Most late-harvest Rieslings have a low alcohol content (6–9 percent) which gives them a lightness and delicacy that the higher-alcohol wines such as Sauternes (12–13 percent alcohol) or Port (18–20 percent alcohol) don't have.

### Sprechen Sie Deutsch?

I don't, but I do speak enough to buy a bottle of German dessert wine. In Germany, wines are put into five categories, according to how sweet they are. You may remember this from our Riesling tasting, but just to make sure, these are the three sweetest dessert wines (from sweet to sweetest).

## YOU'LL NEVER FORGET IT

If you are under the impression that dessert wine is only for dessert, think again. Sweet wines caress supersavory foods and work wonders with spicy bites. I can't think of anything that is more on the savory side than Stilton or Roquefort cheese, so pick up a hunk of blue and a baguette. Then break bread and nibble on some of that stinky blue cheese. Follow it with a sip of sweet sherry or Port and take a moment to absorb the impact on your palate. It's truly a divine pair. Try it, and the next time you are sitting down to a dinner of filet covered in Gorgonzola, you'll think twice before you order that big red—you just might reach for a Sticky with dinner instead.

Auslese

Beerenauslese

Trockenbeerenauslese (or TBA)

The last two are made from nobly rotted (aka botrytis-affected) Riesling grapes that are handpicked one by one at the fullest maturity so they are most concentrated in flavor and sugar. The result is an extremely rich nectar.

TBA is made from the most highly raisined grapes and is outrageously sweet. Some say these are every bit as good as Sauternes, including the famed Château d'Yquem, and they are a lot rarer, since noble rot strikes Germany far less often than Sauternes,

France. Auslese wines range from $20 to $45, Beerenauslese goes for up to $250, and Trockenbeerenauslese is the most expensive, sometimes selling for thousands of dollars a bottle—shazaaam!

### Wine of the Czars

Back in 1647, Hungarian winemakers made a marvelous mistake—a mistake that resulted in their now-famous Tokaji Aszú wine. As lore has it, in that year winemakers delayed their grape harvest in order to keep the Ottoman Turks from stealing their wine. A late bout of botrytis set in, but rather than creating a disaster, the rot

### ★ ★ ★ THE MONA LISA ★ ★ ★

Inniskillin, Oak Aged Vidal Icewine, about $80. It would have been easy for me to place the Château d' Yquem Sauternes in this category, but since it could put you in the poorhouse, I went with something a teeny bit less expensive. OK, so it's not that much easier on the wallet, but this is worth every penny—pitch in with some friends for a phenomenal taste.

I remember the first time I tasted this wine and every time I've sipped it since. It's a mesmerizing wine with its thick, glistening golden legs. It's packed with apricot, peach, and mango aromas and flavors. Succulent swirls of cinnamon and sweet ginger tickle the pockets of your cheeks. It's a honey-covered kiss and the total package when it comes to dessert wine. I love to savor every single sip of this wine—chilly and all by itself.

The vintners at Inniskillin have also succeeded in producing a sparkling Ice Wine (not an easy task!). The wine has all the attributes of an Ice Wine with the added fun of bubbles. It's something else to look for—though somewhat difficult to find.

### ★ ★ ★ THE SALVADOR DALÍ ★ ★ ★

EOS Estate Bottled, Zinfandel Port, Paso Robles, about $30. This month Port lovers and non-Port drinkers alike will want to sample this sinfully divine Zin Port. That's right—if you love the big, jammy fruit frenzy of Zinfandel, you'll love this dessert wine. The aromas of anise, pepper, sweet cedar, and dark chocolate are enough to make this purchase worthwhile. But take a sip, even a teensy-weensy one, and you'll be hooked. The rich walnut and pecan flavors taste as if they've been folded in with ripe blackberries and dipped in chocolate for a dessert wine that leaves you speechless. The finish is rich and deep and stays just long enough for you to start daydreaming of a candyland with flowing dark-chocolate rivers and cotton-candy clouds.

Vin Santo is generally sweet, but some are off-dry or dry. They are all thick, sticky, high in alcohol, smooth, and intensely flavored.

resulted in stellar sweet wines that Hungarians came to call Tokaji Aszú (it's sometimes spelled Tokay Aszú).

When purchasing this little love you may see the words *three, four, five,* or *six puttonyos*. This indicates the number of baskets of botrytis-affected grapes added to each cask of the wine; the higher the number, the sweeter the wine. And the taste? Let's just say that apricot aromas and flavors don't get any more intense than when they star in these wines. With that kind of rich sweetness, it's no wonder these wines have been dubbed the wine of the Czars.

### Wine of the Saints and Sinners

"This is better than sex," says my friend, Marta Leo, an Italian wine specialist who was the first person ever to pour me a glass of Vin Santo.

OK, so that's a lot of weight to put on a wine—but I will say that indeed, I did feel decadent sipping this delectable libation. I loved the rich nutty flavor, and ever since that first sip I've been hooked. Feeling more nice than naughty? Sex comparison aside, *Vin Santo* translates to "wine of the saints," and sipping this wine is said to be like going to heaven.

While Tuscany makes awesome Vin Santo, Umbria, Veneto, and Friuli-Venezia Giulia all reputably produce this elixir. Vin Santo is generally sweet, but some are off-dry or dry. They are all thick, sticky, high in alcohol, smooth, and intensely flavored. The color is like dark butterscotch, and toasted almonds and caramel waft among the aromas.

Vin Santo is often paired with biscotti—Italians dip these cookies into the wine for an irresistible dessert. It's supersimple too—remember the combo next time you want something really intriguing to cap off a dinner party but don't feel like baking all day. Prices of Vin Santo range from $20 to $120 for a half bottle.

### Bubbly for Dessert

While many sparkling wines will do for dessert, Asti and Moscato d'Asti are particularly sweet picks. Made in the Piedmont region of Italy, near the town of Asti, both are delicious, fairly sweet sparkling wines, and both are made from the Moscato grape. The difference between the two is that Asti is a *spumante*, a sparkling wine, whereas Moscato d'Asti is a *frizzante*, a wine with just a slight frisson of bubbles. Both Asti Spumante and Moscato d'Asti are great with dessert and are a good choice to serve with that ever-stately, always-joyous wedding cake. Both are also lower in alcohol than most wines (about 8–9 percent), which makes them nice for an aperitif.

### Ports of Call

Port (or Porto) is the most famous type of fortified wine (see "Feeling Fortified," page 155). Originally from northern Portugal, it's rich, sweet, and high in alcohol. While the ins and outs of the various styles of Port wine are the stuff that Port geeks love to dissect, for now just keep these four basic categories in mind:

**Ruby Ports:** These get their name from their ravishing crimson or ruby hues. Aged in wood for about two years, Ruby Ports are generally the least expensive at about $10–$15 a bottle. When a recipe calls for Port, like Port-poached pears, I grab for a

## ✴ ✴ VIN DE REFRIGERATOR? ✴ ✴

To give us the goods without gouging our pocketbooks, some winemakers now produce Ice Wine by putting grapes in a freezer. The results are good but not great, mainly because the grapes do not get the chance to overripen to sensuous sweetness that they do when the natural process occurs in the vineyard. Muscat Vin de Glaciere from Bonny Doon Vineyard calls on this newfangled freezer process. While it may not rank up there with a $70 Canadian Eiswein, it's yummy, it goes for nearly a quarter of the price, and besides, you gotta love the name: *Vin de Glaciere* means, basically, "refrigerator wine"—I love a winemaker with a sense of humor.

Ruby. Ruby Port tastes like a jumble of ripe berries and vanilla with a dab of tannins.

**Tawny Ports:** These get their name from their tawny color. Made from a blend of grapes from several years, Tawny Ports can be aged in wood for as long as 40 years—when you see a bottle with 10, 20, or 40 on the label, that indicates the number of years it matured before it was bottled. Tawnies range in price from $25 to well over $100. Both Ruby Ports and Tawny Ports are sometimes called "wood ports" or "wood-aged ports" because, unlike vintage port, they're aged in wood.

Port and sherry are often classified as dessert wines; however, their sweetness doesn't come from noble rot or from a chilly harvest. Instead, these two styles of wine are "fortified" (or strengthened) by the addition of grape brandy, which increases the amount of alcohol present in the wine. The point at which the brandy is added during the winemaking process makes all the difference to the taste of the final product. Port is sweet because its fermentation process is cut short by adding the brandy during fermentation. On the other hand, sherry is fortified only after fermentation is completed. The process produces a top-quality wine of great interest and complexity; in addition to being very sweet, the wine also retains a fiery quality from the brandy.

**Vintage Ports:** These are regarded by many connoisseurs as the crème de la crème of Ports. To the rest of us, this means they're the most expensive. Vintage Ports are—as you might have guessed—made from a single vintage of grapes. As with all other vintage wines, the grapes come only from the best sites and from the best vintages. And because not every year is deemed a vintage year, vintage ports are more rare than the others.

The very best Vintage Ports can age 50 years or more, and unlike the Ruby and Tawny Ports, these are aged in the bottle rather than barrel. Vintage Ports bring intense flavors and colors, with tastes ranging from sweet black fruits and chocolate to licorice and coffee.

** THE FOUNTAIN OF YOUTH **
Generally all sherries are nonvintage; what makes the quality consistent year after year is the Spanish "solera" system of topping off older wines with the more recently-made sherry. This process lets the old wines infuse the younger wines with character while the younger wines give their vibrancy to the older wines.

Note: If you do try a Vintage Port, you should be prepared to decant it several hours before drinking—both to remove the sediment that has built up in the more than 50 years of aging and to soften the taste.

**White Ports:** Last (and, I'm afraid, least) of the bunch, White Ports are produced the same way as the Ruby Ports, except they're made from white grapes. If you can find a bottle, White Port is best for making Port coolers (mix it with a bit of club soda). Otherwise, I'd leave this one on the shelf.

### Sherry Baby

Sherry (aka Jerez) comes from the Andalusia region of Spain and ranges broadly in color, flavor, and sweetness. In fact, sherry differs from many of the other dessert wines because it is not necessarily sweet—it's actually very dry in its natural state. There are fundamentally only two types of sherry: dry and sweet. But there are some that fall in between. Here are a few you may spot on the shelves.

**Fino:** These are considered by many to be the world's finest sherry. Pale, straw-colored, light in body, and dry in taste, these are best served as an aperitif. I don't know why this

type of sherry gets a bad rap in the States because it rocks on a hot summer's day! However, these babies are indeed quite dry, so let's leave them here and focus on …

**Oloroso:** These wines range from deep gold to deep brown in color. They're full-bodied with rich aromas like walnuts and raisins and are slightly sweet. Sweeter than fino but not nearly as sweet as an Eiswein, they're still great as a dessert wine and pair perfectly with filet mignon and hearty winter stews. Because olorosos are usually aged longer than most sherries, they're also—you guessed it— more expensive.

**Cream Sherry and PX:** These two are the sweetest of the sherries. They are dark, rich, creamy and divine with dessert or all by themselves.

Beer connoisseurs, listen up: If you love the rich double and triple bocks, or, even better, the chocolate bocks, you're sure to love these wines. That style of beer and these dessert wines share that chocolaty, nutty goodness in the glass.

PX is super-fun to sip. The letters stand for Pedro Ximenez grapes. These little suckers are sun-dried after harvest to concentrate the natural sugars. The effect? You get the sensational flavors of chocolate pecan pie in your glass! You can buy both cream sherry and Pedro Ximenez for under $15 a bottle. You won't have to sweat a hefty price, and you're sure to love this sexy sip.

## If the Glass Fits

Because dessert wines can be so sweet and rich, I don't recommend drinking a lot at one time—usually a few ounces per person is perfect. That's why most dessert wines are sold in the 375 ml size (better known as a half bottle)—a full bottle of the stuff would be just too much to polish off.

Several companies make specific wineglasses for each specific type of dessert wine, but in general dessert wines are served in smaller glasses with a smaller opening, which helps concentrate the rich aromas of these wines. Fill those petite glasses only two-thirds of the way. With these high-alcohol, full-flavored pours, a little dab'll do ya.

Now normally I don't get all giddy over glassware, but I love collecting antique dessert wineglasses. I have supersnazzy glasses, etched crystal, and simple standbys like the sherry "copita." You know the style—it's a tall-yet-small, tapering, straight-sided wineglass traditional for sipping sherry. There are also glasses for Port, similar to the copita but just a little larger, and teensy-weensy wineglasses for those of you who just need a nip or a nightcap.

Not ready to invest? For this tasting you can use your champagne flutes or your all-purpose white-wine glasses. Heck, you could even use little juice glasses. If you have the appropriate glassware, kudos. If not, no biggie. Just remember: no foam or plastic.

## To Chill or Not to Chill

When it comes to stickies—that is the question! Each kind has its own optimum serving temperature—here's what I recommend:

**Sauternes:** Best served cold, but not ice cold (about 52 to 53 degrees).

**Ice Wine:** Keep it in the fridge and serve cool (closer to 43 degrees).

**Late-Harvest, German Sweets, Tokaji Aszú, Sweet Bubbly:** Each of these is best chilly. The recommended serving temp is between 45 and 50 degrees, so just pull them out of the fridge about 10 minutes before pouring.

**Vin Santo, Port, and Sherry:** You'll notice these are all brown, unlike the dessert wines listed above, which are all pale straw to golden in color. Treat them as you would a dry, heavy red and serve them at a cool room temperature. Of course, there are a couple of exceptions, including Tawny Port, which is light enough to chill a little bit, if that's how you prefer it. Dry sherries, too, are usually served chilled. Sweet sherries, on the other hand, are good at room temperature, though you may serve them chilled or even over ice if you like.

## Drink While the Drinking's Good

The only foolproof way to ensure a wine doesn't lose its oomph after opening is to consume it all in one sitting. But just in case that's not going to happen, here are some tips for knowing when dessert wines are best consumed. After a bottle of dessert wine has been opened, consume within the following windows:

**Sauternes:** Polish the bottle off within one to two weeks.

**Ice Wines, Late-Harvest Wines, German Dessert Wines, and Tokaji Aszù:** These are best consumed three to five days after opening but can hang out in the fridge for a couple of weeks.

**Vin Santo:** Can be drunk for up to a year after opening, although I'd be surprised if it lasted that long.

**Port:** Ruby lasts about four weeks, Tawny is best four to eight weeks after opened, and Vintage Port is best consumed within 24 hours—that includes "Vau" Vintage (see "Wine Trend," page 148).

**Sherry:** Finish off that bottle of oloroso or sweet or cream sherry within four to six weeks after opening.

## This Month's Picks

This month, we'll taste three light dessert wines and three dark dessert wines—that way, you'll get to taste the best of both worlds. Because these wines can be steep in price, I suggest the host purchase all of the wines and split the bill among the guests. This will save you money in the long run, because if you purchase a larger quantity of bottles, a wine store is more likely to give you a discount. It is customary to get a 10-percent discount on a case of wine, even if you mix and match. And in this case, you should be able to chat with a wine shop owner and get the best deal the shop has going.

For your tasting include a bottle of each of the following (note that prices are for half bottles):

**Sauternes:** It's expensive. Prices range from $30 to $300 or more a bottle (depending on the vintage). Great Sauternes are Raymond-Lafon and Rieussec; these can range in price from $30 to $70 a bottle.

**Ice Wine:** A bottle of Eiswein from a top German or Austrian Riesling producer will cost more than $70. Some good producers include Dr. Loosen and Robert Weil. Inniskillin, the benchmark for Canadian Ice Wines, costs between $60 and $80. Other less expensive but good Canadian producers include Jackson-Triggs and Henry of Pelham.

**Late-Harvest Riesling:** Late-harvest varietals have a wide price range, and there are many that are very affordable. A few recommendations are Arrowood Vineyards & Winery Riesling Select Late Harvest ($40), Firestone Vineyard Riesling Santa Ynez Late Harvest ($17), and Hogue Late Harvest Riesling ($10).

**10-year Tawny and a Ruby Port:** There are so many great Port producers. Some of my faves are Sandeman, Ferreira, and Taylor Fladgate. Younger Ports are more affordable; for instance, a bottle of 10-year will run you from $15 to $40 a bottle, while a bottle of 40-year Tawny can be upwards of $100 a bottle. For this tasting let's look for a 10-year Port. For the Ruby, look to spend between $10 and $20 a bottle.

**Sweet Sherry:** Go for a bottle of PX. I highly recommend picking up a bottle from the totally awesome Osborne family. You may know the name or even more so recognize the trademark black bull from their other sherry splendors. Their portfolio of wines is full of rock stars, but the PX is out of this world. You'll probably spend about $12 to $16 for a bottle.

## ꙮ LET'S EAT! FOOD AND WINE PAIRING ꙮ

**T**alk about the ultimate fat-free dessert option—dessert wine is it! You may be tempted to have your stickies stand alone as delightful desserts in themselves, but try them alongside some yummy dishes, at least for this month's tasting. They'll surprise you with their abilities to pair with savory foods, and they can be knockout additions to a sweet dessert.

Here are some approaches to pairing food and stickies:

Serve them to complement dessert. For example, think late-harvest Riesling or Ice Wine with a tropical fruit tart. You want the sweetness of your dessert to stand up to the sweetness of the wine; dark chocolate mousse pairs very nicely with very sweet red dessert wines like Ruby Port. Alone each one is rich, sweet,

and decadent, and together they are even more so.

Go for contrast, e.g., a sweet white wine with a spicy Thai curry or fiery Mexican dish. The full body of a sweet wine will massage your palate after being hit with a wallop of spice. Also, the sugar is a natural way to cool down the heat from spicy ingredients. Yes, I know I've said high alcohol intensifies spicy cuisine, so I recommend reaching for a low-alcohol dessert wine like late-harvest Riesling instead of a Tawny Port.

Another natural pairing for dessert wine is that almighty cheese plate or another rich and savory food. For example, Sauternes and foie gras are a classic match offering complements and contrasts all in one mouthful—the wine is sweet and the foie gras is savory, but they are both silky and sinfully rich on the palate.

* * * * * * * * * * * * * * * * * * * *

# ANCHOVY, CARAMELIZED ONION, *and Pimiento Toast Points*

*This is the perfect pair with a sweet sherry. The anchovy, sweet onions, and peppers all work well with the rich sweetness of the wine. It's one of those pairs that you won't believe until you try. So, bon appétit.*

| | |
|---|---|
| 2 | tablespoons olive oil |
| 4 | cups coarsely chopped red onions |
| ⅛ | teaspoon salt |
| 12 | slices white bread |
| 2 | tablespoons anchovy paste |
| 3 | tablespoons thinly sliced pimiento |

**1.** In a medium skillet heat olive oil over medium-low heat. Add onions and salt. Cook for 35 to 45 minutes or until caramelized, stirring occasionally.

**2.** Preheat oven to 425°F. To make toast points, remove the crust from each slice of bread; cut in half diagonally. Arrange bread triangles on a shallow baking sheet. Bake for 4 to 5 minutes or until tops are toasted. Flip triangles over; bake 2 to 3 minutes more or until tops are toasted.

**3.** Spread about ½ teaspoon anchovy paste on each toast point. Top with about 1 teaspoon of the caramelized onions and 1 or 2 sliced pimientos.

**Makes 24 pieces**

# BABY 'BELLOS WITH LEEKS
## *and Goat Cheese*

*This warm goat cheese over melted leeks just melts in your mouth. The earthy mushrooms and the tangy cheese contrast a sweet wine, but the creamy texture stands up to the rich full body of a dessert wine.*

3  tablespoons vegetable oil

2  cups diced leeks

1  tablespoon butter

Salt

Black pepper

25  to 30 baby portobello mushrooms, cleaned and stemmed

3  tablespoons extra-virgin olive oil

2  ounces goat cheese

Cracked black pepper

**1.** In a large skillet heat oil over medium-low heat. Add leeks. Cook and stir about 15 minutes or until translucent. Add butter; season with salt and pepper.

**2.** Preheat oven to 400°F. Place the mushrooms, stem sides up, on a baking sheet. Sprinkle with salt; brush with olive oil. Bake for 6 to 7 minutes. Remove from oven; discard liquid that is inside the mushrooms.

**3.** Preheat broiler. Fill each mushroom with ½ to 1 teaspoon leeks; top with ½ teaspoon goat cheese. Broil for 2 to 4 minutes or until the cheese begins to look golden. Sprinkle with cracked pepper.

**Makes 25 to 30 pieces**

**Note: These mushrooms can be made in advance and kept warm in a 175°F oven until ready to serve.**

# SWEET SHERRY AND CHIPOTLE GLAZED LAMB CHOPS

*The spice of these little chops is divine mixed with a sip of Ice Wine or late-harvest Riesling. Bridge the flavors with the sweet sherry used in the recipe and you'll be grinning from ear to ear.*

2   cups extra-rich sweet sherry (Pedro Ximenez)

2   canned chipotle chile peppers, diced

2   lamb rib roasts (8 ribs each)

2   tablespoons olive oil

Salt

Black pepper

1. For glaze, in heavy saucepan cook sherry over medium-high heat for 20 to 25 minutes or until slightly thickened and syrupy and reduced to about ⅔ cup. Remove from heat; stir in chipotle peppers. Cool. Reserve ⅓ cup of the glaze to serve with lamb.

2. Preheat your grill to medium-high heat. Wrap rib tips with foil. Insert a thermometer into meat without touching bone. Brush lamb with olive oil and season generously with salt and pepper. Grill for 20 to 25 minutes or until 135°F, brushing frequently with glaze.

3. Remove lamb from grill. Cover with foil and let rest for 15 minutes before slicing. Serve with reserved glaze.

**Makes 16 servings**

# SWEET POTATO CROQUETTES

*These sweet and savory nibbles are just yummy when paired with the caramel and molasses flavors of a Tawny Port. Once you pop one of these treats in your mouth, you just can't stop!*

1   cup cooked, mashed sweet potatoes*

1   tablespoon butter

½   teaspoon salt

¼   teaspoon freshly grated nutmeg

⅛   teaspoon black pepper

1   slightly beaten egg

1   teaspoon water

¾   cup fine dry bread crumbs

2   to 3 cups vegetable oil

**1.** Stir together the mashed sweet potatoes, butter, salt, nutmeg, and pepper. Cover and chill for 2 to 8 hours.

**2.** Gently beat egg and water together with a fork; set aside. To make the croquettes, shape a heaping teaspoon of the sweet potato mixture into a ball (any bigger and they will be too mushy). Roll each croquette in bread crumbs. Dip in egg mixture; roll again in bread crumbs. (The double dip in the bread crumbs will give the croquettes a nice crust.)

**3.** In a large deep saucepan or deep-fat fryer heat oil to 375°F. Fry croquettes, 4 or 5 at a time, about 2 minutes or until golden. Remove croquettes with a slotted spoon; drain on paper towels. Keep croquettes hot in a warm oven while frying remaining.

**Makes 16 to 18 croquettes**

*Note: Use 2¼ cups diced, peeled sweet potatoes; cook in boiling salted water until soft.

# GRILLED FIGS
## *with Prosciutto*

*Figs and prosciutto were meant for each other. The salty ham with the sweet fig is a perfect match. This salty-sweetness is playful with a variety of dessert wines. Taste around and find your fave.*

12    large fresh figs, halved

12    pieces proscuitto, halved lengthwise

3    tablespoons olive oil

**1.** Wrap each fig half with a piece of prosciutto; brush wrapped figs with olive oil.

**2.** Preheat your grill to medium-low heat. Grill figs for 2 to 4 minutes or until heated through and prosciutto starts to get crispy.

**Makes 24 pieces**

* * * * * * * **NO-COOK OPTIONS** * * * * * * *

**Chocolate-Covered Pretzels:** I love sweet and salty foods paired with dessert wines. Serve both milk- and dark-chocolate-covered pretzels for a taste test.

**Cheese Popcorn:** This salty snack is often hard to pair with wine, but when you put it in the company of sweet wine—such as the likes of sherry and Port— you may be surprised to see that the combo works.

**Orange-Filled Chocolates:** You could buy a whole box of chocolates to pass around, but these in particular are dynamite with a Tawny Port. The orange filling dances with the caramel of the Tawny, bringing you to your feet for another.

**Biscotti:** These Italian cookies usually come to the table with subtle flavors like anise and vanilla. Dunk one in a glass of dessert wine (Vin Santo is a classic with this cookie) and let it suck up the juice. It's way better than doughnuts and coffee.

**Cookie Tray:** Include some chocolate chips, Linzer tortes, and citrus cookies such as orange tuiles. Sweets with sweets sometimes work and some-

times clash. Only tasting will tell.

**Vanilla Ice Cream:** This is an easy one. Listen to my friend, Janet, and spoon some sweet sherry over the top to treat yourself. Or if you're looking for the ultimate honey and vanilla mix, drizzle a little Sauternes or Ice Wine on top.

**Cajun-Spiced Party Mix:** You've got to try something spicy with your sweet wine—you may like the contrast. But remember, some of these wines are higher in alcohol, so that means they will kick up the heat even more.

**Yogurt-Covered Raisins:** And pick up some Raisinets too! Ports and sweet sherry ooze raisin and chocolate aromas and flavors, so these are the perfect complement.

**Salted Mixed Nuts:** Nutty aromas loom in dessert wines, especially Ports. Having walnuts and pecans on hand helps you home in on those flavors and aromas when tasted side by side. You may also include a walnut loaf or banana nut bread.

* * * * * * * * * * * * * * * * * * * * * * * *

# FIGS
## with Feta

*The bite of the feta is soothed with a sip of Sauternes. Again we're working with salty-sweet fare that behaves beautifully on your palate.*

| | |
|---|---|
| 24 | ¹/₂-inch cubes feta cheese |
| ¹/₄ | cup finely chopped fresh mint |
| 24 | small fresh figs |
| ¹/₄ | cup tupelo honey |
| ³/₄ | cup toasted macadamia nuts |

**1.** Toss the feta cheese cubes with the mint. Score each fig at the skinny top with an X. Place one cube of feta in each fig; press figs back together. Warm the honey in a microwave for 10 seconds; drizzle over figs. Sprinkle with nuts.

**Makes 24 pieces**

# FIGS with Hazelnuts and Dark Chocolate

*Your eyes are sure to glaze over when you follow this warm, gooey sweet with a sip of Ruby Port. Rubies adore chocolate, and I adore this yummy match.*

1   cup hazelnuts

2   tablespoons Godiva liqueur or other chocolate liqueur

12  large fresh figs, halved

24  small pieces Hershey's Special Dark chocolate

**1.** Preheat oven to 350°F. To toast nuts, spread in a single layer in a shallow baking pan. Bake for 8 to 10 minutes or until golden brown, stirring a few times to toast evenly. Remove nuts from oven and place on a clean kitchen towel. Rub vigorously with towel to remove skins.

**2.** Place toasted nuts in a food processor. Cover and process until chopped. Add liqueur; process to form a paste.

**3.** Preheat broiler. Cut a tiny slice off one of the rounded sides of each fig. Arrange figs, cut sides up, on a shallow baking sheet. Spread about 1 teaspoon of the nut paste on each fig half. Top each with a piece of chocolate. Broil for 1 to 2 minutes or just until chocolate starts to melt.

**Makes 24 pieces**

# zinfandel
## for an all-american tailgate

*It was tempting to get you all drinking Zinfandel while you were flag-waving and popping firecrackers around the Fourth of July—from its rags-to-riches heritage to its irreverent spirit, so much about this wine shouts America! But frankly, this big red just isn't my first choice for picnics and porch swingin'*

in summer. Instead, let's bring on the Zin this October for another favorite American pastime: tailgating!

Yes, yes. I've partied in the parking lot a time or two in my life; I know full well that usually there's not a lot of swirling and sniffing (and for that matter, sipping) going on at these things. I know the beverage of choice is usually beer, beer, and more beer. But by now you know that the wine club is all about bustin' loose from the idea that wine is the

exclusive domain of white tablecloths and tuxedoed maître-d's. It's all about fun times. And the best way to put fun into wine is to take wine where the fun is.

I know it's time for a big, warm Zin when I put away the sunscreen and start digging around for my softest sweaters and comfy jeans. That's my traditional tailgate attire. And in the past few years my accessory of choice has become a bottle of this big red. So choose your game day, then grab a designated

driver and pile into the car with your wine club and some great tailgate eats—Zinfandel's a-crashin' the gates.

## Getting to Know Zinfandel

Let's just call it Zin for short, shall we? And when I say Zin, I'm talking red Zinfandel; when we talk about white Zinfandel, that infamous Zin spin-off, we'll call that one white Zin.

Although Zin is often referred to as the all-American grape, it's not exactly native to our shores; how it made its way to California is a bit of a mystery (where's old Sherlock when you need him, anyway?). For a long time, wine experts thought the grape was the same as the Primitivo grape, from Italy; turns out those two are just cousins. After some wine-science sleuths did some fingerprinting—DNA-style—they figured out the real Zin is actually from Croatia, where it's called Crljenak Kastelanski. Right—it just rolls off your tongue.

Italian immigrants are credited with planting the grape, wherever it came from, in California in the mid-19th century, and

> The great thing about Zin is that it's not expected to imitate or aspire to anything in the Old World.

Zinfandel's popularity soared during the gold rush, when miners were looking for a hearty and substantial quaff. That fits—that rough-and-tumble crowd wasn't going to be drinking any flowery Viogniers or elegant Rieslings!

For decades Zin was used in blending or for inexpensive wines; in fact, anyone who drank jug wines in the 1970s probably drank

* * * * * * * * * * * *

## WINE TREND

### ZAP and the Zin Zealot

Watch out, wine world—the Zin zealots are making waves!

While it's true that Zin fans have been lingering in the wine world for some time now, their legions grow stronger every year. Want proof? Take a look at ZAP, an association of Zin Advocates & Producers: At the first tasting held by this organization in 1992, a mere 22 wineries and a handful of Zin fans showed up. Fast-forward to the ZAP festival in January 2005—more than 10,000 people attended and 275 wineries poured their Zins.

If you find yourself falling into the Zin-nut category, check out the ZAP organization. Based in (where else?) the heart of Zin country,

California, this educational organization comprises Zin growers, winemakers, and more than 6,000 fans. In addition to the huge annual bashes, ZAP organizes tastings in major cities around the country (they're open to the public) and even at sea, offering crash courses on cruise ships. Find ZAP at www.zinfandel.org.

I've never been to the big California ZAP fete, but I hear it's quite the party. It's a wine tasting, yes, but it's no pinky-in-the-air affair. So next year, I'm in. In the world of wine, I'm not usually a follower, but this is one bandwagon I don't want to miss. These people have fun with their wine. Any wonder why I chose this bunch for a tailgate party?

* * * * * * * * * * * * * * * * * * * * * *

Zinfandel without even knowing it. The label may have said "Burgundy," but the wine inside was often Zin. Who knew?

Times have changed—these days, the grape has transcended such humble origins (how American is that?). Today's bottles command more cash, allowing winemakers to invest in the vines and do what it takes to make some pretty killer wines. But while bottles can fetch a pretty penny, worry not—there are still some good buys to be had. Best of all, while times have changed, Zin's anything-but-snooty, rough-and-tumble rep has not. Zin's all about keepin' it real.

### Zin's No Wannabe

Great American Merlots and Cabs are often expected to measure up to grand French Bordeaux; American Pinots often get examined through the lens of those ever-noble Burgundies. The great thing about Zin is that it's not expected to imitate or aspire to anything in the Old World. In fact, aside from a spattering of patches in South Africa and Australia, few winemakers bother much with it outside of California.

That's right, we own this game. There's simply no contest.

And it's not just because we're the only player that makes American Zin such a winner. This wine rocks! Just by looking at the out-there labels that pop up in the Zinfandel aisle—Cardinal Zin, Seven Deadly Zins, Sin Zin, and the like—you know this one's a real character. Though there are fresh and fruity styles of this wine, the ones people go nuts for are often the deeper, more in-your-face styles.

Not for the faint of heart, these Zins are known for their backbone, coming on strong with intense fruit flavors (think of the richness of a juicy plum at the peak of ripeness) and often hitting you with a punch of pepper.

You'll find, too, that the Zin drinker is a special breed of wine lover. Many wine drinkers turn to Merlot, Cab, or Chardonnay out of habit; they may have a favorite grape, but in a pinch, most can switch back and forth among varietals without a lot of separa-

* * **BANG FOR YOUR BUCK** * *

Ravenswood, Vintners Blend Zinfandel, $10 a bottle. I gotta love a wine that says "No Wimpy Wines" right on the label. This wine delivers a great value for the price year after year. It's totally purple and totally fun. It's got the berries, it's got the bod, and it's got the backbone of a great wine. There may be a svelte price tag, but don't be deceived—this is a big-boy wine. So open it up, let it breathe, and then dig in.

tion anxiety. Not so with Zin zealots—they're die-hard fans. There's something about this renegade grape that demands fanatical following, and if you take their juice away, some would rather not drink any other wine. (For more information on these wine-world renegades, see "Wine Trend," page 168.)

### White Zin's No Sin

Most wine drinkers have probably sipped white Zinfandel, that infamous pink wine, at least once in their lives, and whether you love it or hate it is not my concern. However, there is one thing I do want you to know: There is no such thing as a white Zinfandel grape.

White Zinfandel wine was invented by Bob Trinchero of Sutter Home winery more than 30 years ago. He left the pressed juice of Zinfandel grapes (which are a red variety, remember) in contact with the grape skins for a much shorter time than normal for a red wine. Because red wines get their color from the skins, the result of this too-brief intermingling of juice and skins was a pink wine instead of a red one. And it was a very light pink one at that.

Well, guess what. This little experiment (or mistake, depending on whom you talk to) became a runaway best-seller; in fact, white Zin became the number-one-selling varietal until the mid-1990s, when Chard ascended the throne. Even now, white Zinfandel is the second-best-selling varietal, though every year it loses a little more steam.

Why the popularity? Here's my theory: White Zin is simple, and although some can be on the dry side, most are quite sweet, smelling of strawberries, raspberries, and even cream. Americans like sweet things—

### ✳ ✳ ✳ THE MONA LISA ✳ ✳ ✳

Mara Marquise Reserve Zinfandel, about $35 a bottle. Some Zin freaks would argue that the famous Turley Zin is by far the *Mona Lisa* of this category, and though it is all things Zin, the cook in me yearns for a less aggressive wine to pour with my meal. By all means, if you are searching for that monster Zin, Turley's got it. But my *Mona* is the Mara Zinfandel. Now, they make fewer than 500 cases of this wine, so you are more likely to find it on a restaurant wine list than in the stores. But that's all part of having fun with the wine club. When you go out to dinner and spot this on the list, it's a must-order! I fell in love when I sipped this wine alongside a grilled veal chop at one of my favorite Atlanta restaurants, Dish. It's an intense purple wine with intoxicating aromas of cassis and black cherry. I love how elegant it feels as it flows across my tongue. It's layered with flavors of fresh-cracked black pepper and licorice and softened by a hint of vanilla. It always finishes with full finesse and makes every meal memorable.

### ✳ ✳ ✳ THE SALVADOR DALÍ ✳ ✳ ✳

Roshambo Winery Dry Creek Zinfandel, about $21. I love the name, the label, the winery, and most of all the wine. The name is California slang for that classic tie-breaking game Rock, Paper, Scissors. The winery is totally hot, complete with its own funky art gallery. In fact, all the way around, this winery just gets it! Its own words of wisdom could be right from my mouth: "Visiting a winery should never be intimidating. It requires no special language, clothing, or attitude." Darn straight! The wine and the people behind it are all about having fun. And while you're kickin' up your heels in full party fashion, you'll be quaffing a mouthful of rich red berries, with sensual tannins. This Zin is jam-packed with sweet, ripe fruit and all the fun and funk worthy of this category.

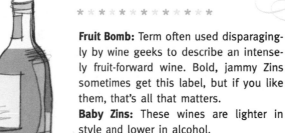

* * * * * * * * * * *

**Chewy:** I use this to talk about big, meaty Zins. These are wines with super-huge body, alcohol, and fruit. They feel like you could eat them instead of drink them—these are the ones you could drink with a fork.

**Jammy:** Describes wines with superconcentrated ripe fruit flavors.

**Hot:** Describes wines that leave a burn in your mouth and throat when the alcohol taste is too intense and not in balance with the fruit.

* * * * * * * * * * *

**Fruit Bomb:** Term often used disparagingly by wine geeks to describe an intensely fruit-forward wine. Bold, jammy Zins sometimes get this label, but if you like them, that's all that matters.

**Baby Zins:** These wines are lighter in style and lower in alcohol.

**Monster Zins:** These are the big-boy wines. They are full-bodied, rich, and high in alcohol—sometimes as high as 17 percent, which means that they have a lot of legs too.

* * * * * * * * * * * * * * * * * * * * * * * * * * * * * *

after all, we eat lots of sweets when growing up, from fruit juices and sodas to sugarcoated cereals and candy bars. For people who weren't used to drinking wine—which would describe many Americans in the late '70s and early '80s—sweet white Zin was any easy way to get in on the wine-drinking action. They loved it because it was just like the sweet stuff they grew up on.

Mention white Zin to any wine snob and he will promptly put his nose in the air. Fancy Bordeaux it's not, but there's no reason white Zin can't have a place in your glass if it tastes good to you. Women, especially, relish this fruity, light drink as a refreshing summer quaff. A glass of lightly chilled white Zin on a hot and muggy night in August makes perfect sense. And when I'm sweating over a hot grill, it makes for a great sip.

Frankly, I'm grateful to white Zin for a couple of reasons: First, let's not forget who brung us to the dance! White Zin brought a lot of Americans to the wine-drinking party, and from there, their taste buds tingled and their wine curiosity was piqued.

Second, if it weren't for white Zin, we wouldn't have so much excellent red Zin. You see, after those Zin-based jug wines and

* * * * * * * * * * * * * * * * * * * * * * * * * * * * * *

### IF THE GLASS FITS ...

If you find yourself turning into a Zin nut, you may want to invest in stemware specifically made for this wine. There's one available from—yup—Riedel. It is designed to enhance your experience of the wine's aromas and flavors, blah-blah-blah. But since I'm a no-nonsense girl, I think an all-purpose red-wine glass for red Zinfandel will do just fine; for white Zinfandel, use an all-purpose white-wine glass.

* * * * * * * * * * * * * * * * * * * * * * * * * * * * * *

blends fell out of fashion, the race was on to plant the up-and-coming varietals like Cab and Merlot. California winemakers were ripping up Zinfandel vines left and right. Fortunately, when white Zin busted onto the scene, that all screeched to a halt.

Now that the white Zin craze is waning, more and more winemakers with Zin in their vineyards are turning their talents to producing killer red Zins. Good thing they kept those vines!

## Speaking of Vines ...

Zin likes warmer climates but not necessarily hot climates; the grape loves California. In fact, after Cab, Zin is the most widely planted red grape in the state. While it's grown in many Cali regions—Mendocino-Lake, Sierra Foothills, Napa, Central Coast, Central Valley, Bay Area, and Southern California—it's Sonoma County that has time and again shown itself to be one of the finest regions (if not *the* finest) for growing this grape. And within Sonoma County, the Dry Creek Valley produces especially yummy Zins.

## Old Vines

When buying Zin, you'll sometimes run into *Old Vine* prominently splashed on the label. This means the wine comes from vines that

* * * * * * * * * * * *

### YOU'LL NEVER FORGET IT

When learning about wine, you'll find much of the information repetitive, with a lot of wine "experts" saying just what the guy before them said. But when you come across someone totally dynamic with something real to contribute—You'll Never Forget It! This is the case with the ever-more-eccentric winemaker from Bonny Doon Vineyard, Randall Graham.

A couple of years ago my editor at *The Wine Report* magazine, Gil Kulers, and I sat down to lunch with Randall. He pulled a few tricks from his sleeve—literally—to teach us about *terroir*.

Randall poured us each a glass of Bonny Doon's Big House Red. We swirled and sniffed and sipped to our delight. Then he sprinkled a little something into our glasses and prompted us to drink again. I was a little wary, but I thought, hey, this isn't such a bad way to go out—drinking yummy wine with the coolest winemaker I've ever met. But no, I was not about to meet my maker.

Instead Randall showed us what he called "poor man's *terroir*"; I know the concept of *terroir* can be a bit obscure, but by pulling this parlor trick you'll see how something in soil (like, in this case, high levels of sodium) can completely alter the final juice.

When we sipped there was a noticeable difference in the wine with the tiny tablets. It was just plain table salt. Yet adding it to the wine changed the mouth feel and the tannin structure on the palate. With this little trick Randall taught us that high levels of sodium tend to transform blocky tannins and give them much greater length on the palate—and that's a characteristic of Old World wine's *terroir*.

So take a glass of big, red, tannic American Zin and season with a sprinkling of table salt. See if you notice the tannin change. Is your New World wine seeming a bit old school? Sodium is just one of the many factors that come into play when it comes to *terroir*. This simple experiment will quickly show you how one element can change the entire tasting game.

* * * * * * * * * * * *

Most of those "wine coolers" you buy at the store are usually not wine at all, but a beverage made with malt liquor. Actually, a real wine cooler—made with wine and club soda with a twist of lemon served over ice—may not make a wine geek swoon, but it can be just the ticket served dockside on a scorching day. When made with white Zin, it's light, a little sweet (mixing with club soda helps cut down that sweetness), and refreshing. It's also a relatively low-alcohol drink—which makes it the perfect pick for a garden party or hanging out by the pool.

★ ★ ★ ★ ★ ★ ★ ★ ★ ★ ★ ★ ★ ★ ★ ★ ★ ★ ★ ★ ★ ★

One reason Sonoma County is so famous for its Zins is because it claims the most old vines in the state; these vineyards are some of the most celebrated in the country.

are at least 50 years old—though some are even a century old. By the time vines get that old, the grapes they produce are smaller, but what the grapes lack in size, they make up for in flavor, resulting in big, bold wines Zin zealots love. One reason Sonoma County is so famous for its Zins is because it claims the most old vines in the state; these vineyards are some of the most celebrated in the country.

You guessed it—an old-vine Zin is a must for this month's tasting.

### Time and Temp

Like Cab and other full-bodied reds, big Zins should be served between 63 and 66 degrees. But don't go bonkers—just aim for room temp (the variable being the room—lean toward basement temp, not hot kitchen temp). However, those fresh-and-fruity lighter-bodied Zins can be served a little cooler—it won't hurt to chill them just a bit before you uncork them. How do you know if you have a lighter-bodied Zin? Look at the label; alcohol content (listed on every label) says a lot. Those with higher alcohol content (above 14 percent) are bigger, and those with lower alcohol content (below 14 percent) are mostly lighter.

### ✱ ✱ ✱ PURPLE HAZE? ✱ ✱ ✱

You can always spot someone who's been drinking Zin—the stuff leaves your lips and teeth stained like no other wine. This means Zin's not a great pick for a romantic dinner with someone you're just getting to know, unless you both have a good sense of humor!

As for aging Zin, in general you don't need to. This wine should be enjoyed within three to five years (give or take); otherwise, it will lose its luscious signature fruit and just become "hot" (see "Wine Speak," page 171).

White Zin? Drink it chilled and drink it young. Treat it like a white wine. Keep it in the fridge and pull it out about 10 to 15 minutes before serving it. I've seen this wine more than any others festooned with ice, so if you like it superchilled, drop in a couple of cubes.

## October's Picks

Frankly, Cali's at the top of the Zin game, so there's just no reason to go outside of the state for this tasting. You've already tasted how *terroir* shows differently in wines from country to country; now let's see if we can detect some differences among wines grown in particular regions within one state and in particular regions within one county. Sonoma wins my vote for best Zinland, but we'll sip picks from other well-known areas for the grape, and you can pick your poison. Here are my picks from each region:

**Sonoma County—Dry Creek Valley:** Choose an old-vine Zin; you'll pay $24 to $35.

**Sonoma County—Russian River Valley or Alexander Valley:** Choose a Zin priced $14 to $25.

**Central Valley–Lodi:** You'll spend about $14 to $18 a bottle.

**Napa Valley:** Priced from about $14 to $22.

**Central Coast–Paso Robles:** Ask your wine merchant for a "claret-style" Zin—one with less alcohol (12–13 percent) so you can sample a lighter side to this wine. Spend $13 to $19.

**Ringer:** Buy a Primitivo from Italy. As we discussed earler, it was once thought that America's Zinfandel and Italy's Primitivo were the same thing, and though that's no longer the story, the Italian winemakers certainly haven't minded cashing in on the Zin craze and marketing this wine stateside. The two are related, and the good news is that Primitivo is generally cheaper than Cali Zins (you can definitely find them for less than $15 a bottle and sometimes even less than $10), so if you end up liking Primitivo better, lucky you.

# GET YOUR DRINK ON

*Ready? It's time to see if you're a Zin zealot or not—some people really go gaga with this grape. Even if you don't become a die-hard fan, you'll likely find a lot to love, especially if you're into intense, fruit-forward styles of wine. Since it's all New World juice we're tasting, the styles will vary, mostly depending on producer. So call your wine store clerk into action when you're looking for a specific style—like a big, jammy Zin. I always say this is the wine you can drink with a fork—so dig in!*

**COLOR:** There's nothing subtle about Zinfandel, especially the first impression it makes. With Zin the ride begins with a glance. This wine can range in color from deep ruby red to a plummy dark purple. Sometimes it may even appear black with the right lighting. You may think red wine comes from red grapes, but in fact the grapes' color is closer to black. And Zin showcases just how deep and dark the wines from "black" grapes can be.

**AROMA:** Zin usually brings big, ripe fruit flavors—thus the term *jammy*. You can smell raspberry, blueberry, cherry, and blackberry aromas. And when I said spice I meant it—you might sniff black pepper or nutmeg. Also, since we're talking about a Cali wine, you can bet there's oak, so scents of vanilla, smoke, and cedar can find their way into the glass. To help detect jammy aromas, you can create a Smell–O–Rama by putting out a few small ramekins of jams including those from the berries listed above. Smelling the jams next to the wine helps to identify the different berry aromas and is a fun little exercise for you and your guests.

**TASTE:** The hallmark flavors of Zin range from fruity to spicy, so if you like spicy, peppery flavors mixed with dark cherries, you'll like Zin. In general, the juicy fruit flavors can be everything from blueberry to fig. Of course there's some chocolate to be had too, and, in true Zin fashion, you may also get a hint of sweet brown sugar. However, on the opposite end, Zinfandel can be a bit bitter. Depending on the *terroir* you may taste mineral notes. The exaggerated, highly alcoholic Zins can taste hot, even burnt, and will show a more raisiny palate. If you get a lot of layered flavors versus just big fruit, you are more likely tasting old-vine Zin.

**BODY:** Zin can range from a soft, lighthearted sip to those superhuge hearty wines. Some Zin makers come from the school of thought that bigger is better, making wines with alcohol as high as 17 percent (most reds top out at 14 percent—and that's usually the big Cabs); in these cases, Zin brings a gigantic mouth feel. The tannins can also range from softly present to full-blown tannic attacks—only firsthand knowledge of the winery or the winemaker will key you in to which style will be in the bottle, so ask your wine shop expert when you're browsing.

**FINISH:** Big-style wines can leave an unbelievably long finish, but again some of the softer styles will leave a more soothing feel for the finale.

**RINGER:** Primitivo is just like Zin in color variation and taste profile. The major difference: that Old World versus New World thing. Primitivo should have that Old World charm and show a bit more *terroir* and layers of mineral along with big, bold fruit and spice. It is still high in alcohol, but nowhere near the whopping 15 percent and up for some of the New World styles.

## ❧ LET'S EAT! FOOD AND WINE PAIRING ❧

Because Zin has such an all-American identity, we'll be pairing it with some typically American foods. And note that if you're not a sports fan, you don't need to drive to a stadium parking lot for this tasting as long as you get into the tailgating spirit wherever you rest your rump.

Zin loves robust flavors, so the first thing that springs to mind is big, bad barbecue fare—perfect for tailgating. A word of caution: You might be tempted to drink 'cue-friendly Zin at summertime gatherings, but because it's full-bodied and high in alcohol, I prefer to reach for something else during the season's dog days. However, because Zin has less tannin and great fruit, it is said to be the all-weather wine, and for sure it's a better warm-weather choice than Cab or Merlot. That's right: It's a great transition wine—good stuff when we're pulling out those fall sweaters but still frolicking in that sunshine.

# TROPICAL SALSA

*This dip brings a lot of flavor with fresh-picked cilantro and a touch of sweetness with tropical fruit. It works for both Zin and white Zin fans. Serve it with grilled chicken and you've got an all-star dinner.*

| | |
|---|---|
| 2 | cups diced mango |
| 1 | cup diced papaya |
| 1 | cup diced pineapple |
| ½ | cup diced red bell pepper |
| 2 | tablespoons fresh lime juice (1 medium lime) |
| 2 | tablespoons chopped fresh cilantro |
| 1 | jalapeño chile pepper, seeded and minced* |
| ½ | teaspoon ground cumin |
| 1/2 | teaspoon salt |
| ⅛ | teaspoon cayenne pepper |
| | Blue tortilla chips |

1. In a large bowl combine mango, papaya, pineapple, bell pepper, lime juice, cilantro, jalapeño pepper, cumin, salt, and cayenne pepper. Serve with tortilla chips.

**Makes 3½ cups**

*Note: Because hot chile peppers, such as jalapeños, contain volatile oils that can burn your skin and eyes, avoid direct contact with chiles as much as possible. When working with chile peppers, wear plastic or rubber gloves. If your bare hands do touch the chile peppers, wash your hands well with soap and water.

# 3-CHEESE BABY BURGERS
## with Paprika-Lemon Aïoli

*Nothing's more American than burgers from the grill at halftime. With a glass of Zin in hand and one of these little babies in your mouth, you'll think you died and went to tailgate heaven.*

| | |
|---|---|
| 1 | pound ground round |
| 2 | tablespoons minced onion |
| 1 | tablespoon Worcestershire sauce |
| 1 | teaspoon dried Italian seasoning |
| ½ | teaspoon salt |
| ¼ | teaspoon freshly ground black pepper |
| 2½ | **to 3** ounces Brie |
| 4 | slices Cheddar cheese, quartered |
| 4 | slices smoked Gruyère cheese, quartered |
| 4 | mini-pita bread rounds, quartered |
| 1 | recipe Paprika-Lemon Aïoli (see below) |

**1.** In a bowl combine ground round, onion, Worcestershire sauce, Italian seasoning, salt, and pepper. Shape beef mixture into 16 patties. Make a thumbprint in the center of each patty. Set aside.

**2.** Roll ¼ teaspoon Brie into a ball; repeat with the remaining Brie, making a total of 16 balls.

**3.** Preheat your grill to medium-high heat. Grill patties thumbprint sides down for 2 to 3 minutes. Flip the patties and place the Brie balls in imprints. Top each with a slice of cheddar and a slice of Gruyère. Cover and grill for 1 to 2 minutes more or until cheese melts and the burgers are cooked through (160°F). Place each burger in a pita quarter. Serve with Paprika-Lemon Aïoli.

**Makes 16 mini burgers**

**Paprika-Lemon Aïoli: In a food processor combine 1 cup mayonnaise, 2 tablespoons fresh lemon juice, 3 cloves smashed garlic, 1 teaspoon sweet or smoked paprika, and ⅛ teaspoon salt. Cover and process until smooth.**

**Makes about 1 cup**

# MUFFULETTA SUBS

*"Holy cow, this olive salad rocks," says my friend, Vanessa. The smoked meats topped with olive salad make the ideal date for a chewy Zin. And this sizable sub is perfect for a crowd.*

¼  cup red wine vinegar

¼  cup loosely packed fresh Italian (flat leaf) parsley

1  teaspoon dried oregano, crushed

½  teaspoon freshly ground black pepper

2  garlic cloves, crushed

½  cup olive oil

½  cup pimiento-stuffed green olives

½  cup kalamata olives, pitted

½  cup marinated artichoke hearts, drained and coarsley chopped

½  cup roasted red sweet peppers, drained and coarsely chopped

1  tablespoon capers, drained

2  12-inch sub rolls or soft Italian hoagie rolls

¼  pound Genoa salami, thinly sliced

¼  pound smoked Virginia ham, thinly sliced

¼  pound prosciutto, thinly sliced

¼  pound provolone cheese, thinly sliced

**1.** For the olive salad, in a food processor combine vinegar, parsley, oregano, black pepper, and garlic. With the processor running slowly, drizzle in oil, processing until combined. Add green olives, kalamata olives, and artichoke hearts to the processor; pulse 3 or 4 times only—don't overprocess this or it will be mush!! Scrape down the sides. Add the red peppers and capers; pulse 3 or 4 more times.

**2.** To make the sandwiches, cut the rolls in half horizontally. Spread about one-fourth of olive salad on each roll half. Evenly top the roll bottoms with the salami, ham, prosciutto, and cheese. Put tops back on each sandwich. Cut each sandwich into twelve 1-inch pieces and secure with fancy toothpicks to help hold the pieces together.

**Makes 24 pieces**

# ROASTED RED PEPPER DIP

*You gotta have dip at a tailgate! Here a little mint goes a long way to bring this dip up to snuff. It's got a cool mouth feel that works with a spicy Zin. Outta the parking lot and into the garden, this dip also makes for yummy finger sandwiches.*

| | |
|---|---|
| 1 | 8-ounce package cream cheese, cut up |
| 6 | ounces feta cheese, crumbled |
| 6 | roasted red sweet peppers, drained |
| 1 | teaspoon salt |
| ½ | teaspoon freshly ground black pepper |
| 2 | tablespoons fresh mint |
| | Pita chips, crackers, or toast points |

1. In a food processor combine cream cheese, feta cheese, roasted peppers, salt, and black pepper. Cover and process until combined. Stir in mint. Serve with pita chips, crackers, or toast points.

**Makes 2½ cups**

### ★ ★ ★ ★ ★ ★ ★ NO-COOK OPTIONS ★ ★ ★ ★ ★ ★ ★

Really, how hard is it to throw something on the grill? Go for juicy burgers, barbecued chicken, sausages (chorizo would be good), ribeye steak — anything robust and meaty. Chances are there's a grilling guru in your crowd who will be more than happy to take over the tongs and show off his or her grilling prowess, so, in fact, something grilled actually morphs into a no-cook option for you. The sweetness of white Zin is a no-brainer with spicy sauces. It gives that perfect balance of heat and sweet. Serve spicy coleslaw and baked beans from a good deli; if it's a really good deli, maybe you can score a roasted potato salad too—a great choice with Zin.

Some other fun no-cook bites:

★ Peanut Butter and Jelly on Ritz crackers: These sandwiches remind me of my childhood. That jammy Zin thing is a great complement to PB&J; it's sure to bring out the kid in you, along with some laughs.

★ Fruit Chutneys: A store-bought, spicy pineapple chutney served with crackers or cured meats like prosciutto is deee-lish when paired with Zin.

★ Fondue: If you've got the pots, both cheese and chocolate dipping are great with a big Zin. Go for full-flavor cheeses. This wine can definitely handle it.

★ Ham and Cheese Sandwiches: You can't get more American than ham and cheese, but for this no-cook option kick it up a notch (thank you, Emeril). Pile thinly sliced Black Forest ham with a stinky blue cheese and smush them between two pieces of crusty baguette. These nibbles take a twist on the all-American sandwich and make a swell sidekick for Zin.

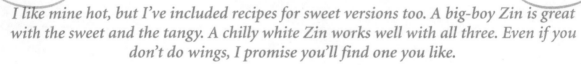

# WINGS

*I like mine hot, but I've included recipes for sweet versions too. A big-boy Zin is great with the sweet and the tangy. A chilly white Zin works well with all three. Even if you don't do wings, I promise you'll find one you like.*

## Hot Wings

¼    cup butter

20    chicken wings (about 3 pounds)

¾    cup Frank's Red Hot Sauce

Crumbled blue cheese

Bottled blue cheese salad dressing, celery and carrot sticks

**1.** Preheat oven to 400°F. Place butter in a baking pan and warm in oven until it melts.

**2.** Meanwhile, place chicken wings in a large bowl. Pour ½ cup of the hot sauce over the wings; toss to coat. Arrange wings in a single layer in the melted butter. Bake for about 30 minutes or until no longer pink.

**3.** Flip wings over and brush with the remaining ¼ cup hot sauce. Sprinkle with blue cheese. Serve with salad dressing and celery and carrot sticks.

**Makes 20 pieces**

## Teriyaki Wings

¼    cup butter

20    chicken wings (about 3 pounds)

¾    cup bottled teriyaki glaze

1    tablespoon sesame seeds

**1.** Preheat oven to 400°F. Place butter in a baking pan and warm in oven until it melts.

**2.** Meanwhile, place chicken wings in a large bowl. Pour ½ cup of the teriyaki glaze over the wings; toss to coat. Arrange wings in a single layer in the melted butter. Bake for about 30 minutes or until no longer pink.

**3.** Flip wings over and brush with the remaining ¼ cup teriyaki glaze. Sprinkle with sesame seeds.

**Makes 20 pieces**

## Honey Mustard Wings

¼    cup butter

20    chicken wings (about 3 pounds)

¾    cup bottled honey mustard sauce

**1.** Preheat oven to 400°F. Place butter in a baking pan and warm in oven until it melts.

**2.** Meanwhile, place chicken wings in a large bowl. Pour ½ cup of the honey mustard sauce over the wings; toss to coat. Arrange wings in a single layer in the melted butter. Bake for about 30 minutes or until no longer pink.

**3.** Flip wings over and brush with the remaining ¼ cup honey-mustard sauce.

**Makes 20 pieces**

# S'MORES

*The concentrated fruits of Zin are the perfect complement to this gooey, bitter, dark-chocolate treat. These rule when toasted over the campfire and rock on the grill for any tailgate. I mean, seriously—who doesn't love s'mores?*

24    graham crackers

12    large marshmallows, cut in half

1    4-ounce bar Hershey's Special Dark sweet chocolate, cut into 12 triangles

**1.** Preheat oven to 300°F. Line a baking pan with parchment paper. Place 12 graham crackers on the prepared baking sheet. Place one chocolate triangle on each cracker and top with marshmallow. Bake for 5 minutes.

**2.** Remove from oven. Top each with another graham cracker to make a sandwich. Serve immediately.

**Makes 12**

Note: These are fine at room temperature for 1 hour; after that they get hard but are still good for another hour. Any longer than that, and they will be too hard. They can be reheated in the microwave in 5-second intervals. Also, they can be made ahead, cooled completely, then put into a 170°F oven for up to an hour or wrapped in a foil pack and heated on a barely warm grill.

# waxing poetic with pinot

**Wine** lovers often describe their connection to Pinot Noir (PEE-noh nwahr) in the most passionate terms. A great bottle of this seductive wine is like a great love affair itself: thrilling and elusive, each one utterly unique unto itself. Yup, I did it. I waxed poetic about Pinot. Sooner or later, nearly every

Pinot lover does. You see, you can talk all you want about grand cru and premier cru; you can learn to pinpoint the Côte de Nuits on a map and memorize the famous winemaking villages of Burgundy. But in the end, wine lovers respond to Pinot in the most emotional ways. Sorry to get all sappy.

So before we get into those crus and villages and other things that are nice to know about Pinot (but not necessary to know to love it), let's wax poetic some more. Because

really, it's the best way to get to the heart and soul of this grape.

## A Love Story

Tamie Cook, a member of the original book/wine club, tells the story of the first time she ever tasted Pinot Noir. I thought this was important to share so you could see just how Pinot invokes passion in its prey.

"We were sitting in Chez René, a restaurant on the Left Bank of Paris. All the guidebooks

said that this was the place for Coq au Vin, so we knew we had to order this classic French dish. However, when it came time to order the wine, we were at a total loss, so we asked our server for a recommendation. For him, the only option was a Pinot Noir from Burgundy; after all, the dish we had ordered was made with this wine. We took his advice.

"He came to the table, opened the bottle, and my husband took a taste. I could tell from his expression that we had made the wrong choice. But wanting to fit in—and not wanting to be rude—he nodded his approval and the waiter poured me a glass as well.

"My husband told me to brace myself. Of course, not ever having heard of Burgundy or Pinot, I had no preconceived notion that this wine was supposed to taste like some sort of elixir from the gods. Not knowing what to expect, I took my first sip.

"It took everything I had not to spit it out. The first thing that came to mind was my Uncle Elmer's farm, with chickens scratching the dirt in the barnyard. Combined with this

On occasion, Pinot from France has lovingly been said to have the perfume of a barnyard. Yes, that's right: wet hay, horses, and straight-up manure. Doesn't that sound delicious?

was a pinelike flavor, a little like furniture polish. To top it off, it was sour and bitter and made me pucker.

"After a lengthy but relaxing wait, our dinner arrived. Much to my surprise, the aroma was heavenly. The smells of onions and bacon and browned chicken were familiar and mouthwatering. If there can be richness in an aroma, this was it. There was, however, something else—something intoxicating in the sauce that was unfamiliar but enticing.

"One bite was all it took. I grew up in the

* * * * * * * * * * * **WINE TREND** * * * * * * * * * * * *

By now you know that I love to explore up-and-coming wine regions. I wouldn't say that South Africa is exactly new to the world of wine, but the selection of juice is new to our wine shop shelves. South Africa makes fabu wines but not a lot of them hit our shelves. However, I am thrilled to say that the intrigue of the country's little Pinotage grape has created a demand in our marketplace. So head out and pick up a Pinotage. You may have to hit a few shops before you find one, but don't be discouraged.

Don't let the name fool you (often people do). This South African grape is no Pinot Noir, but it is related—it's a crossbreed of Pinot Noir and another grape, Cinsault. It's a meaty red, much fleshier than our delicate Pinot Noir. It is big and chewy and deserves some street cred among the big-boy reds. With a dark and ominous allure, its inky juice is full of blackberries and currants. This is not a wine for the faint of heart. It is one of my faves from South Africa, and I think you'll agree it's well worth the search. Look for one from around the Cape, Stellenbosch, or Paarl.

* * * * * * * * * * * * * * * * * * * * * * * * * * * * *

South, where everyone knows that sauce equals gravy. So when I took that first bite and the velvety sauce containing the wine glided across my tongue, I was overwhelmed. I had never tasted anything this good in my life.

"Next up: the wine to wash it down. Hesitantly I took a sip, and much to my surprise and amazement, it was delicious; a lot of those barnyardy tastes I didn't like had blown off, and some wonderful flavors revealed themselves. The butteriness of the sauce was accentuated and complemented by the astringency and sharp Pinot-ness of the wine. At the same time, while the flavors contrasted each other, they seemed to be married on a much deeper level.

It was a bond that rarely forms quite this profoundly, but when it does, one steps back and takes notice. You never forget it."

### Vin de Barnyard?

Yes, Tamie was dead-on with her description. On occasion, Pinot from France has lovingly been said to have the perfume of a barnyard. Yes, that's right: wet hay, horses, and straight-up manure. Doesn't that sound delicious? Although these traits, when present, are usually found in French reds, don't dump your wine if you smell a little funk. The juice beneath the aroma (or should I say "stench"?) can be some of the most succulent you've

* * * * * * * * * * * *

## YOU'LL NEVER FORGET IT

Along our tasting travels we've talked about minerality in wine. Certain wines taste minerally and others show mineral notes when you sniff. Minerality is part and parcel of that elusive *terroir* and gives a wine structure, complexity, and layers of flavor. If you haven't yet been able to figure out what I'm talking about, this is a simple little exercise for your senses.

I mentioned in October that I've learned a thing or two from Randall Graham, winemaker at Bonny Doon Vineyard. This is another one of his exercises that I've never forgotten. At a tasting, he discreetly pulled a tiny bottle from his inside jacket pocket. He poured me a glass of red, then opened the mysterious bottle and added a few drops. "Taste it," he said. I was a bit wary, but I figured I'd lived through the salt episode, so what the heck. It was simply a bottle of trace minerals (available in health food stores). He explained that it is the greater concentration of minerals in Old World wines relative to New World wines that gives them

their distinctive taste profile, as well as their ability to age well. You can't simply add minerals to wine to give them an Old World quality, but you can get some of that *terroir*.

So take two glasses of New World Pinot. Put in a couple of drops of trace minerals and compare them side by side. See if you can tell the difference minerals make in wine. For Randall, and now me too, the minerals in wine are their organizing principle, their moral center, as it were, and tend to give the wine a much greater presence on the midpalate.

Randall brings us to another noteworthy wine mention. When I recently chatted with him via the information superhighway, he was jazzed to share that the Bonny Doon winemakers been farming their vineyard biodynamically for the last two years. He thinks they've made real breakthroughs in obtaining true minerality in their wines. What the *^#@$% is biodynamic winemaking? Check out this month's Dalí pick for a little more insight.

* * * * * * * * * * * *       * * * * * * * * * * * *

ever sipped. I have to be honest and tell you it took me a couple of times to get used to this aroma. OK, so it was more like a couple of years. I kept going back to the comfort of those luscious fruit-forward reds. I just

couldn't bear having my wine smelling like horse manure. But when I finally did get over my Pinot phobia, I, too, fell hard for this delicate wine.

So don't be afraid to sip even if you don't love the sniff. Besides, most often once you swirl a few rounds, this smell will lessen and even go away or "blow off" (see "Wine Speak," page 188). Give it a fair chance. It's not everyone's cup of tea. If you're not an animal lover (or at least don't love those barnyard aromas), stick to Pinot from the New World, especially California and Oregon.

## That Pinot Epiphany

Just about everyone who has come to love Pinot has a story like Tamie's—an instant in which the grape's true wonders were revealed. She was lucky—it happened with her first experience. For other Pinot lovers, it may not have happened with their first bottle or even their 10th. But somewhere along the line, an amazing bottle of Pinot will come along and rock your wine-loving soul.

Or maybe not. There are some wine lovers who never take to Pinot, just as there are wine lovers who never go grapes over Zin, Cab, or Chard. And that's fine too. Wine wouldn't be

---

## IF THE GLASS FITS ...

As you probably know by now, I'm not a "glass snob"; generally, I feel that if you have all-purpose red- and white-wine glasses, plus some narrow champagne flutes, you're good to go. However, it's no surprise that Pinot Noir—the wine that demands kid-glove treatment in the vineyard, barrel, and bottle—desires its own style of glass. Made to enhance the enjoyment of this delicate and refined wine, the traditional Pinot glass is larger than other red-wine glasses, with a grand bulbous shape that allows more flavor and aroma to develop. If you're not yet sure you're going to fall in love with Pinot, use an all-purpose red-wine glass until you're ready to invest.

much fun if we all loved the same one, right?

For those ready to journey forth on a quest for a great Pinot epiphany, Tamie's story should help, because it tells you everything the newcomer needs to know about Pinot:

**1. Burgundy is key.**

**2. Pinot's charms are elusive.**

**3. Pinot loves food.**

Stay with me. The lessons are brief, the rewards divine.

### The Noble Grape of Burgundy

Cultivated in France for more then 2,000 years, Pinot Noir is often called the "noble grape of Burgundy" because it is the red grape of this world-famous winegrowing area; that is, if the wine is red and it's from Burgundy (or Bourgogne in French), then the grape is—with few exceptions—Pinot Noir.

Pinot Noir is a bratty grape to grow. It needs a cool climate, yet because it has an exceptionally thin skin, it can rot easily in too-cool spots. Pinot Noir grapes require extra care in the winemaking process, and this temperamental wine absolutely must be stored properly. All this adds up to Pinot's pricey price point. But as with most types of wine, there are delish bargain Pinots to be

### ✷ ✷ ✷ THE MONA LISA ✷ ✷ ✷

2002 Joseph Drouhin, Nuits Saint Georges; about $45. This is the perfect example of a solid red Burgundy. The grapes come from the heart of the Côte de Nuits, and if this wine doesn't tug at your heartstrings, I don't know what wine will. She has a killer stare with those ruby red eyes, and she dances across your palate with cherry, black currant, and a lick of truffles. Her perfume exudes scents of ripe plums with a nudge of spice. Her touch is more subtle than strong, but one twirl around with this stunning beauty inevitably leaves a lingering allure. These wines are consistently great with a harmonious blend of clean fruit flavors and fine tannins. This pour is pure elegance.

### ✷ ✷ ✷ THE SALVADOR DALÍ ✷ ✷ ✷

Robert Sinskey, Carneros, Pinot Noir, $30 a bottle. You know this category brings something different to the table, so this month I want you to check out an organic biodynamic wine. You probably know what organic means when it comes to food, and it holds true with wine too. The first time Rob Sinskey, winemaker, explained biodynamic to me, I was thinking, this guy is nuts. He talked about the cycles of the moon, harvesting in the middle of the night, and all this other weird stuff. But then when I really listened, I understood why it is so important to him and his family and should be to us as consumers. Part of the winery philosophy is to encourage natural farming and winemaking practices by employing sustainable organic techniques influenced by biodynamic methods. I love that Rob's business card titles him the resident Daydream Believer. That title means he makes awesome wine with a sound philosophy. There's a lot more to it—actually it could be another book. Check out www.robertsinskey.com for more info on biodynamics. In the meantime grab a bottle of this delish, mouthwatering wine—ruby red-colored; strawberry-, cranberry-, and orange-tinged; and tannin-balanced.

* * * * * * * * * * * *

**To Blow Off:** Sometimes when a wine smells a little funky at first, the funky smell will lessen or disappear after the wine breathes awhile. In wine speak, that's what it means for a smell to "blow off."

**Silky:** Refers to a smooth and rich mouth feel—often used to describe Pinot.

**Velvety:** Another term often used to describe the mouth feel of Pinot—it's soft yet intensely rich.

**Bright:** Refers to a wine that's translucent enough for light to shine through it. While this is usually a descriptor for the look of a white wine, Pinot can

often be described as bright as well. Bright can also refer to the taste of a wine—if the acidity is well balanced, you can describe it as bright.

**Shimmering:** Descriptor for a wine that reflects light as well as lets light shine through it.

**Umami:** This refers to the fifth flavor (the other four are sweet, sour, salty, and bitter). Umami is that earthy, dirty flavor you get from mushrooms. It's evident in a lot of Asian cuisine and in a lot of Pinot Noir. It's a *terroir* taste if there ever was one.

* * * * * * * * * * * * * * * * * * * * * * * *

found—you just have to look.

So if Chardonnay is Queen and Cab is King, Pinot is a prince—a petulant little prince that commands the kid-glove treatment. But he's sheer royalty nonetheless, for when he's ready—as long as he's treated right—he'll reward you with a glass overflowing with grace and quality. You know

### ＊＊ PINOT—DÉJÀ VU? ＊＊

Truth be told, you've already sampled some Pinot Noir in your wine club this year. Remember? It was a while back. In January, to be exact—that's when you sampled blanc de noir, a sparkling wine made strictly from the Pinot Noir grape. And some of those other bubblies probably had the Pinot pizzazz as well. Remember, along with Chard and Pinot Meunier it's one of the big three used in blending bubbly.

how little girls dream of marrying a prince? One of the girls in the wine club said she wished that finding a prince to fall in love with was as easy as falling in love with a Pinot. Well, you may not be able to marry a bottle of wine, but you can sure cuddle up with one at night.

The grape is just as difficult to grow outside of Burgundy, and yet, producing a superior Pinot has become a Holy Grail-like quest for winemakers around the world. Some have succeeded. Outside of Burgundy, Pinot seems to express itself best in the northwest United States, specifically in the Oregon Willamette Valley. In fact, Pinot Noir put Oregon winemaking on the map.

In California, Pinot makes up a mere 5 to 10 percent of the total grapes grown in the state; Carneros, Sonoma Coast, Russian River Valley (my fave spot for California Pinot), and Santa Lucia Highlands are known for their divine Pinots.

Most Pinot should be sipped young. Usually it has some time in the bottle before it is released, so when you buy the wine it's ready for tonight's dinner or, even better, today's lunch.

### Soaking in Pinot

Pinot Noir is grown throughout Burgundy, but the superstars hail from the Côte d'Or, a 30-mile-long, half-mile-wide swath of land that's divided into two subregions. The southern half—the Côte de Beaune—is most famous for its Chards, while the northern half—the Côte de Nuits—is Pinot Noir heaven. Dotting this narrow strip of breath-takingly beautiful vineyards are world-famous wine-producing villages, including Gevrey-Chambertin, Morey-Saint-Denis, Nuits-Saint-Georges, Chambolle-Musigny, Vougeot, and Vosne-Romanée.

So, if you want a great Pinot Noir from Burgundy, all it takes is to choose a bottle from one of those world-famous wine-pro-ducing villages, right?

Oh, please, it's never that simple.

This moody bunch of grapes doesn't always produce awesome wines even when grown in the precious patches of these world-famous vineyards. I hate to say it, but vin-tage certainly matters. And yet, it's not enough to say that a particular year was a great year for Burgundies, because even within a great year, the quality can vary greatly from vineyard to vineyard within each winegrowing region. Unfortunately when it comes to Pinot, when there's no pain there's no gain.

Pinot Noir is the "heartbreak grape" because it's so difficult to grow, but it's also a heartbreak for the wine lover; you can plunk down some major cash on premier cru wine (see "The Crux of Cru," page 191) and be entirely bummed out. Another day, you'll roll the dice on a simple Bourgogne rouge for under $15 that will make you jazzed for the bang you got for your buck. But when you go back to the store to buy a case, it's gone. Boo-hoo. Anyway, I'm all for exploring your wine options.

### Time and Temp

Most Pinot should be sipped young. Usually it has some time in the bottle before it is released, so when you buy the wine it's ready for tonight's dinner or, even better, today's lunch. There are some Pinots that can stand the test of time, but I wouldn't go much past five to seven years after the vintage date. That's just my personal opinion. This wine doesn't give the gusto of a big red, so I don't think a nap longer than that does it much good. Yet, you should know that some producers do say their poison can be cellared for decades. Again, those wouldn't be wines I'd be lining up for, but if that's your cup of tea, by all means give it a try. When you do decide to pour this prince, serve it a teensy bit cooler than your big reds. Aim for 60 to 62 degrees.

### Your New Best Friend

So, given the roll of the dice when it comes to finding a sublime Pinot, did my friend Tamie just experience an incredible case of beginner's luck?

Yes—and no.

She was lucky (I mean after all, she was in Paris, right?), but the odds were in her favor because she was in the hands of people who knew Pinot. The waiter surely knew the wine list; moreover, the person who selected wines for this Parisian restaurant—famous for its coq au vin—surely knew a good Burgundy when he tasted one, and no doubt he or she had tasted every wine on the restaurant's list.

This is not the month to walk down the aisles of the wine megamarket and go "eeeny-meeny-miney-mo." This is the month to get close and cozy with someone who knows great Pinot.

That someone would be a passionate wine shop owner or manager. Most major towns have a handful of these quirky little shops. The owners know the qualities of the villages and vintages they stock, and if they're truly wine geeks worth their salt, they've stored the bottles with the loving care needed to keep this wine's magic intact.

Sniff a few of these places out, tell the shop owners you want to book a trip to Pinot paradise, and see what they suggest. I'll also give a few specifics for my faves.

### The Elusive Charms of Pinot

Of all the grape varieties, it's most difficult to make flavor generalizations about Pinot Noir because the wine so transparently demonstrates its *terroir*; depending on where it's grown, its charms can vary greatly.

In fact, while Pinot is often described as offering the aromas and flavors of bright red fruits, mushrooms, and certain spices, it's more often nonfood terms that come to mind when describing Pinot: The wine, especially those from Burgundy, can exhibit earthy, musty, piney, or resinlike qualities. Yes, we're talking about soil again, and in Pinot that earthiness is generally considered a good thing—it's a quality that makes Pinots complex, layered, and interesting.

And yet, as Tamie's story shows, it's hard to appreciate this earthy quality at first sip. If your first pour of Pinot has a certain barnyardy smell, swirl it for a while and let the wine breathe. What you're seeking is a magical mar-

In Burgundy there's no question: The answer is a resounding NO. While the best wines of Bordeaux are blends, white Burgundy (Chardonnay) and red Burgundy (Pinot Noir) are never, ever blended. Well, at least the top wines stay 100 percent true to the varietal. A red Burgundy is synonymous with Pinot Noir, and a white Burgundy is always 100 percent Chard.

★ ★ ★ ★ ★ ★ ★ ★ ★ ★ ★ ★ ★ ★ ★ ★ ★ ★ ★ ★

riage of fruit and earth in one heavenly sip. And when you find it, you'll be addicted.

## Pinot Begs for Food

Pinot, above all other reds, is a true food-loving wine.

While some wines stand on their own—the greats that make you think of nothing else but having another glass—Pinot is a wine that is made to enjoy with food. It shines brightest when at the table. In fact, a great Pinot without food is like the ultimate sexy lover without someone to love.

## November's Picks

This month we'll focus on Burgundy, the spiritual home of Pinot Noir—sorry if I'm getting too gushy again. Don't worry, I won't have you buying a grand or premier cru—for those you'll need a second job! But let's see what the other rungs bring and whether you can tell a marked difference between a village wine and a vin de Bourgogne (see "The Crux of Cru" for an explanation of this cru stuff). Of course, if you're feeling splashy, by all means, splurge on a premier cru—get recommendations from a reliable wine shop, or try a bottle from one of

★ ★ ★ ★ ★ ★ ★ ★ ★ ★ ★

## THE CRUX OF CRU

Understanding how Burgundy wines are ranked in terms of quality is challenging even to veteran wine lovers. Below is a rough guide to the classifications, going from lowest to highest. As the rankings climb, so do the prices, because the grapes are coming from smaller, more well-defined vineyards, and these precious patches of land are in limited supply. No need to memorize, but if you're watching your wallet, it's worth a once-over.

**Bourgogne Rouge:** These simple, basic regional wines are generally blended from various lots of grapes grown anywhere in Burgundy. "*Bourgogne*" or "*Vin de Bourgogne*" will generally appear on the label.

**Village Wine:** These wines are made entirely from grapes grown in and around a specific village. The village's name will appear on the label.

**Premier Cru (or "First Growth"):** All the wines in this classification are made from grapes grown in a specific vineyard. The name of the village, followed by the name of the vineyard, will appear on the label.

**Grand Cru ("Great Growth"):** All the wines in this classification are made from grapes grown in one of Burgundy's highest-ranked vineyards. Only the name of the vineyard (and not the village) will appear on the label. Grand cru wines are extremely rare, representing only 2 percent of the total production in Burgundy. You know what rare means, right? Bring the big bucks to the shop if you're up for a splurge.

★ ★ ★ ★ ★ ★ ★ ★ ★ ★ ★ ★ ★ ★ ★ ★ ★ ★ ★ ★ ★

the producers I've recommended below. We'll also sip Pinots from Oregon and California and see what the New World has to offer. I'm asking you to shell out a little more dough on these selections, but I'm having you buy just four bottles instead of five (plus the ringer, of course).

This month is unique in that I'm suggesting you look for specific producers and/or wholesalers (called *negociants* in France) for the wines you taste. In the Pinot game, choosing wines from a tried-and-true *negociant* or producer is often more reliable than choosing based on village, vineyard, or price. And of course, ask for other recommendations from your wine merchant.

**Burgundy, France—Vin de Bourgogne:** Look for wines from Louis Jadot. The wine will say "*Bourgogne*" on the label.

**Burgundy, France—Village Wine:** The name of the village will appear on the label; these are often hyphenated (e.g., Gevrey-Chambertin, Morey-Saint-Denis, Nuits-Saint-Georges, Chambolle-Musigny, and Vosne-Romanée), though Vougeot is not. Again, look for wines from Louis Jadot.

**Oregon Pinot Noir:** Great producers include Domaine Drouhin, Adelsheim, Archery Summit, Erath Vineyards, Sokol Blosser, and Rex Hill Vineyards.

**California Pinot Noir:** Try Acacia, Au Bon Climat, Calera, Gary Farrell, Iron Horse, La Crema, Pepperwood Grove, Steele, Sanford, or Tantara.

**Ringer:** This month we're throwing in another French kiss: Beaujolais (Boh-zh-LAY). Produced in the Beaujolais region of Burgundy, Beaujolais is the exception to the

> In the Pinot game, choosing wines from a tried-and-true *negociant* or producer is often more reliable than choosing based on village, vineyard, or price.

rule that all red Burgundies are Pinot Noir; this one is made from the Gamay grape. You might be able to pick up a particular style of Beaujolais, the famous Beaujolais Nouveau. The third Thursday of every November, winemakers release the latest vintage—which is meant to be drunk young—with a huge celebration. If you find you enjoy Beaujolais, you might want to consider laying in a supply for your upcoming holiday fetes—often you can buy a case of this wine for the price of one bottle of Pinot from the same side of the globe. Consider buying a mixed case of Beaujolais Nouveau from an assortment of producers to see which you like best. Look to spend about $10 a bottle. Throw this one in the fridge before serving; it shows well on the chilly side.

# GET YOUR DRINK ON

*The levels of price in Pinot don't always predict the final product. There's no guarantee a village wine is going to be a lot better than a vin de Bourgogne, and a grand cru isn't always better than a premier cru. So in general, if you sip something you just get sappy over, you've picked a winner. On the other hand, if what you swallow tastes more like Pine Sol® than wine, well, better luck next time. Describing Pinot Noir is a bit like describing someone you love. Where do you start? With a great Pinot, sometimes the food comparisons (cherries, blackberries, etc.) just don't do it justice, so when you're rhapsodizing on this grape, don't be surprised if more captivating words come to mind: silky, sensuous, seductive, complex, layered … in a word: spellbinding.*

*If you're at a loss for words, see if these are some of the attributes you're noticing in the wine:*

**COLOR:** Pinot shimmers in a ruby red dress. It varies from a strappy, sheer number to a rich and velvety robe with a touch of violet. A see-through sheath is not always a sign of something insipid, so don't be fooled by the looks that your Pinot may flaunt.

**AROMA:** New World wines again will be fruitier, with sweet red berries, plums, and cherries. Pinot Noir from Burgundy can be barnyardy, mushroomy, earthy, and musty. American Pinot shows its oak, so look for that creamy vanilla in the New World juice. Other Pinot profiles from both the New and Old Worlds include a hint of smoke or leather, herbs like rosemary and thyme, and scents of pine, eucalyptus, and peppermint. Last but not least, Pinot's bouquet of flowers can include lilacs, roses, and violets. Remember Tamie's ever so delicate description of her first Pinot experience? OK, so it was pretty brutal, but that's the point. You can't be wrong!

**TASTE:** French Pinot tends to be less alcoholic, lighter-bodied, and more subtle and earthy than American Pinot. It's like the difference between a French manicure and painting your nails a racy red. The American Pinots are bigger, bolder, and more fruit forward. While Old World Pinot shows its earth, American Pinot shows its oak with a ripple of sweet

spices. The fruits of this wine are usually red berries like strawberries, raspberries, and cranberries.

**BODY:** Pinot is the lightest-bodied of the reds we've sipped thus far; generally, it is softer than big Cabs and has more finesse than Merlot. Pinot is silky smooth and melts in your mouth—it tickles your palate instead of storming it. Keep in mind, though, that there are fuller-bodied babes from California. And while those from Burgundy may not bring the big guns, they are still rich with grace.

**FINISH:** Its color may not be brash, but the finish of Pinot can be big. Pinot's light tannins and bright acidity make for a mouthwatering finish that will have you begging for more.

**RINGER:** Our Beaujolais beauty will be a transparent, pinkish/pale purple juice; it's a light and juicy wine, thanks to the Gamay grape from which it's made. These wines are made to be drunk young—very, very young! So pop the cork now and talk technical later. You'll be able to spot this ringer by the difference in temp (it's cooler, if you put the chill on as I suggested earlier), the difference in body (it's lighter), and the difference in color (again, it's lighter). Plus, all those earthy qualities found in Pinot are absent in Beaujolais.

The great thing about Pinot is that it rarely lets you down in the food-and-wine pairing department. However, to best show off the delicacy and texture of Pinot, try a good cut of plain roast beef or roasted/braised lamb or duck. Meaty fish such as salmon, shark, and swordfish are also good choices. In fact, Oregon's Pinots were the first to break the hallowed and predictable rule "Red with meat; white with fish and poultry." These wines have good acidity and are loaded with fruit flavor, two attributes of a flexible, food-loving wine.

Of course, you can't go wrong with dishes specifically created for Burgundy wines: coq au vin and boeuf bourguignonne.

However, since it's November, for this tasting let's think Thanksgiving. Pinot pairs well with the many flavors on this feast's table. But let's face it—a family gathering can be a weensy bit stressful; you can't pick your family, but you can pick your friends. So after the family has packed up and left, let's transform those leftovers into unbelievable hors d'oeuvres. Invite the people you wish you were related to, pop open a few Pinots, and enjoy a friends' Thanksgiving.

\* \* \* \* \* \* \* \* \* \* \* \* \* \* \* \* \* \* \*

# LEFTOVER PUMPKIN PIE PARFAITS

*I love the way this simple transformation of pumpkin pie pairs with Pinot Noir. The pie's spices work so well with this earthy wine, and the cream is a perfect complement to the silky Pinot.*

| | |
|---|---|
| 1 | leftover 8- or 9-inch pumpkin pie |
| 2 | cups dairy sour cream |
| ¼ | cup pure maple syrup |
| 2 | tablespoons orange juice concentrate, thawed |
| ½ | teaspoon pumpkin pie spice |
| 2 | cups whipped cream or frozen dessert topping, thawed |
| ¾ | cup crumbled graham crackers |
| 1 | orange, peeled, with peel cut into thin strips |

1. Remove pumpkin filling from piecrust; discard the crust.

2. In a medium bowl whisk together sour cream, maple syrup, orange juice concentrate, and pumpkin pie spice.

3. In the bottom of 10 small parfait or aperitif glasses, place 2 to 3 tablespoons pumpkin pie filling. Add a layer of the sour cream mixture to each glass. Top with a layer of whipped cream. Repeat each layer until glasses are full.

4. Top each with a sprinkle of graham cracker crumbs. Garnish each serving with orange peel. Serve immediately or cover and chill overnight.

**Makes 10 servings**

Note: You may use 2 partial leftover pies with different fillings—apple and pumpkin, for example—and make half of the parfaits with each.

# CRANBERRY BRUSCHETTA

*This is such a simple morph for your leftover cranberry sauce. The cranberry flavors and colors of the wine and this hors d' oeuvre create a feast for the eyes as well as the palate. A smooth Pinot brings out the best in this tart bite.*

| | |
|---|---|
| 1 | 7- to 9-inch baguette-style loaf of French bread |
| 2 | tablespoons butter, melted |
| ⅔ | cup diced red onion |
| ½ | cup rice wine vinegar |
| ⅓ | cup sugar |
| 2 | tablespoons pickled ginger, coarsely chopped, or 1 tablespoon grated fresh ginger |
| ½ | teaspoon crushed red chile pepper flakes |
| 1 | cup leftover Cranberry Sauce or leftover purchased cranberry sauce |
| ½ | teaspoon minced fresh rosemary |
| 6 | ounces cream cheese, softened |
| ¼ | teaspoon minced fresh rosemary |

**1.** Preheat oven to 375°F. Bias-slice baguette into twelve ½-inch-thick slices. Arrange bread on a baking sheet. Lightly brush 1 side of each baguette slice with melted butter. Bake about 10 minutes or until toasted. Let cool.

**2.** In a heavy saucepan combine onion, vinegar, sugar, ginger, and red chile pepper flakes. Simmer over medium-high heat until the vinegar is reduced by more than half and the sugar begins to caramelize (the red onion will become pink and translucent). Reduce heat; stir in Cranberry Sauce and the ½ teaspoon minced rosemary. Bring to a boil. Remove from heat; cool completely.

**3.** To serve, smear each toasted baguette slice with about 1 tablespoon cream cheese. Top with 1 to 2 heaping tablespoons of the cranberry mixture. Garnish with the ¼ teaspoon fresh rosemary.

**Makes 12 bruschetta**

**Cranberry Sauce:** In a heavy saucepan combine 2 cups fresh cranberries, 1 cup sugar, 1 cup water, and 1 tablespoon finely shredded orange peel. Bring to a boil over high heat. Reduce heat to medium; simmer until the cranberries pop. Stir as necessary to prevent sugar from burning or sticking to the bottom of the saucepan. Cook until sauce is thick and coats the back of a wooden spoon. Cool completely. Cover and chill for up to 1 week. Makes about 3 cups

# ALMOND AND PUMPKIN SEED BRITTLE

*My grandpop is a brittle connoisseur and he gives this one a big thumbs-up. This is stick-to-your-teeth goodness. With a little swishing of Pinot you'll experience a sweetly spiced, nutty palate pleaser.*

³⁄₄   cup blanched or slivered almonds

¹⁄₂   cup raw pumpkin seeds, shelled

    Nonstick cooking spray

1   cup sugar (superfine preferred)

¹⁄₄   cup water

2   tablespoons fresh lemon juice (1 medium lemon)

2   tablespoons honey

¹⁄₂   teaspoon baking soda

¹⁄₂   teaspoon lemon extract

¹⁄₄   teaspoon salt

1. Preheat oven to 300°F. To toast almonds and pumpkin seeds, spread out in a single layer on a large baking sheet. Bake about 10 minutes or until slightly golden, stirring once or twice. Remove from baking sheet; let cool.

2. When the baking sheet is cool enough to handle, line it with foil and spray foil with nonstick cooking spray.

3. In a 4-quart heavy saucepan combine sugar, water, lemon juice, and honey. Dip a clean pastry brush in water. Brush down the sides of the saucepan until there are no visible sugar crystals above the candy mixture. Clip a candy thermometer to the side of the saucepan.

4. Bring candy mixture to a boil over medium-high heat. Do not stir. (If necessary, brush the sides of the pan with the wet pastry brush to prevent sugar crystals from forming.) Once the candy mixture begins to caramelize, reduce heat to medium. Continue to cook until the temperature reaches 260°F. Add the almonds and pumpkin seeds. Stir in baking soda, lemon extract, and salt. The mixture will begin to foam up once the baking soda is added. Stir vigorously with a wooden spoon until nuts and seeds are coated and the foaming begins to subside. Continue to cook until temperature reaches 300°F. Remove pan from heat. Quickly pour mixture onto the prepared baking sheet. Spread evenly and quickly because brittle will begin to set up immediately. Cool completely; break into pieces.

**Makes 12 to 16 cups**

Note: Store in an airtight container for up to 1 month.

# MASHED POTATO–APPLE BLINI

*These li'l pancakes are so very cute and yummy. When I was creating this recipe, my husband was eating them faster than I could make them. With a Pinot in hand and sour cream on his face, he was one happy man.*

1   to 1½ cups grated apples (such as Gala or Red Delicious)

2   tablespoons butter

2   teaspoons minced fresh thyme

½   teaspoon black pepper

¼   cup all-purpose flour

1   teaspoon kosher salt

1   to 1½ cups mashed potatoes

    Nonstick cooking spray

¾   cup dairy sour cream

    Finely chopped fresh chives

1. In a skillet cook apples in hot butter until soft (apples will begin to turn pink as the sugars start to caramelize). Stir in thyme and pepper. Remove from heat.

2. For blini, in a large bowl combine flour and salt. Add the mashed potatoes and apple mixture; stir until just combined. (Depending on the consistency of your mashed potatoes, you may need to add a little more flour—the mixture should not be runny.) Shape into 2-inch pancakes about ¼ inch thick; set aside.

3. Spray a nonstick skillet with nonstick cooking spray. Preheat skillet over medium to medium-low heat. Add as many blini to hot skillet as will fit without crowding. Cook about 2 minutes or until edges begin to brown. Gently flip blini; cook about 2 minutes more or until done in the middle. Repeat with remaining blini. Serve with a dollop of sour cream. Garnish with chives.

**Makes about 30 blini**

## * * * * * * * * NO-COOK OPTIONS * * * * * * * *

Buy a piece of smoked salmon and set it out with crackers and bowls of lemon wedges, fresh dill, capers, finely chopped red onion, and sour cream. The richness of the salmon is a perfect match for the earthiness and acidity of a typical Oregon Pinot.

**Epoisse Cheese:** When in doubt, go for foods and wines from the same region. Made in Burgundy, this strongly flavored cheese goes beautifully with a French Pinot.

**Mixed Nuts:** An earthy Pinot works with many nuts. Buy a variety—spiced, barbecued, plain, and salted mixed nuts—and see which you prefer with Pinot.

**Tortilla Chips and Salsa:** I love thin, crisp tortillas and a fresh salsa with Pinot. Pinot is also awesome with most Mexican cuisine.

**Angel Food Cake and Chocolate Sauce:** Mix Pinot into a ramekin of chocolate sauce and break out the angel food cake. Bridging the Pinot in this sauce with a glass of Pinot Noir is heaven in your mouth.

**Crudités:** A simple platter of fresh-cut veggies and a chilled creamy dip works with an earthy Pinot. Just be sure to have mushrooms on your platter for the ultimate umami (see "Wine Speak," page 188).

* * * * * * * * * * * * * * * * * * * * * * * * *

# SPICED PUMPKIN SEEDS

*This snack embraces the flavors of fall. The spicy, sweet seeds love the black cherry fruit of Pinot. Before you realize it you'll be reaching for another handful and your glass will need refilling.*

Nonstick cooking spray

2 egg whites

½ cup sugar

2 tablespoons vegetable oil

1 tablespoon finely shredded lemon peel (optional)

1 tablespoon kosher salt

1 teaspoon ground cinnamon

½ teaspoon ground nutmeg

½ teaspoon ground allspice

½ teaspoon cayenne pepper

½ teaspoon chili powder

¼ teaspoon black pepper

1 8-ounce bag unsalted pumpkin seeds (in the shell)

**1.** Preheat oven to 325°F. Line a baking sheet with foil; spray foil with nonstick cooking spray.

**2.** Place egg whites, sugar, oil, lemon peel (if desired), salt, cinnamon, nutmeg, allspice, cayenne pepper, chili powder, and black pepper in a large bowl. Whisk together until egg whites are frothy and sugar is mostly dissolved. Add pumpkin seeds; toss to coat evenly.

**3.** Spread pumpkin seeds evenly on the prepared baking sheet. Bake about 25 minutes or until pumpkin seeds are dry and crisp. Cool completely; break into pieces. Store in an airtight container for up to 2 weeks.

**Makes about 4 cups**

# LEFTOVER TURKEY
## and Stuffing Pot Stickers

*Usually I look for the dipping sauce as soon as I get a dumpling in hand. But these are awesome as is. Until you nibble these you'll never know how good turkey and stuffing can be.*

| | |
|---|---|
| 1 | egg white |
| 2 | tablespoons toasted sesame oil |
| 2 | teaspoons soy sauce or tamari |
| 2 | teaspoons grated fresh ginger |
| ½ | teaspoon black pepper |
| ¼ | teaspoon kosher salt |
| 1¼ | cups finely chopped leftover turkey |
| ½ | cup finely chopped leftover stuffing |
| ½ | cup chopped green onions |
| 30 | to 35 wonton wrappers (round or square) |
| | Vegetable or peanut oil |
| | Toasted sesame seeds |

**1.** For filling, in a bowl combine egg white, sesame oil, soy sauce, ginger, pepper, and salt. Stir in turkey, stuffing, and green onions.

**2.** On a clean work surface, lay out several wonton wrappers. With the tip of your finger or a small pastry brush, very lightly brush some water along the edges of each wonton wrapper (this will help the edges stick tightly together once you form the dumplings).

**3.** Place about 1 tablespoon of the filling in the middle of a wrapper. Fold the wonton in half. Gently press out any air from around the filling and seal the edges of the wonton by pinching together with your fingertips.

**4.** Brush a small amount of water along one side of the flat edge of the wonton. Fold in the sides so that the two points overlap like an envelope; press firmly to seal. Repeat with remaining filling and wrappers. (At this point, the pot stickers can be frozen for future use.)

**5.** Bring a large saucepan of water to a rapid boil over high heat. Drop in several of the pot stickers and swirl them around so that they do not stick together or to the bottom of the saucepan. Once they rise to the surface of the water, remove with a slotted spoon. (At this point the pot stickers can be cooled, covered, and chilled until ready to fry.)

**6.** Heat 1 tablespoon oil in a large nonstick skillet over medium-high heat. Add as many pot stickers as will fit in skillet without crowding. Fry for several minutes on each side or until golden and crisp. Repeat with remaining pot stickers. Sprinkle with sesame seeds. Serve immediately.

**Makes 30 to 35 pot stickers**

★ ★ ★

★ ★ ★

***Can*** *you believe a whole year of tasting wine has gone by? Time flies when you're having fun and drinking wine. You've already tasted some major reds, some major whites, dessert wines, and Champagne. And each time you've headed to the store to buy the month's picks, I bet you've marveled at the*

rows and rows of mystery bottles from around the world—from the romantic-sounding Vermentino di Gallura and the intriguing Carmenere to strange and exotic ones like Xynomavro. You might have even spotted a Chenin Blanc from Tennessee and thought, maybe next time. Well, now's the perfect time!

This is the month to quench your curiosity and go exploring. I'll tell you a little about some of my faves among the wines we've not yet covered. Read a bit and simply pencil in a

little star by the ones that pique your curiosity. Then I'll give you some pointers on organizing a tasting so you can break out on your own, homing in on the varietals or winegrowing regions that tempt your taste buds.

Numero uno this month: BE CONFIDENT. Stick around and learn how to set up a wine and cheese party that's perfect for any occasion. You'll learn about cheeses— the hard, the soft, and the stinky too. And I'll

fill you in on the best-kept secrets of dynamite party planners: The world's great cheeses are a shortcut to throwing a fabulous, foolproof fete. First let's get our bottles in line.

## EUROPE

As you know, we've been sampling sips from quite a few winegrowing regions of France; we hit up German Riesling and got into Primitivo from Italy. But as you've probably guessed, this is only scratching the surface! For this month, consider sips from European countries we haven't yet visited and/or get a little deeper into those that we have.

### France

First, you've got to give yourself some serious credit—just look at everywhere we've been this year! We've sipped Riesling from Alsace, Cabernet- and Merlot-based wines from Bordeaux, Sauvingon Blanc and Chenin Blanc from the Loire Valley, Pinot Noir and Chardonnay from Burgundy, Champagne from Champagne, Viognier from the Rhône, and Syrah from both the Rhône and the Languedoc regions. Oh, yes—and how can we forget those succulent sweet wines from Sauternes?

That's my kind of Tour de France!

Now, if you're ready to delve a little deeper into some other great French grapes, take a look at these:

**Marsanne and Roussanne:** From the northern Rhône Valley come these two famous white-wine grapes. Both of these whites are mixed with Syrah in parts of the Rhône to soften out those huge reds. But on their own they can be quite interesting. Marsanne makes deep-colored white wines that are fairly full-bodied and sometimes described as waxy. The wines generate aromas of almond paste mixed with a citrus perfume. The best ones have concentrated orange marmalade and peach flavors. Acid's not this wine's strong point, so to get it while it's good, drink it when it's young. I like mine when summer nights just start to get that whip of fall wind in the air.

Roussanne is often blended with Marsanne. You can find bottles that are straight-up Roussanne, but it's a little hard-

* * * * * * * * **A BASIC CHEESE VOCABULARY** * * * * * * * *

Here are some words you'll hear tossed around when you start talking to serious cheese lovers:

**Aged:** Allowed to ripen or mature.

**Fresh or Unripened:** Non-aged, such as ricotta and mozzarella.

**Artisanal:** Made by hand, usually by small independent cheesemakers who use time-honored traditions and produce high-quality products.

**Bloomy Rind:** An edible outer coating, as found on Brie and Camembert.

**Blue-Veined:** Having streaks of blue, like Gorgonzola and Roquefort.

**Pasteurized:** Made with milk that has been heated and sterilized.

**Raw-Milk:** Made with milk that has not been pasteurized. Many of the best imported cheeses and fullest-flavored artisanal cheeses are made from raw milk.

* * * * * * * * * * * * * * * * * * * * * * * * * * * * * * * *

er. Look to California for this Rhône varietal all on its own. These wines can smell like herbal tea; like Marsanne, they have fla-

For this month, consider sips from European countries we haven't yet visited and/or get a little deeper into those that we have.

vors of peach with a slip of earthiness and a slightly unusual waxy texture. The yummy ones taste like fresh pears and honey. Instead of iced sweet tea on a hot summer day, try this for brunch, lunch, or teatime.

Remember—French labels can be tricky. Marsannes and Roussannes from the Rhône are not labeled by the grape but by the appellation: Look for a white wine from Croze-Hermitage, Hermitage, or Saint Joseph. Unless you know that a specific producer is making white with all Marsanne or all Roussanne, if you get a white from one of these spots you're most likely sipping Marsanne with a kick of Roussanne. To make it easy, pick up a bottle of California's take on this lovely white Frenchy.

**Grenache:** No doubt Syrah's the big kid on the block in the northern Rhône, but it's not the only gangsta red grape in that valley. Grenache gets plenty of play in the southern Rhône—it's the godfather grape in most all of the red blends from this area, including Côtes-du-Rhône Villages and the very famous Châteauneuf-du-Pape wines. This grape makes rich, low-tannin wines with ravishing red-berry flavors.

**Muscadet:** If you enjoyed the white wines from the Loire Valley you sampled in August, try this little number. It's crisp-tart and dry, with a jangle of apples and minerals and occasionally a nuzzle of grapefruit. Helpfully, major French Muscadets have the word *Muscadet* in their titles—in this case, the appellation includes the name of the grape. Examples include Muscadet, Muscadet de Sèvre-et-Maine, and Muscadet des Coteaux de la Loire. *Merci.*

### Germany

If you dug the German Rieslings you tasted in June, give Müller-Thurgau a go. A cross between Riesling and Sylvaner, Müller-Thurgau is the most commonly grown grape in Germany. The wines it produces are generally semidry and light. You could also pick up a bottle of this guy from Oregon or Washington for this month's shindig.

### Italy

I love all things Italian. Even Italy's simplest food is fantastic, and its wines are true heartthrobs. If you didn't love the Primitivo wine you tasted alongside Zins in October, don't give up! There's so much more to explore. Good places to start:

**Chianti (Tuscany):** This wine is more famous than Italy's flag. Chianti is made from at least 75 percent Sangiovese, Tuscany's darling little red grape. In general this juice is medium-bodied, with mild tannins, cherry-strawberry fruit, and earthy spice. This very dry red is typically acidic and tannic. Tart foods balance that tannic acidity, so you'll find it works with most food—especially Italian fare.

When buying Chianti, look for the phrase *Chianti Classico*, which means the wine comes from the heartland of Italy's Chianti region. Chianti Classico Riserva is even more prized; it signals the wine has been aged longer in oak barrels and has aromas of smoke and spice. One of the nice things about this wine is that it is cheap: You can find good Chianti for around $10 a bottle. Even better, when you're in Italy it will only cost a couple of euro per bottle.

**Grillo (Sicily):** Grillo is the white-wine grape usually used to make Marsala, a wine that's fortified with the addition of spirits. However, it's now coming to you courtesy of Feudo Arancio winery, and it rocks for a summer barbecue, a day at the beach, or a poolside afternoon. It's a supercrisp summer sip.

**Nero d'Avola (Sicily):** Watch out—Sicily is seriously getting in the wine game. And it has its game face on with its signature red grape. This little number produces deep red wines with dark fruit and nutty flavors. If you dig Zinfandel, this month reach for a gutsy Nero d'Avola.

**Vermentino di Gallura (Sardinia):** Doesn't it sound so sexy? Vermentino is a tough little grape. It grows in adverse conditions, which gives it a little edge in the glass. The hallmark feature of this white wine is its herbaceous aromas (think mint, sage, oregano, etc.), which it picks up from other plants grown in the area. If you don't do fruity whites, this wine's for you.

**Vernaccia di San Gimignano (Tuscany):** Love, love, love this little white. We turned friends on to this a few years ago and it's still

* * * * * * * * * **A ROSÉ IS A ROSÉ IS A ROSÉ—SORT OF** * * * * * * * * * *

Now's a good chance to tune you into one of the most misunderstood styles of wine of all time: rosé. No, rosé is not made from pink grapes. You need red grapes to make a rosé; in fact, any red grape can be used to make rosé.

How then do red-wine grapes make pink wines? One of two ways: The first is when the winemaker lets the skin of the red grape come into contact with the wine for only a short time. Because the skins are what give the juice its color, this brief contact between skin and juice results in a lighter color of wine. The second method of making a rosé merely involves adding white wine to a red wine.

Because white Zinfandel is the first wine people think of when they think "pink," many wine drinkers assume that all rosés are sweet. That's just so not so! Unlike white Zin, rosé is designed to have less sugar. Also, because the skins don't hang out too long with the juice, the wine doesn't have a lot of tannin; however, because rosés are made from red grapes, they have more body than whites.

France is the unofficial headquarters of rosé—they produce amazing versions in the south. Among the most famous and delightful is Tavel, from the Rhône region. It's a little pricey, but you can find other Rhône rosés—as well as some good finds from Languedoc—for a good price. Also look for Rosado from Spain and Rosato from Italy. Again, Sicily's in the game with one of my faves, Rosé di Regaleali. Drink rosé on a hot summer day or as a light, vibrant aperitif any time of year.

* * * * * * * * * * * * * * * * * * * * * * * * * * * * * * * * * * * *

## YOU'LL NEVER FORGET IT

Like wine, cheese should be served at just the right temperature. For cheese, just right is room temperature, so be sure to pull your cheese out of the fridge about a half hour to an hour before serving. Cold temperatures diminish the flavor and aroma of cheeses; they also can make the texture of soft to semisoft cheeses hard and waxy when they should be creamy and supple. Don't think temp really matters that much? Try this simple exercise:

Slice a few pieces of a good, flavorful artisanal cheese from a hunk in the fridge; let the slices sit out on the counter about a half hour but refrigerate the rest of the cheese. After the time is up, slice a few pieces from the cold hunk in the fridge and taste them side by side with the slices that have been sitting out. See? You're cheating yourself of some great flavors when you eat cheese directly from the fridge.

their favorite white. This bit's a little textbooky, but it may help you remember the name: There are various white grape varieties called "Vernaccia" that grow throughout Italy; the word is related to *vernacular*, implying a local or native vine. Vernaccia of San Gimignano, however, is what you want. It's grown nowhere else but around the town of San Gimignano in Tuscany. Often blended with a splash of Chardonnay, these wines have a distinctive almond and spice flavor that totally rocks with or without food.

**Gavi (Piedmont):** With all this Italian wine vocabulary, you're almost fluent. Well, after a few glasses no one will know you're just rattling off names of grapes and wine- producing towns. This one is named for the Gavi winegrowing region in Piedmont— not the grape. The wine is a dry, acidic white wine made from the Cortese grape and has a straw color and a neutral, mild aroma. Gavi di Gavi (meaning Gavi from Gavi) is the ultimate. If you're a Sauvignon Blanc die-hard, you need to branch out; I

promise you will add this to your list of faves. I love it as an aperitif before a big Italian dinner.

### Spain

Spain's going gangbusters in the wine world! Until recently, Spanish wines were mostly pooh-poohed as plonk, but in the past 20 or so years, Spanish winemakers have moved from making cheap wines in bulk to putting out quality juice. The wine world is taking notice, and you should too. Some good places to start dabbling:

**Rioja:** Reds, whites, and rosés come from this northern winemaking region; I suggest you start with the red Rioja, an utterly classic Spanish wine made mostly from the saucy Tempranillo grape. Wines at the top end can taste full, rich, and velvety—a bit like a great Bordeaux but less expensive. Riojas have their charms too—they can be lighter, with bright berry flavors; like Pinot Noir and Chianti, these lighter versions are great summer reds and behave beautifully with food.

You'll notice Rioja is classified three ways. "Crianza" brings the lightest, least oaky, inexpensive wine—I consider it a good house red. Next up is "Reserve"; this is a little more oaky, heavy, and a little pricier. At the top of the heap are the "Gran Reserves"; these are the heaviest, oakiest, and most costly and are made only in the best years.

**Albarino (Alvarinho in Portuguese):** This grape makes one of Spain's and Portugal's most prized white wines. Medium- to full-bodied, it makes your mouth water with citrus fruits, flowers, and peach, and sometimes it is stitched with mineraly wet stone flavors. It tastes somewhat similar to Chardonnay, but since it's not usually fermented in oak barrels, it doesn't have the sweet vanilla aromas that a Chardonnay does, and it's much lighter than those big butter-bomb styles.

**Carmenere:** For years, these vines in Spain were thought to be Merlot. This grape used to be common in Bordeaux but is no longer used for these blends. Merlot drinkers especially should like Carmenere—it's dark, rich, and smooth, with nice plum flavors. Merlot lovers could also pick up the popular Carmenere from Chile and do a little side-by-side tasting.

### Portugal

Go to Portugal. Seriously, if you're planning a European vacay, this is where you should go to sip light, spritzy white wines alongside fresh seafood and finish off the meal with an array of Ports. They have great coffee too. So what could be better? Like Spain, it's coming up in the wine world. Which means the prices are still great. To get a taste, check out Alvarinho (above) as well as:

**Vinho Verde:** *Verde* means "green," and the term doesn't describe this wine's color but the fact that you're supposed to drink it young. I love these whites all summer long. Their crisp lemony flavors with a hint of fizz are so much fun to sip. Usually this is lower in alcohol, so it's a great lunch wine. And you'll love this: With the average cost of wine between $4 and $5 a bottle, you can't go wrong.

### Greece

Although Greece practically invented wine, these days the country is considered merely an "emerging wine region"—probably because people think of the wretched Retsina (in short it's Greek white wine mixed with pine resin and, in my opinion, is nasty). But there are some respectable pours coming from the mainland as well as some of the Greek islands. When going Greek check out these regions and what they do best:

**Macedonia:** Look for reds from this region, especially wines from that mysterious Xynomavro grape. These wines will be intense

> Go to Portugal. Seriously, if you're planning a European vacay, this is where you should go to sip light, spritzy white wines alongside fresh seafood and finish off the meal with an array of Ports.

raisiny reds with a slightly medicinal twang.

**Peloponnese:** This spot makes divine dessert wine called Mavrodaphne from its famed black Muscat grape. If you like Tawny Port, you'll be happy you picked up one of these.

**Santorini:** This sexy Greek Isle is known for its black beaches (from volcanic soil) and, for me, breakfast. On a family trip to see my brother, we sipped the light white wines from the Assyrtico grape in the mornings. We called it breakfast on the black beach. If you like light, dry whites, I highly recommend sipping one from Santorini.

# UNITED STATES

Let's take a look at a few lesser-known California regions as well as some of the up-and-coming American contenders.

## California

Over the months, most of the United States wines your wine club has been sipping have come from California—and for good reason! Almost nine out of every ten bottles in America come from this state. But remember, there's a lot more to Cali wines than Napa and Sonoma. Some interesting wine-growing areas to explore next:

**Livermore Valley:** This little winegrowing region lies south of Oakland. Wente Vineyards is one of the oldest producers in the area. If you've enjoyed the Zinfandel and Sauvignon Blanc months of your wine club, pick up some bottles of those juices from this Livermore winery. My favorite Wente wine is a fun little redhead called Nth Degree Shiraz. It's enough to whet your palate for more

from Livermore Valley.

**Lodi Valley:** Near Sacramento, this wine-growing region produces delicious wines for half the price of those from the state's more better-known regions. Try Syrah, Zinfandel, Petite Sirah, and Viognier.

## Other States

In this year's wine club, our domestic tastings have favored Cali, New York, Oregon, and Washington. But did you know that wine is now being produced in all 50 states? I swear I bought a decent Syrah from Arkansas. There may even be a winery near you, so give the home team a chance—the more you support them, the better they'll get, and that can only be good for everyone. I find the best way to learn is to look for local wines when traveling—sipping regional products helps me learn the lay of the land. Here are just a few suggestions when it comes to buying wine from the states, along with what varieties to look for in each.

**Virginia:** Stick with whites in this state, especially Viognier, Chardonnay, Sémillon, and Riesling.

**Alabama:** Look for wines made from the Cynthiana grape—often called the "Cabernet of the South." This wine is rich, full-bodied, and intensely flavorful.

**Oregon:** As you gleaned in November, this is a place for Pinot; the state's also showing superb Chard.

**Ohio:** Go for Pinot Grigio or Riesling.

**New York State:** The two main growing regions here are the Finger Lakes (you tried the area's Riesling in June) and Long Island. Best varietals are Chardonnay, Cabernet,

Merlot, and of course Riesling.

**Texas:** Although the wine industry in Texas is only about 25 years old, the Lone Star State has emerged as the fifth-largest wine-producing state in the country. Cab, Chard, and Sauvignon Blanc are all grown here; a few top producers include Llano Estacado and Becker Vineyards.

**Tennessee:** Look for white Zinfandel, Chenin Blanc, and Viognier.

## SOUTH AMERICA and MEXICO

We're headed south of the border. South American wines are good buys for the American wine drinker. Lately, however, their popularity and prices have been climbing, but so has the quality. A few highlights:

### Argentina

Argentina is known mostly for putting out lots and lots of cheap juice. Most good wines from this country come from the Mendoza region. Look for yummy Malbec from Mendoza; it's rich with tannins and oak, dark in color, and very juicy and spicy.

### Brazil

Look for Chard and Pinotage. And pick up Cabs and Merlot that are blended with Tannat (a very dark, tannic red wine usually used to beef up blends).

### Chile

Chile makes all-star Cabs and those green, grassy, and inexpensive Sauvignon Blancs you tasted in August. Also look for good buys on Merlot, and if you've become a Viognier nut, try one from this country too.

### Mexico

There's more to Mexico than sombreros, including Cabernet Sauvignon, Pinot Noir,

* * * * * * * * * * * * * *

### ODE TO FUNKY FROMAGE

You've smelled some funny things in your wine over the past year—cat pee, barnyardy aromas, dirt, and the like. As you now know, these are often considered expected (and even desirable) attributes in certain wines. Well, get ready for some major stink in your cheese! Some cheeses really put out a whiff—and some cheese lovers can't get enough of it (for them, the smellier the better). I for one love stinky cheese! So when you hear a cheesehead describe a pick as "pungent," "smelly," or even "stinky," he or she is not dissing the cheese! Earthy, funky, and dramatic flavors are the hallmark of some of the world's best.

If you're not yet on the boat with smelly cheeses, give one a taste next time the cheesemonger is offering samples. A few super whiffers include Muenster from Alsace, Epoisse from Burgundy, and Taleggio from northern Italy. Note that when you buy these, you should always try to get a taste first, or at least check the expiration date if samples aren't available. Strong cheeses should be smelly but should not reek of ammonia—a scent that signals the cheese has gone over the edge. Also, be sure to team smellier cheeses with less funky cheeses for good variety. Manchego, Saint André, Camembert, Gruyère, and Compté would all provide a good contrast to the more assertive cheeses you choose.

* * * * * * * * * * * *      * * * * * * * * * * * *

Zinfandel, Chardonnay, and Riesling. Some say the North Baja California area is Mexico's answer to Napa. Good Cab, Chard, and Pinot are also coming from the Queretaro region. And for those of you with sticky fingers, Mexican winemaker Hans Backhoff of Monte Xanic is producing some awesome Ice Wine, so check it out.

## Shall We Keep Going?

Yes—I could go on and on, because so many countries produce wines. I'll stop with just a few more mentions of some wine producing countries that might interest you in light of what we've tasted so far this year. Now if there is a wine or region I haven't hit upon

If you loved the Aussies' big, bold, fruit-forward style of Shiraz, look for Cabernet and Cabernet-Shiraz blends as well as Sauvignon Blanc.

and you want to venture out on your own, all I have to say is—you've made me proud. Remember, it's up to you to pick your poison.

**Australia:** As you learned in March, Shiraz is Australia's darling grape. If you loved the Aussies' big, bold, fruit-forward style of Shiraz, look for Cabernet and Cabernet-Shiraz blends as well as Sauvignon Blanc. Seriously, it's hard to go wrong with wine from down under. I haven't met an Aussie I didn't like.

**New Zealand:** I can't say it enough: I love the zippy and zingy Sauvignon Blancs from NZ. If you prefer a cleaner, leaner Chardonnay, you'll love theirs. And Pinot fans—watch out,

because the juice flowing from NZ rocks.

**Israel:** This country grows a versatile mix of grapes, including Cabernet Sauvignon, Merlot, Chardonnay, and Sauvignon Blanc. Israel has a reputation for high-quality California-style varietals, with influences from France, South Africa, and Australia. While Israel still makes a variety of kosher wines, they aren't all sweet and blah. The wines of this country are finally getting in the game with the big boys.

**Croatia:** This is believed to be the birthplace of the original Zinfandel grape, Crljenak Kastelanski; its descendant is called Plavac Mali. So if you're super into Zin, seek out a bottle and see what its Croatian cousin has to offer. Zin zealots: This is no easy find. You'll need to make a few phone calls and maybe even a special order to get some Plavac Mali.

**South Africa:** We talked Pinotage last month. Aside from this red grape, most of the grapes planted in South Africa are white varieties—Chardonnay, Sauvignon Blanc, and Steen (aka Chenin Blanc). The Chardonnay Sémillon blend from Vergelegen, now available in the United States, is one of the best whites I have ever tasted. It is so unbelievably elegant and seductive, it takes you to a deeper level in wine appreciation. Though the country does produce some expensive wines, in general wines from South Africa are still a pretty good buy, if you can get your hands on them.

Hey—it's your turn to choose the juice! I'm retiring from this gig for a while (at least until the next time we meet between the pages). After all, the wine club isn't about learning to love wines I happen to love. It's about helping you discover the wines you love. This month is all you, baby—be brave and delve deeper into the wide world of wine.

Here are a few ways you could organize this mess of wine info I've thrown at you. Some tasting options:

1. **Mixed Bag:** Share the preceding pages with your wine club buddies and get everyone to bring one wine that piques his or her interest.

2. **Heritage Tasting:** Have everyone in the club bring a wine from a country or state their ancestors lived. Or taste wines from places you've traveled and loved.

3. **American Heritage Tasting:** Jump the California state border and look for wines from lesser-known winegrowing regions.

4. **Choose-a-Country Tasting:** But not France—you've been all over that one. Try wines from a variety of regions within Italy, Spain, Germany, Chile, Australia, New Zealand, or any other country whose wines have been wowing you.

5. **Explore Your *Terroir*:** Do a tasting of wines from your state or nearby states. Ask your local wine shop for recommendations—you may be surprised by what you will find.

6. **Delve Deeper into Your Favorite Varietal:** Love Chard or gaga for Syrah? Round up a sampling of wines from the more obscure countries and regions known for your grape.

7. **La Vie en Rosé:** I would be especially proud of you if you tried a tasting of rosés from around the world—there are some dynamite dry, crisp styles being made out there, and you can officially march in the rosé revolution with a small but growing band of people who truly get what rosé is all about!

8. **Name the Grape:** Here's a test no one

### ✸ ✸ CHEESE SPEAK ✸ ✸

At a loss for words when it comes to describing these great cheeses you're tasting? See if any of these hit their mark:

**Aroma:** Descriptors include earthy, floral, fresh, fruity, nutty, oniony, smoky, pungent, sour, sweet, subtle, and stinky.

**Taste:** Descriptors include buttery, citrusy, complex, creamy, earthy, grassy, herbaceous, musty, peppery, ripe, sharp, smoky, spicy, sweet, tangy, tart, zesty, and truffly.

**Texture:** Useful descriptions here include crumbly, dense, firm, hard, silky, soft, smooth, and velvety.

should mind taking. Round up five different reds (Syrah, Merlot, Cab, Pinot, Zin) we've tasted over the year, or five different whites (Chard, Viognier, Riesling, Sauvignon Blanc, and a Vouvray, (aka Chenin Blanc—it was the ringer in August, remember?). Wrap them up and see if you can guess which varietal is which. It's a fun exercise to see if you're getting the hang of these different grapes. And if you don't pass with flying colors, don't worry—even the pros have been fooled. Also remember that practice makes perfect.

Feel free to lose any of these takes on tasting. You may be inspired to branch out and find your own way—the cool part about this is that there are no rules when it comes to this month's tasting!

### What's to Eat?

With all the cooking we have looming on the horizon this holiday season, let's take a load off and tap into the simplest way to put on a party. We're getting cheesy for this wine club meeting. Seriously, I know of no quicker shortcut to getting together a buffet of amaz-ing flavors than a great cheese selection. World-class cheeses turn heads and get conversations going so much more easily than just about anything you can cook up.

Of course, we're not talking about buying the usual yellow and white supermarket cheeses we all grew up with—you stepped it up with your wine knowledge, so let's get a little more cheese-savvy too. What you're looking for this month is a sampling of artisanal cheeses (see "Cheese Speak," opposite) or other off-the-beaten-path varieties.

The first step in putting together a cheese

plate is to figure out where you're going to buy all this fancy-pants *fromage* (that's Frenchy for cheese). If you can find a specialty cheese shop in your area, great! It's a good time to make friends with the cheesemonger (aka the person behind the counter). Ask questions, be curious—just like you've done in your local wine shop. Most of all—you guessed it—experiment. Cheesemongers are usually quick to offer samples, so taste away!

If you're lucky enough to live in an area with a big specialty food store, like Trader Joe's or Whole Foods Market, check its cheese selection—it's usually extensive. And these days, even local grocery stores are tapping into more and more varieties. Just roll that cart right on past those individually wrapped processed American cheese slices. In fact, you might have to ask where the gourmet cheeses are kept—they're sometimes separate from the mass-produced brands and displayed in a special deli section or case.

## I'll Have a Little Cheese with That Whine

That's what an old boss I had used to cleverly say to whining employees. But there is something to this whole wine and cheese thing. Since this is the wine club, I know you're thinking about how to make sure the cheeses you choose go with the wines you're pouring, but don't get too stressed out about that. One general rule of thumb is that wines and cheeses from the same regions go together well. Doing a tasting of Italian wines? Taste them alongside Italian cheeses. Spanish wines? Spanish cheeses. California wines? You got it. Another way to go about it is to try to match the inten-

sity and mouth feel of the cheese and wine; for example, a tangy goat cheese will go nicely with a crisp, acidic Sauvignon Blanc, while rich, triple-crème cheeses mingle well with thick, opulent dessert wines. Aged cheeses go well with wines that generally age well, and fresh cheeses go pretty well with zippy whites, so reach for big reds when tasting big, bold cheeses and refreshing whites with light and tangy cheeses.

However, if you're doing an eclectic wine tasting with wines from all over the world, don't feel you have to chase down cheeses from the same exact regions—or with the same exact mouth feel—of the wines. Frankly, it's not very likely you'll come up with a horrible gotta-spit-it-out cheese/wine pairing, although you may get a wine or a cheese that just won't pass the palate. Stick to serving cheeses that intrigue you alongside wines that interest you and notice how they go together. If a cheese and wine don't pair well, take note and move on to the next cheese or the next wine (after all, you'll be serving a number of both). And isn't it nice to move from having *moi* tell you exactly what to pair with what to noticing how you think things pair? That's right—you've got your wine club wings now; it's time to take off on your own!

## Choosing Cheeses

When putting a cheese platter together, you'll want a range of cheeses from soft or fresh to semihard to hard; you also might want to include cheeses from the three types of milk (goat, sheep, and cow). A good cheesemonger can help you find just the right mix, but here are some of my favorite picks in various categories to get you started.

## 1. FRESH CHEESES

**Cow's Milk:** Mozzarella (look for fresh mozzarella, packaged in water), ricotta, queso fresco, and feta (which can be made with sheep's, goat's, or cow's milk).

**Goat's Milk:** Fresh goat cheese.

## 2. SOFT TO SEMISOFT CHEESES

**Cow's Milk:** Brie, Camembert, Morbier, Epoisse, Muenster (try the real one, from Alsace), Explorateur (a superrich triple-crème cheese), and Taleggio.

**Goat's Milk:** Crottin or Chabichou (can also be firm, depending on age).

## 3. FIRM TO SEMIHARD CHEESES

**Cow's Milk:** Compté, Gruyère, Asiago, New England cheddar (Cabot cheddar from Vermont is delish), Irish cheddar, Emmentaler, fontina, and Gouda—I'm a total sucker for smoked Gouda.

**Goat's Milk:** Crottin or Chabichou (can also be soft, depending on age).

**Sheep's Milk:** Manchego, Ossau-Iraty, Vermont Shepherd.

## 4. HARD CHEESES

**Cow's Milk:** Aged Gouda, Parmesan (real Parmigiano-Reggiano from Italy—not the stuff you shake from a canister), aged Cheddar, dry Vella Jack.

**Sheep's Milk:** Pecorino Romano.

## 5. BLUE CHEESES

For me, at least one piercing blue is a must on a cheese tray. A few of my favorites include Montbriac, a Camembert-like blue cheese from France; Roquefort, the quintessential French blue; Gorgonzola from Italy, a rich and creamy blue; Cabrales from Spain, an awesome blue made from a mix of cow's, goat's, and sheep's milk; and Shropshire Blue from England. United States cheesemakers are putting out some amazing blue too. Try Maytag Blue, Point Reyes Blue, Great Hill Blue, and Jersey Blue.

### Serving and Savoring Cheese

A mix of three to five cheeses is more than adequate for a sampling—you don't want to overwhelm your palate. Plan on about four to six ounces total cheese per guest. However, if you're planning to serve a cheese course after a meal, about three ounces total per guest will suffice.

Serve the cheeses with a good variety of crackers, crusty bread, dried fruits such as figs and apricots, and nuts. Try to avoid anything that will overpower your cheese. Also, when eating bread with your cheese, don't mush the cheese into the bread—just place it on top (the idea is to use the bread as a vessel for the cheese, not to make the bread and cheese into one!).

Tasting cheese is similar to tasting wine. If you are tasting a variety of reds, you would start with the lightest—say, Pinot Noir, and end with a big gun like Cab. Always taste cheese from mild to pungent and from soft to hard. If you taste the stinky blues before the subtle crèmes, you're sure to still have stink lingering and won't be able to taste the nuances of the crèmes. Wine and cheese are both complex in flavor, aroma, and texture. You'll want to taste and smell cheese to appreciate the full flavor.

# mind your manners

*Emily Post may not grace each of our nightstands, but etiquette is far from dead. Here are some tips my mother taught me, and you should know, when it comes to minding your manners with wine.*

**Lipstick:** Avoid it altogether if you can. Lip stains and long-lasting lipwear can really be a bear to remove from glassware. Also, if you cake on the lipstick, liner, gloss, and all that other goop, you may taste more of that than the wine.

**Perfume:** Do yourself and your friends a favor and go *au naturel* for the evening. A big waft of Chanel can ruin your nose for the night, and the same goes for heavy aftershave. Instead, let the aromas of wine perfume the evening.

Your guests are there to see you, so get out of the kitchen! It's rude to be gone for more than a few minutes at a time—guests will think they've put you out, and that makes them feel uncomfortable. So do as much prepwork as you can in advance so you can enjoy the party too.

## Sending Back Bad Wine

Once a restaurant opens a bottle of wine, the staff may fail to store it properly after that first pour. When you've been served the wine, you should swirl and sniff and make a decision on whether or not it has gone bad right away—don't wait until you've finished off half a glass or half a bottle before deeming it unsuitable. Same goes for wines you buy from stores and wineries—the management is much more likely to accept the return of a fuller bottle than a near-empty one.

If you just straight up don't like the taste of the wine you ordered by the glass, regardless of whether you chose it or someone recommended it, a polite request to try another is totally acceptable. If you spit it out and arrogantly demand something palatable, you're likely to offend not only your server but also your dinner companions.

However, if you've chosen a bottle and simply don't happen to love it, you may have to live with it. The exception is if you feel you have been misled by the waiter, sommelier, or wine merchant—that is, if he or she sold you on a wine that was not what you expected. If you're feeling a little uneasy about it, put the pressure on the server; politely ask him or her to smell it or taste it. If you end up with a bottle of wine you don't love, find something you do enjoy about the wine, learn something about it, and move on.

### Choosing Wine for Everyone

Once people find out you're in a wine club you will be presumed the wine know-it-all, and ordering wine from a wine list may become your task. Make it easy on yourself and ask your dining companions what they like and dislike. Next, think price point. Are you splitting the bill, is someone else hosting, or do you plan to pick up the tab? Narrow it down to a few bottles and ask your server which is his or her favorite. See? That wasn't so painful!

### Wine for the Host

A bottle of wine makes for the perfect host or hostess gift. Here are a few tips to ensure you keep making the guest list.

Remember, this is a gift. Do not expect the recipient to open the bottle and share it with you. If he decides to do so, that is completely his choice.

If indeed the host or hostess has requested you bring a bottle to be opened at the party, bring a conversation starter. Avoid that same old white wine you always buy and choose something new, like a Viognier—I promise it will get people talking.

Give a bottle of something you love and cherish. Include a card saying why this wine is so memorable to you or share a little knowledge about the wine on a gift card and tie it to the neck of the bottle.

When giving the gift of white wines, should you bring it already chilled? I would recommend bringing it at room temperature—don't assume your host is going to serve it that evening. And if she doesn't have room to keep it in the refrigerator, the wine will not be exposed to fluctuating temperatures.

### Ice—Naughty or Nice?

It is never polite to scoff at a guest request, even if someone asks for ice cubes in her wine. True, when ice melts, it waters down the drink. However, if an ice cube or two will encourage someone to sip a chilled glass of Sauvignon Blanc rather than a Bartles & James, I'm all for it. So be a good sport and bring out the cubes if a guest requests it.

For learning purposes, encourage your guests to leave the cubes in the trays and sip the wines straight up. Politely explain that just as you should always taste your food before adding salt, you should sip your wine before adding ice. They may be pleasantly surprised.

*Whether you prefer to Google™ or thumb through a book, there's a lot of great info out there for the taking. Here are some of my faves to get you started.*

## INTERNET SITES

**Bonappetit.com:** This site gives you the goods on all things great in food and wine pairing, the latest and greatest gadgets for wine lovers, and bargain wines.

**Bonnydoonvineyard.com:** This site rocks. Winemaker Randall Graham gives an insightful rant that makes frequent visits to the site well worthwhile. He always says that "wine should be as fun as government regulations allow." He's a breath of fresh air in the often stuffy wine world.

**Freethegrapes.org:** This site is all about shipping laws. You may be of legal drinking age and a taxpaying adult, but you may not be able to order wine to your door. Log on and find out if you're one of the lucky ones living in a state allows, and, if not, how to become active in the fight.

**Koeppelonwine.com:** The coolest guy in Memphis pens this lively site. Fredric Koeppel is hip but with the utmost reverence for the drink. You'll find a good mix of reviews on "Refrigerator Door Wines" and those lovelies that require a little more patience.

**Thewinedoctor.com:** No bells and whistles here. Just good advice and a fab glossary. Any wine-speak ailment you can't cure? The doctor's got just what you need.

**Vinesugar.com:** Here's the place for all of you up-and-comers in the wide world of wine. It's free, it's fun, and there's no fancy-shmancy wine talk. Head here for a lighter take on the juice. Log on and you'll get a variety of articles, links to other wine web sites, travel talk, and tasting notes.

**Whitleyonwine.com:** This is a serious site for those of you jonesing for more wine info. Robert Whitley knows more about wine than anyone I've ever met. He's also the host of the Internet-based *Wine Talk*, two weekly radio shows that explore great food and wine.

**Wine.com:** Search for top-rated bang-for-your-buck wines, splurges, and everything in between via region, type, winery, and price.

**Wineaccess.com:** You can search among 45,000 wines on this shop-till-you-drop site. It's a good spot to check out before you shop. You can compare this site's prices to your local vendors' prices and see which wines fit into your budget.

**Wineforall.com:** W. R. Tish is a charmingly witty author of monthly rants and raves on the wine world. This site is all about feel-good wine stuff, from Desperate House Wines to an undying battle against numerical wine ratings.

**Wineloverspage.com:** Log on for articles, reviews, and info on wine travel. There are tons of fun stuff to explore on this site, so get off eBay and spend your hours clicking through wine info galore.

**Wineskinny.com:** Look no further "for the inside skinny on wine." From bargins under $15 to pricey splurges to reads on wine and health, they've got ya covered.

**Winexwired.com:** This is my kind of site. It's targeted at you twentysomethings but could teach the old-school wine snobs a thing or two. You can also expand your horizons into the world of beer, cocktails, and bit on coffee and tea.

**Zinfandel.org:** If you've gone grapes over America's favorite redhead—Zinfandel—this site is all you, baby. Join ZAP, check out what's happenin' in the world of Zin, and get more info on the heritage of the grape in America.

# BOOKS

**Exploring Wine.** This is the official textbook used at the Culinary Institute of America. It's what the pros need to pass their wine courses. So if you're interested in going pro, it's a must-have.

**Great Wine Made Simple.** My favorite wine girl, Andrea Immer, sets up simple guides for learning about wine the right way—by drinking it. There are lots of helpful tasting notes and tips in this super-cute red book.

**Oldman's Guide to Outsmarting Wine: 108 Ingenious Shortcuts to Navigate the World of Wine with Confidence and Style, by Mark Oldman.** After getting into the wine club, this is a great next step to pick up pointers on everything from super Tuscan wines to "Insider Cred" when it comes to the famed Pinot Grigio.

**Sparkling Harvest, The Seasons of the Vine.** Learn about one of my very favorite California wineries, Shramsburg Vineyards, while taking in all things romantic about bubbly including breathtaking photography, divine recipes, and menu ideas perfect for sparkling wine.

**The New Sotheby's Wine Encyclopedia: A Comprehensive Reference Guide to the Wines of the World, by Tom Stevenson.** This book has awesome colorful maps of wine-growing regions and stunning pictures of enchanting châteaux and vineyards. It's a big honker at 600 pages but a great go-to reference book, containing everything from historical information to authoritative assessments of individual wines.

**The Oxford Companion to Wine.** This is all things academic. This is not a cuddle-up-and-read book. It's loaded with heavy-duty wine info. You'll get everything from information on wine regions to glassware history.

**The Wine Bible, by Karen MacNeil.** A giant weighing in at 910 pages, this will surely answer just about any question a wine lover could ask. And although it's amazingly comprehensive, it's also a fun read, full of tips, anecdotes, and fascinating asides.

**The Wine-Lover's Companion, 2nd Edition, by Ron Herbst and Sharon Tyler Herbst.** This is like a dictionary of wine—a quick reference to have on hand when you can't remember, for example, what grape is in a Condrieu or what the heck Johannisberg Riesling Is. The Glossary of Wine Tasting Terms in the back of the book gives you words to use to describe wines you like (and don't).

**Wine and War: The French, the Nazis and the Battle for France's Greatest Treasure, by Don and Petie Kladstrup.** This is for those of you who love a little history with your wine. It's the incredibly true tale of how the Frenchies saved their beloved wine from the German pillaging in WWII. Pour a big glass of Bordeaux and cuddle up for a fantastic read.

**Wine for Dummies.** Even the pros can learn from this easy-to-use wine information source. It's a great book to have in your library for quick bits on buying, storing, and all-around learning to love wine.

**Wine for Women: A Guide to Buying, Pairing, and Sharing Wine, by Leslie Sbrocco.** Sorry, guys, this book is a light read for all you gals who are into sipping with your gal pals. It's all things chick with fun and informative wine stuff including wines to go with that little black dress.

*Popular varietals and places that make yummy wine from them:*

## WHITE GRAPES

### Chardonnay
★ Burgundy and Champagne (France), southern France, northeastern Italy, Tuscany (Italy), California, Oregon, Washington State, New York State
★ Western Australia, South Australia, Hunter Valley (Australia)
★ Stellenbosch (South Africa)
★ Marlborough and Gisbourne (New Zealand)

### Sauvignon Blanc
★ Bordeaux and Loire Valley (France), northeastern Italy
★ Marlborough and Hawke's Bay (New Zealand)
★ California and Washington State
★ Stellenbosch (South Africa)
★ Maipo Valley and Casablanca (Chile)

### Riesling
★ Mosel-Saar-Ruwer, Rheingau, Rheinhessen, Pfalz (Germany)
★ Alsace (France)
★ Austria
★ Northeastern Italy
★ California, Washington State, New York
★ Southern Australia

### Gewürztraminer
★ Alsace (France)
★ Trentino (Italy)
★ California, Washington State, New York State

### Chenin Blanc
★ Loire Valley (France)
★ California
★ South Africa—where they call it Steen

### Pinot Gris
★ Alsace (France ) (Tokay d' Alsace Pinot Gris)
★ Northeastern Italy (Pinot Grigio)
★ Baden (Germany) (Grauburgunder or Rulander)
★ Oregon

### Viognier
★ Northern Rhône Valley (France)
★ California
★ Southern France

## RED GRAPES

### Cabernet Sauvignon
★ Bordeaux (France) (especially Medoc and Graves)
★ North and central Italy
★ Southern France
★ California, Washington State, New York State
★ Western Australia, South Australia, Victoria (Australia)
★ Penedes and Ribera del Duero (Spain)
★ Maipo Valley (Chile)
★ Mendoza (Argentina)

### Merlot
★ Bordeaux (France) (especially Pomerol and St. Emillion)
★ Northern and central Italy
★ Southern France
★ California, Washington State, New York State
★ Maipo and Rapel (Chile)

### Pinot Noir
★ Burgundy and Champagne (France)
★ California, Oregon, New York State
★ Marlborough (New Zealand)
★ Tuscany and Alto-Adige (Italy)

### Sangiovese
★ Tuscany (Italy)
★ California

### Syrah
★ Rhône Valley (France)
★ Southern France
★ Barossa Valley (where it's called Shiraz), South Australia; Hunter Valley, New South Wales; Victoria (Australia)
★ California, Washington State
★ South Africa

### Zinfandel
★ California
★ Washington State
★ Brazil
★ South Africa

# tasting notes

**Complete Name of Wine**
*(e.g., Gallo Vintner's Reserve Chardonnay)*

_____

_____

**Grape Variety**
*(e.g., Cabernet Sauvignon, 80% Shiraz/20% Cabernet Sauvignon)*

_____

_____

**Vintage:** _____

**Tasting Date:** _____

**Price Value:** _____

_____

**Aroma:** _____

**Color:** _____

**Taste:** _____

**Body:** _____

**Finish:** _____

**Notes on Food Pairings:** _____

_____

**Overall Thoughts:** _____

_____

_____

_____

_____

# INDEX